France during World War II

Abba Queens Gate Hotel
31 34 Queens Gate, Kensington

Gloucester Road Tube Stop
(Cromwell Road)

Paul,
Best of luck
Tom

France during World War II

From Defeat to Liberation

Thomas R. Christofferson with
Michael S. Christofferson

Fordham University Press | New York 2006

World War II: The Global, Human, and Ethical Dimension, No. 10
ISSN 1541-0293

Library of Congress Cataloging-in-Publication Data

Christofferson, Thomas Rodney, 1939–
    France during World War II : from defeat to liberation / Thomas R. Christofferson with Michael S. Christofferson.—1st ed.
        p.   cm.—(World War II—the global, human, and ethical dimension, 1541–0293; no. 10)
    Includes bibliographical references and index.
    ISBN 0-8232-2562-3 (hardcover : alk. paper)—ISBN 0-8232-2563-1 (pbk. : alk. paper)
    1. World War, 1939–1945—France.   2. World War, 1939–1945—Campaigns— France.   3. France—History—German occupation, 1940–1945.   4. France—Social conditions—20th century.   I. Title: France during World War Two.   II. Title: France during World War 2.   III. Christofferson, Michael Scott.   IV. Title.   V. World War II—the global, human, and ethical dimension; 10.
    D761.C48   2006
    940.53'44—dc22

                                                                                    2006006872

Printed in the United States of America
08 07 06   5 4 3 2 1
First edition

To Pablo

Contents

Abbreviations

BBC	British Broadcasting Corporation
CFLN	Comité français de la Libération nationale
CFTC	Confédération française des travailleurs chrétiens
CGT	Confédération général du travail
CGQJ	Commissariat général aux questions juives
FFI	Forces françaises de l'intérieur
LVF	Légion des volontaires français contre le bolchévisme
MUR	Mouvements unis de la Résistance
NRF	*Nouvelle Revue française*
OCM	Organisation civile et militaire
OSE	Oeuvre de secours aux enfants
OSS	Office of Strategic Services
PPF	Parti populaire français
PQJ	Police aux questions juives
RNP	Rassemblement national populaire
SA	Sturmabteilung
SFIO	Section française de l'Internationale ouvrière
SOL	Service d'ordre légionnaire
SS	Schutzstaffel
STO	Service du travail obligatoire
TC	Témoignage chrétien
UGIF	Union générale des Israélites de France

Preface

This is a book about France during the Second World War, a subject that has been discussed and debated passionately by the French for the past sixty years, replacing the French Revolution as the event that most seriously divided the nation into warring factions. Today, however, it seems that the divisive debate on Vichy has reached a point of exhaustion, maybe even a conclusion of sorts. Maurice Papon's 1998 trial and conviction for crimes against humanity committed during World War II seems to have ended a long, arduous period in which the French judicial system attempted—not always successfully—to bring the remaining French and German violators of human rights to justice. No more trials are in the offing, mainly because no one is left to be tried. The World War II generation is rapidly dying off in France and with it the memory of what occurred during that dark age.

In any case, the issues that divided France during the war are no longer relevant today. The European Union and the economic modernization of the past sixty years have put an end to the "True France" of peasants, folklore, rural values, and the like that produced Vichy's nostalgic, vicious counterrevolution, better known at the time as the National Revolution. Vichy's motto, "Work, Family, Fatherland" [*Travail, Famille, Patrie*] no longer applies to a France in which cohabitation has replaced marriage, the thirty-five-hour week has redefined work, and the broader European community has changed the meaning of the nation state. Vichy's total failure to impose its vision on France during World War II discredited its ideology, preparing the way for an urban nation with social, political, and economic structures radically different from those of the past. Today, the National Front is the only serious political remnant of the old regime in France. Its strength should neither be underestimated to encourage complacency in the face of extremism nor exaggerated to raise a false specter of fascism gaining power. Nevertheless, in the 2002 election, the French people rejected the Front's candidate for president by a margin of 82 to 18 percent, proclaiming loudly and clearly that the extremist ideas upheld by the Front did not represent France.

Finally, thanks to advances in historical scholarship, including careful studies on collaboration, anti-Semitism, resistance, and the like, we can make judgments and reach conclusions with a complexity of perspective that historians did not possess until recently. As this book will show, France was a potpourri of resisters and collaborators, anti-Semites and philo-Semites. There was no French exceptionalism, no shining Resistance movement that stood head and shoulders above the other such movements in Europe. Nor was France notorious as a nation of collaborators or anti-Semites. Put simply, France's record on these issues was no better or worse than that of other western European countries under Nazi rule, although it should be noted that such comparisons are difficult since each country faced unique situations, including moral dilemmas leading often to surprising outcomes.

Nevertheless, certain judgments can be made about this period of French history. We know, for example, that institutions failed miserably during World War II, including the military, the political system, the Vichy government, the Church, and the educational system. As we proceed, we will see that France could have won the opening battles of World War II had it not been for the total failure of military and political elites to act properly and decisively. In the Vichy regime and the National Revolution (which is the subject of the second chapter) elites offered the French little more than collaboration and exclusion as principles of governance. As a result, millions of French men and women suffered severe hardship under the draconian terms of the armistice and collaboration, while Jews, Gypsies, Freemasons, and communists were excluded from French society, incarcerated in concentration camps, and—especially in the case of the Jews—even killed. Sadly, the French Catholic Church went along with much of this, although a few members of the hierarchy spoke out against Vichy and the Nazis.

The heroes in France during World War II were not institutions but individuals and communities that acted upon their convictions, whether secular, religious, ethical, or cultural in nature. Collaboration, as the third chapter argues, was popular among only a small minority of the French. Almost from the beginning—certainly from the Montoire meeting between Pétain and Hitler in late October 1940—the French people rejected collaboration between France and Germany. Regardless of public opinion, collaboration remained a French government policy to the bitter end of the war. Nor did the French accept Vichy's anti-Semitic acts, even though the vast majority thought ill of the Jews, as numerous polls revealed during the 1930s and 1940s. As chapter 4 points out, although French gentiles were mostly unconcerned by the anti-Semitic legislation of 1940 and 1941, they overwhelmingly opposed the roundups of Jews and other anti-Semitic actions undertaken by the Vichy government beginning in 1942. Individual acts to protect the Jews helped save thousands from the Nazi extermination camps. Even Vichy listened to the outcry against the roundups of Jews and changed its policies after 1942 to thwart the Germans somewhat from achieving their goals. And finally, as the last two chapters argue, the Resistance provided the means for French men and women of all political cultures and backgrounds, from extreme right nationalists to extreme left members of the Communist Party, to oppose collaboration and the Nazis and fight for France's independence. In the end, these individuals played a major role, with the support of General de Gaulle's Free French, in liberating France from Nazi occupation and creating a renewed republic under de Gaulle's leadership. They were tarnished, imperfect heroes who made mistakes. Some of them remained ideologically close to Vichy or Pétain while others seemed more like bandits than members of an idealistic political movement. Certainly, very few of them resembled the idealized Resistance figures that de Gaulle and the Communist Party depicted after the war ended.

Whether we historians realize it or not, we search for meaning in history. We make moral judgments about the past; we evaluate people and events; and we try to tell a story that holds together. These are the objectives that we have tried to realize in the essay that follows. It is not a comprehensive account of France during World War II. For that we direct the reader to other works in the bibliography and footnotes. Instead, we have tried to tell a complex morality tale for an audience of interested lay readers and scholars who might want a succinct historical account, although not one that oversimplifies what are difficult issues. What follows is based on the best and the most recent scholarship about the period. It is not primarily a summary of that scholarship, but rather an interpretation, one that does not deviate greatly from the mainstream, but which assumes—whether rightly or wrongly—that scholarship on Vichy has come to an end point where we can say: "This history is over; its lessons can now be fully assimilated." This is one minor attempt to understand what those lessons are, based on the magnificent body of historical scholarship produced in the past forty years or so.

Finally, a note on the authorship of this book. This book is primarily the intellectual product of Thomas R. Christofferson, but Michael S. Christofferson has been given some authorial credit in reflection of his significant contribution to it. Thomas researched and wrote a draft of this book that passed Fordham University Press's peer review. At this point, Michael began to work on the project. In consultation with Thomas, Michael checked facts and revised the manuscript to reduce its size, improve its clarity, and address issues of fact and interpretation raised by Robert O. Paxton. He also researched and wrote a few additions to the text. The most important of these are discussions of interwar politics, diplomacy, and rearmament in the first chapter and the Epilogue's paragraphs on contemporary France. He also shepherded the manuscript through the production process, including bringing it into conformity with the Press's stylesheet, reviewing copyedits and page proofs, and creating the index.

Last but not least, the authors would like to thank Robert O. Paxton for his extensive and detailed comments on the manuscript. Although the authors have not always followed his expert advice, it has made this book significantly better. He, of course, is not responsible for any errors and shortcomings of this work.

This book is dedicated to Pablo and, with him, a brighter future.

France during World War II

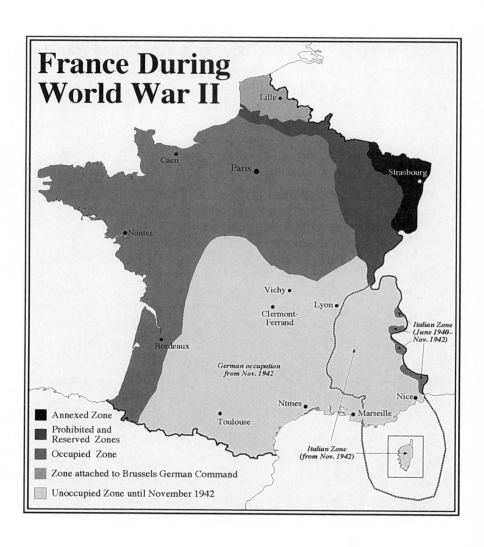

France During World War II

Lille

Caen

Paris

Strasbourg

Nantes

Vichy

Lyon

Clermont-
Ferrand

*Italian Zone
(June 1940–
Nov. 1942)*

Bordeaux

*German occupation
from Nov. 1942*

Nîmes

Nice

Toulouse

Marseille

*Italian Zone
(from Nov. 1942)*

Annexed Zone

Prohibited and
Reserved Zones

Occupied Zone

Zone attached to Brussels German Command

Unoccupied Zone until November 1942

1   **Defeat of France**

In the spring of 1940 France suffered the most humiliating defeat in its modern history as the German military overran it in a few weeks, leading to a demoralizing armistice in June. No one had expected such a devastating outcome. The western democracies, England and the United States, were stunned. Nazi Germany was ecstatic. The long, defensive war that France and England had anticipated, in light of World War I, did not occur. Instead, blitzkrieg prevailed—at least in the short run.

The effort to understand why France fell so easily to the Germans has concentrated on specific French circumstances, ranging from the thesis of internal decay to the failure of the military to prepare for the right kind of war and to respond effectively to the German invasion. Today most historians place the primary blame on the military, but in 1940 the thesis of internal decay dominated interpretation. Marshal Philippe Pétain, who became head of state in the summer of 1940, focused attention on national decadence as the cause of defeat, dismissing any criticism of the military for the national catastrophe. The so-called Vichy regime that the Marshal created in July 1940 was based solidly on the perceived necessity of rejuvenating traditional morality in order to realize national salvation.

On June 25, 1940, Marshal Pétain explained the harsh provisions of the armistice with Germany in terms of the need for a new order in France, one based on peasant values ("The earth does not lie," he exclaimed) and the rejection of the "spirit of pleasure," which had undermined the "spirit of sacrifice" during the interwar years. France's leading intellectual, André Gide, supported Pétain on this, despite his

having openly embraced homosexuality, which was considered decadent at the time. Gide wrote in his diary that the Marshal's statement
was "simply admirable." Others, more inclined to rightist views, such
as the Catholic writer Paul Claudel, expressed open disdain for the
discredited republic: "this foul parliamentary regime that for years has
been eating away at France like a generalized cancer." And Church
leaders such as Cardinal Gerlier viewed defeat as an opportunity for
spiritual renewal: "If France had been victorious it would have remained the prisoner of its errors." To most intellectuals on the Right
and some on the Left the Third Republic and its apparent decadence
were responsible for the debacle of 1940.[1]

How much truth is there to this argument? Did France lose the war
in 1940 because of internal rot, which made it unprepared for battle?
The answer is simple: Rot existed, but it explains more the reaction to
defeat than defeat itself, which was due primarily to the errors of the
military high command. To understand what this means requires more
detailed explanation.

France during the Interwar Years: An Interpretation of Some Reasons for Defeat in 1940

France came out of World War I a victorious but exhausted nation.
The war had taken such a heavy toll that the vast majority of the
French had no stomach for another. Out of a population of slightly less
than 40 million, over 1.3 million soldiers were killed, an average of 890
per day for more than four years. Another 2.8 million—40 percent of
all soldiers—were wounded one or more times. The dead soldiers left
behind approximately 600,000 widows, 760,000 orphans, and 1.3 million grieving parents. Nearly all of France mourned the loss of someone, a fact that contributed powerfully to interwar pacifism. Birth
rates, already troublingly low before 1914, suffered greatly from men
being at the front, creating "hollow years" in the late 1930s when those
born during the war reached the age of military service. Concern about
population stagnation that continued into the interwar years contributed to a postwar backlash against women and laws repressing abortion and contraception. To make up for wartime losses, France

imported laborers to work in factories and mines in the prosperous 1920s such that France surpassed the United States as the industrialized nation with the largest percentage of its population comprised of immigrants. Meanwhile, the native population was disproportionately made up of war veterans, widows, and old people. Youth comprised a definite minority in this gerontocratic society.[2]

The material costs of World War I were also important. The ten invaded departments of northern France, which had been the industrial heartland of France before the war, were devastated and had to be rebuilt. France had paid for the war by massive borrowing, turning France from a creditor into a debtor nation and unleashing inflation. By October 1920 retail prices were more than four times higher than in July 1914. France's bourgeois *rentier* class was devastated as its bonds lost much of their value. Although inflation hit workers' wages less severely than bourgeois savings, workers felt exploited by arms manufacturers who had made huge wartime profits. Peasants, in turn, resented having paid a "blood tax" in casualties that workers in factories escaped. These resentments would fuel the fascist and communist political extremes, yet bridging class differences was the consensus that the Germans should pay for the war.[3]

Disillusionment with France's victory in 1918 eventually followed from the lack of proportion between the death and destruction and France's gains.[4] At first glance, the treaties that ended World War I were extremely favorable to France. France's empire expanded with the addition of mandates in Africa and the Middle East. Alsace and Lorraine, lost in the Franco-Prussian War of 1870–71, were returned to France, and the coal-rich Saar was given to France for fifteen years in compensation for damage to French coal mines. Substantial reparations payments from Germany promised to finance reconstruction. The threat from Germany seemed much reduced due to its territorial losses, serious limits placed on its military's size and equipment, and the permanent demilitarization of the German Rhineland bordering France.

Despite these gains, the fact remains that France had won World War I only with the help of allies, and these allies were hard to find after the war. The alliance with Russia had collapsed following the

Bolshevik Revolution of 1917. Great Britain became increasingly convinced after the war that France was too harsh on Germany. France was, British Prime Minister Lloyd George remarked in March 1919, "a poor winner" that "does not take her victories well."[5] In the 1920s and 1930s France could not count on either Britain or the United States. The United States' failure to ratify the Treaty of Versailles and its retreat into isolation after the war effectively nullified an Anglo-American guarantee of French security made at the Paris peace conference. As France would learn in its unsuccessful attempt to force Germany to pay reparations by occupying the Ruhr in 1923, without allies France's victory of 1918 could easily be reversed. Given Germany's larger population and stronger economy, the prospect of German revival was frightening.

Although social and political tensions abated in the prosperity of the mid 1920s, the Great Depression gave them new life. The impact of the depression in France was somewhat different from that in other industrialized countries. It became serious in France only beginning in 1931—later than elsewhere—was less sharp, and resulted in lower levels of unemployment. Workers, whose real wages fared well as prices declined, were not hit as hard as farmers and the lower middle class of artisans and small businessmen. The depression also lasted longer in France than it did elsewhere. While Britain and Germany saw recovery in the mid-1930s, France did not until the acceleration of rearmament in late 1938.[6]

The long duration of the depression in France was partially due to the political response to it. With the exception of the Popular Front period of 1936–37, the government followed a policy of deflation and refused to follow other countries in devaluing its currency, thereby rendering French exports uncompetitive. This orthodox remedy comforted a bourgeoisie fearful of a return to inflation, but only worsened an economy that needed demand stimulation. Political crisis resulted. Following the success of the Left in the 1932 elections a second wave of fascist agitation, after that of 1924–26, hit France. Older fascistic groups such as Action française and the Jeunesses patriotes gained new support, and new ones emerged such as Solidarité française, founded in 1933, and Croix de feu, a veterans organization turned into a politically ambitious fascist league by Colonel de La Rocque after he took charge of it in 1931. The mobilization of these and other protest groups against the left-center governments of 1932–34 culminated in the riots of February 6, 1934, in which seventeen people were killed, the most deaths in Parisian political violence since the 1871 Commune.[7] The February 6 riots intensified the political crisis. Although the violence resulted in the resignation of the government and the return of the Right to power, this did not diminish the strength of the extreme right, as the Right's return to government had in 1926. Croix de feu, in particular, grew dramatically from 35,000 members before the riots to 500,000 members in February 1936 to become the most important fascist movement in France.[8] On the Left, the riots were interpreted as an attempted fascist coup d'état and created a dynamic favorable to a Popular Front coalition against fascism. This was given a crucial push forward by the Comintern and French Communist Party's June 1934 abandonment of "class against class" politics, which saw the main enemy as social democracy, in favor of forging a United Front against fascism. Ultimately bringing together the Communist, Socialist, and Radical parties, the Popular Front would win the May 1936 elections on a reformist and antifascist program, which notably called for an end to deflationary economic policies.[9]

The 1936–37 Popular Front government led by the socialist Léon Blum was a mixture of successes and failures. Following massive June 1936 strikes by workers seeking to capitalize on the Left's electoral victory, workers gained a forty-hour work week, two weeks of paid vacation, union and collective bargaining rights, and significant pay raises. The Popular Front's dissolution of the fascist leagues and more generally its commitment to the defense of democracy over the promotion of revolution helped prevent fascism from taking power in 1930s France. But the Popular Front was less successful in dealing with the depression. Its efforts to stimulate the economy were hindered by Blum's initial refusal to countenance a devaluation of the currency without which exports could not be revived. Further, the forty-hour week had the unintended consequence of hindering French industry from meeting domestic demand. Also, although the Popular Front had stymied fascism in the short term, it further polarized French politics. Many in the middle class saw a breakdown of social order in the strikes and reforms of the Popular Front. Anticommunism grew within both the Right and the Left in reaction to the Communist Party (PCF) electoral breakthrough in the 1936 elections and out of fear that the communists might push France into an antifascist war. Particularly notable was the Radical Party's shift from Popular Front ally of the communists in 1936 to vehement anticommunism by 1938.[10] One beneficiary of the rise of anticommunism was Colonel de La Rocque's arguably fascist Parti social français founded in 1936 after the Popular Front banned the fascist leagues including Croix de feu. Feeding on fear of the Popular Front, it became France's largest political party with perhaps as many as 1 million members in 1938.[11]

The Popular Front government, in the true sense of the term, lasted barely a year, as the Radicals deserted the cause and the Socialists under Léon Blum squabbled among themselves over policy and gave up hope of continuing in office in the face of a financial crisis they could not resolve. The Popular Front came to a definite end when the radical Edouard Daladier formed a government without socialist members in April 1938, which proceeded to reverse key Popular Front reforms in late 1938. In the name of national defense, Daladier's Minster of Finance Paul Reynaud issued decrees in November 1938 that restored the forty-eight-hour workweek and increased taxes on salaried employees. The unions' general strike of November 30, 1930, to protest Reynaud's policies failed miserably and led to a massive decline in union membership: the largest union, the Confédération générale du travail (CGT), lost 1 million members within a year.[12] Daladier's successful assault on labor led capital, which had fled France during the Popular Front, to flow back into the country. This plus a massive increase in rearmament spending helped pull France out of the depression in 1939.

Especially on the Right, World War I, the Great Depression, and the Popular Front fueled a critique of decadent France and a defense of "True France"[13] that was key to defining the agenda of the Vichy regime that emerged from France's defeat in 1940. For many, this critique of decadent France focused on the interwar crisis of rural France, which was quite real. Facing declining commodity prices and starved of needed capital, agriculture suffered in the interwar years. Cultivated land declined by 1.7 million hectares in the 1920s and 1930s, and the agricultural workforce fell from 42 to 36 percent of all workers between 1921 and 1936. The rural commune lost its reason to be as rural industries shut down and schools and churches closed their doors. Village festivals and customs, such as the evening social gatherings at home, known as the *veillée,* faded away as only the old were left to carry on tradition. Radio, the press, the cinema, and other forces of modernity undermined peasant society and culture.[14]

To many, the decline of peasant France meant the decline of True France, of France itself. World War I had been won by the peasants who comprised half of the frontline troops by 1918. Super nationalists, such as Maurice Barrès, marveled at the eternal spiritual traits that these men displayed and imagined the joy that they would experience in future commemorations of the war. Yet the interwar reality was quite different as joy turned to pacifism and the eternal values of the countryside, such as patriarchy, collapsed. Tradition-minded Catholics tried to counter this trend, creating the Catholic Agricultural Youth movement (JACistes) to preserve the traditional Catholic nature of the countryside. Various corporatist groups emerged, such as the Semaines sociales de France and the Union nationale des syndicats agricoles. They opposed both socialism and parliamentary government, favoring instead a union of peasants and landowners in one corporate body that would make decisions for all rural interests. In a more radical vein, the peasant party led by Henri Dorgères used quasi-fascist violent direct action to achieve its objectives. The common thread running through all of these organizations was the failure of normal institutions to deal with the crisis of agriculture. Political parties, parliamentary government, and the State were incapable of resolving this crisis, according to them. Only a rupture—a radical break from past practices—could preserve the values of True France.[15]

The peasant France that these groups projected as a model was a static France for the most part, opposed to capitalism, the Republic, and modernity. They did not understand that World War I and international economic forces had irreparably damaged their model. But this blindness was not confined to the countryside. Many urban intellectuals also suffered from nostalgia for the archaic. Behind debates about the school system, the Americanization of French culture, immigration, and parliamentary government lurked a vision of utopian, rural France. Decadence was urban; authenticity was peasant and rural. Or at least this was true among those on the Right, the defenders of the old order against the new. In the 1920s and 1930s, however, it seemed that most were on the side of tradition and nostalgia.

The republican school system was a particular target of conservatives, who attacked it for undermining traditional values. Marshal Pétain complained that the schools had abandoned spirituality. Many, including Charles Maurras, the leader of the quasi-fascist Action française, agreed with him. Others focused on what the schools taught. The 1902 law that allowed secondary students to opt out of learning Greek and Latin became the focus of conservatives who feared that the French language would atrophy without ties to the Latin mother tongue. Still others, like Abel Bonnard, author of *In Praise of Ignorance* who became minister of education under the Vichy regime, linked the republican system of education with a "civilization of half-breeds." Bonnard deplored the pernicious influence of primary school teachers who encouraged students to have high expectations. He wanted the schools to teach students to be content and accept their station in life in order to revive the pre-1789 hierarchical social order. Alexis Carrel, recipient of the Nobel Prize in biology, supported Bonnard's views on education. Carrel believed in rule by a genetically selected scientific elite of which peasants and workers could never be part due to their biological inferiority. Only the elite could be educated, he claimed. Carrel and the opponents of the republican school system believed that universal education was not only unnecessary but also destructive. To them egalitarianism was nothing but demagoguery; all societies needed educated, ruling elites to preserve the social order against the forces of egalitarianism and anarchy.[16]

The fear of modernity also prevailed among those who warned against the danger of Americanization, which emerged during the interwar period as one of the main enemies of True France. The anti-Semitic novelist Louis-Ferdinand Céline found nothing but materialist vulgarity in Henry Ford's America. His virulent fictional attack was matched by such popular nonfiction works as Georges Duhamel's *Scènes de la vie future* (1930), which depicted the United States as a barbaric and soulless threat to French civilization, and Robert Aron and Arnaud Dandieu's *Le Cancer américain* (1931), which called for a French spiritual revolution to overcome the cancer of American culture. These writers and many others searched for some third way, between American capitalism and Soviet communism, beyond France's failed liberal parliamentary form of government. Spiritual renewal comprised a major part of their answer to the crisis of modernity, whether in the form of Emmanuel Mounier's personalism, which placed the individual before society, or Thierry Maulnier's corporatism, which was based on a strong state. "Neither Right nor Left" served as an appropriate slogan for many of the new intellectuals who emerged on the French scene in the early 1930s.[17]

Scapegoating became increasingly common in the 1930s to explain how and why the True France of the peasantry or the Church or social cohesion or the nation had been undermined. In the simplistic analysis of some, the nation's ills could be cured only if the Jew, the communist, or the capitalist were eliminated. The Republic turned from welcoming outsiders—especially if they were European in origin—in the 1920s, to virtually complete intolerance toward them by the end of the 1930s. As early as 1927, the year in which the government passed a liberal naturalization law, the geographer André Siegfried published an academic work which warned that France risked becoming a decadent polyglot nation, like the United States, if it continued to allow immigration. Once the depression began, the slogan "France for the French" became common, and hundreds of thousands of immigrant workers were forced to leave to open up jobs for the native-born. The watchdogs of citizenship increasingly insisted that immigrants who wanted to be naturalized had to be assimilated into the culture. But they doubted this was possible in light of the failure of colonial subjects to do so. Beginning in 1933 the minister of the interior required prefects to keep detailed records on all foreigners, similar to those kept on criminals. By World War II, the French police possessed five times more dossiers on foreigners than Mussolini had on his political enemies.[18]

The nation's elites were hardly immune to this anti-immigrant mood. During the 1930s, doctors and lawyers successfully lobbied for laws that prevented newly naturalized citizens from practicing medicine or the law. French civil servants also succeeded in keeping immigrants out of jobs in the state bureaucracy. By the mid-1930s the naturalized French were effectively second-class citizens because the law excluded them from a large part of French life.[19]

As World War II approached immigrant Jews were singled out for harsh treatment. Although the nation had welcomed Jewish refugees in 1933, by 1938 this was no longer the case. Even French Jews went along with the new restrictive policies of the Daladier government, which created internment camps in November 1938 to handle those refugees who could not be deported. Jews made up many of the internees, but they were soon outnumbered by the flight of nearly 500,000 Spaniards into France after the end of the Spanish Civil War. In desperation, the Daladier government planned to settle thousands of refugees in the colonies, notably in Madagascar and New Caledonia.[20] Although the vast majority of immigrants in France were Italians and Spanish—they were 2.2 million in 1936—the 60,000 Jews who obtained asylum after the Nazis seized power became the focus of abuse by the late 1930s. For one, most were German. As one journalist noted: "French Jews complain that the newcomers have brought with them the particular faults of the Germans. Too noisy, too convinced of the superiority of German civilization. In brief—veritable 'Boches.'" For another, they were associated with the war party in France. In the late 1930s a number of pacifist philo-Semitic publications turned against the Jews in their advocacy of peace at any price. The radical newspaper *L'Ère nouvelle,* which had a Jewish editor, was one of the most prominent of these. Even socialists espoused anti-Semitic views. The leader of the pacifist wing of the Socialist Party, Paul Faure, attacked the party's Jewish leader, Léon Blum, claiming that he "would have us all killed for his Jews." In 1938, with France on the verge of war with Germany, mobs attacked Jewish communities in Rouen, Dijon, Lille, and Nancy. In this climate of growing pacifist anti-Semitism, Prime Minister Edouard Daladier refused to condemn the Nazi pogrom of *Kristallnacht* because his government valued good relations with Germany above concerns for German Jews. Daladier's foreign minister, Georges Bonnet, replied to press attacks on the government's silence by accusing the Jews and the communists of trying to undermine him.[21]

The banality of anti-Semitism in the late 1930s meant that no one feared ostracism for expressing the most outlandish sentiments about Jews. Robert Brasillach, a leading intellectual, could write in the extreme right journal *Je suis partout* that all Jews should be deprived of citizenship, yet remain respectable enough to be nominated, on the eve of World War II, for the Goncourt literary prize for his pro-fascist novel *Les Sept Couleurs.* Sadly, French elites in the 1930s did not view anti-Semitism as a serious problem; in fact, most French leaders accepted, at a minimum, a mild form of it. Even a majority of non-Jews who supported Dreyfus in 1898 had become anti-Semitic out of pacifism by the late 1930s, revealing clearly that Vichy France cannot be understood adequately as the revenge of the anti-Dreyfusards.[22]

The mentality of an isolationist, peasant France infused these misguided attitudes about Jews and immigrants during the 1930s, blocking out the inevitable reality that France was part of a broader world, one that included not only the rest of Europe but also the forces of modernization, industrialization, and urbanization. Although not everyone fell into the xenophobic, racist style of analysis, many accepted a fundamentalist form of pacifism, which was as much a part of the True France mentality as anti-Semitic or anti-immigrant attitudes. In 1936 Roger Martin du Gard, the well-known and respected novelist, wrote: "Anything rather than war! Anything! . . . even Fascism in Spain . . . even Fascism in France: Nothing, no trial, no servitude can be compared to war: Anything, Hitler rather than war!"[23] He was not alone. In the same year, the Provençal novelist Jean Giono wrote: "For my part, I prefer being a living German to being a dead

Frenchman."[24] For the pacifist philosopher Alain, whose ideas shaped the Radical Party, rearmament represented a form of fascism. For others on the extreme right, such as Thierry Maulnier, war against Germany was out of the question for it would weaken the one major bulwark against the spread of communism in Europe. Except for the Communist Party, no political party or major institutional force overcame pacifist reservations before the Munich agreement of 1938 to assert unambiguously the need to stand up to fascism in Europe. Pacifism contributed to the shortcomings of French foreign policy in the run-up to war.

When France went to war in 1939 it had only one major ally, Great Britain. This was, in part, a reflection of the inherent difficulties of France's diplomatic position when Hitler began to threaten the peace in the mid-1930s. The Bolshevik Revolution had brought an end to the Russian alliance, which had been key to France's survival in World War I. The alliances France constructed in the 1920s with the successor states of the Habsburg Empire (Poland, Czechoslovakia, Romania, and Yugoslavia) were of limited utility given these states' weaknesses and quarrels among themselves. Getting Great Britain to commit to an alliance with France was itself a difficult chore and indeed a real accomplishment, but the nurturing of relations with Britain was clearly a drag on the rest of French foreign policy. Yet, if France entered World War II with too few allies, this was only partially due to the difficult constellation of international forces. In addition to pacifism, internal French political dynamics and military weakness in the early years of Hitler's foreign policy offensive contributed to France's deteriorating international position. We can see how French foreign policy came up short by looking at its failure to secure alliances with Italy and the Soviet Union and to resist both Germany's remilitarization of the Rhineland in March 1936 and Germany's demand to take the Sudetenland from Czechoslovakia in 1938.

Although Italy was the "least of the great powers,"[25] it was a valuable potential ally of France. It had proven helpful after entering World War I on the French side in May 1915. An alliance with Italy would allow France to move resources from protecting its southeastern border and North African empire to the front with Germany. It would also facilitate linkages with central European allies such as Yugoslavia. Shared concerns about German rearmament made a Franco-Italian rapprochement seem possible in 1934–35. Talks in January 1935 between French Prime Minister Pierre Laval and Italy's fascist dictator Benito Mussolini resulted in a preliminary agreement that only the French communists opposed. Germany's announcement of extensive rearmament in March 1935 was met by France, Britain, and Italy uniting in the Stresa Front to condemn Germany's violation of the Treaty of Versailles and Franco-Italian discussions regarding military cooperation. This progress in Franco-Italian relations was reversed by Italy's invasion of Ethiopia in October 1935. Although the French government did not wish to oppose the invasion, Britain's importance as a potential ally compelled it to support the British initiative to impose League of Nations sanctions on Italy. The subsequent election of the Popular Front in France and Italy's intervention in the Spanish Civil War resulted in the collapse of Franco-Italian relations, after which an alliance was impossible. It may be that Mussolini's desire to inject dynamism into Italian fascism through external aggression made a Franco-Italian alliance unlikely, but what little chance there had been for it was clearly lost over the sanctions issue. In any event, the Ethiopian affair marked the beginning of a shift in the domestic politics of French foreign policy. While some on the Left were moving away from pacifism out of antifascism, a significant pacifist current emerged for the first time on the Right which rejected sanctions out of sympathy for fascism and fear that the Left would drive France into an antifascist war. Many on the Right would continue to push for an Italian alliance long after it had lost any prospect of success. This pacifist turn of right-wing opinion would remain important at least through 1938 and influence French foreign policy choices.[26]

This ideological dimension of French foreign policy contributed to France's failure to secure an alliance with the Soviet Union. The French elite had many grievances against the Soviet regime: its refusal to honor Czarist bonds (which the French bourgeoisie had purchased in large quantities), its exit from World War I, and its advocacy of world

revolution. Consequently, although France recognized the bolshevik regime in 1924, the hostility of the Right and the issue of the bonds
prevented a significant improvement in relations during the 1920s. The
rise of Hitler resulted in more serious Franco-Soviet discussions, especially under French Foreign Minister Louis Barthou in 1934. After Barthou's assassination in October 1934, Laval concluded the negotiations
and signed a Franco-Soviet Pact of Mutual Assistance in May 1935, but
Laval, along with the military and Quai d'Orsay foreign policy establishment, did not follow up on it. Laval reportedly said that a further improvement of Franco-Soviet relations would bring "the International
and the red flag" to France, a view echoed by the large right-wing vote
against the pact when it came before the Senate in March 1936, just
days after Hitler had remilitarized the Rhineland. The conservative military's General Staff blocked staff talks out of fear of communist subver-
sion and a conviction that the Soviet military was weak and useless.
The Popular Front, despite its antifascism and the Soviet Union's eager-
ness to secure a military alliance, did little to further it. The military
and the Quai continued to obstruct it, and the cabinet was divided.
Many on the Left, like the Popular Front Foreign Minister Yvon Delbos
and Paul Faure, shared with the Right the fear that the Soviet Union
sought to drag France into an antifascist war. Thus the progress of relations with the Soviet Union stalled until Hitler's March 1939 occupation
of Prague led to new talks. Even then, Franco-British negotiations with
the Soviets continued to be dilatory and marked by mistrust. They
floundered on the issue of Red Army access to Poland. It was too little
too late. In August the Nazi-Soviet Pact was signed.[27]

Germany's March 1936 remilitarization of the Rhineland was its
first territorial revision of the Treaty of Versailles. France's failure to
resist it was of enormous importance. Remilitarization deprived
France of the ability to assist its central European allies by easily occupying the Rhineland, and France's inaction cast doubt on its willingness to resist German aggression. France's passive reaction was
overdetermined by a series of diplomatic, political, economic, and military factors. France was certainly weakened by lack of support from
its Stresa Front partners, Britain and Italy, but the tendency of French

politicians to blame Britain disguised more profound domestic issues. France's pacifist population was firmly opposed to war in 1936. How could the caretaker government of the time risk going to war on the eve of the 1936 elections when, as the satirical *Le Canard enchaîné* joked, the Germans had invaded Germany? Further, given the perilous state of French finances, mobilization for war would almost certainly have sparked a financial crisis. Military factors loomed large. The French military grossly overestimated the strength of the invading German army and had a keen sense of France's lack of military preparedness. Budget cuts in the deflationary early 1930s had resulted in the cancellation of weapons orders and field maneuvers as well as a reduction of personnel and their pay. Finally, the military lacked the capacity to fight a limited war. Mobilization plans for total war called for active divisions to split in three to form the core of new divisions of citizen soldiers. If the active divisions were thrown into a limited war, this risked compromising any future general mobilization. Thus France's top general, General Gamelin, told the government that military action could be taken against the Germans only if the reserves were called up first. Of course, this was not done. The remilitarization of the Rhineland was followed by Belgium's declaration of neutrality in October 1936, making 1936 a disastrous year for France's strategic position.[28]

Germany's annexation of Czechoslovakia's Sudetenland, which France and Great Britain accepted at the infamous Munich Conference on September 30, 1938, was an even greater setback. In 1938 Germany and Czechoslovakia had, we now know, roughly equivalent armies. The German tank divisions and air support that formed the basis of the blitzkrieg tactics of 1939 were not yet ready for combat, and Czechoslovakia's frontier fortifications were formidable. The Czechs were prepared to got to war, and the Soviet Union—like France—was bound by treaty to fight with them, but neither would fight without France. France's failure to break with Britain and stand by Czechoslovakia left it without important continental allies and alienated the Soviet Union, which was not consulted on the matter. It also strengthened Hitler domestically, effectively bringing an end to army coup plots against him. Finally, it allowed Germany to seize Czechoslovakia's substantial military and industrial resources, including tanks used against France in 1940.[29]

France's failure to support Czechoslovakia was due to many of the same factors that influenced its decision making in 1936: pacifist public opinion, a sense of military weakness, and—more so than in 1936—deference to Britain. Only two deputies outside of the Communist Party voted against the Munich Accords in the Chamber of Deputies. The rest followed public opinion, which initially favored Munich—57 percent approved and 37 percent disapproved of the agreement according to one poll. Prime Minister Daladier and his government were more conflicted than the Chamber of Deputies or the public. One faction led by Foreign Minister Georges Bonnet favored appeasement, and another led by Colonial Minister Georges Mandel and Justice Minister Paul Reynaud was ready to go to war. Daladier eventually sided with Bonnet in this case, but did not share his illusions. He understood that Munich had only bought France time to prepare for war. Met by cheering crowds on his return from Munich, Daladier called them "blind fools" and said: "This is only a respite, and if we don't make use of it, we will all be shot."[30]

Daladier's acceptance of the Munich agreement was due in large part to military and strategic considerations. The French military told him that it was not ready for war, and that if war were declared, it would be two years before a serious offensive was possible. Particularly troubling was the prediction of General Vuillemin that the French air force he commanded would be wiped out in the first fifteen days. These grim reports only reinforced Daladier's conviction that France could not go to war without Britain. Thus Daladier allowed British Prime Minister Neville Chamberlain to take the lead in discussions with Hitler and accepted the capitulation to Hitler that resulted.[31]

After Munich, France's posture changed dramatically. Opinion immediately began to shift against pacifist refusal of war. An October 1938 poll showed 70 percent in favor of resisting further German demands. Most of those on the Right who had turned to pacifism out of anticommunism moved away from it after Daladier's government

crushed the French labor movement. Hitler's seizure of Prague solidified this turn away from pacifism. In the course of 1939, veterans,
school teachers, and peasants—all of whom had been overwhelmingly
pacifist—mostly resigned themselves to the necessity of war. In July
1939, 76 percent of those polled believed that France should use force
to stop a German seizure of Danzig. When Paul Faure proclaimed that
Danzig was not worth "the death of a single Macon *vigneron*" and the
fascist leader Marcel Déat rejected war in his famous article "To Die
for Danzig?" they were in the minority. This turn in opinion mirrored
a shift in government policy. A huge increase in rearmament spending
followed Munich. Finally, in the spring of 1939 the Franco-British alliance came together. In late March, following Hitler's occupation of
Prague, serious joint military planning began, and a joint Franco-
British guarantee of Poland's security was issued. When war broke out
in September 1939 following Germany's invasion of Poland, France
was reasonably well prepared for it. Its population was resigned to its
necessity; no more dodged the draft than in 1914 (1.5 percent). France
had secured an important ally, and its rearmament effort had, as we
shall see, been largely successful. Nonetheless, France's pacifism, military weakness, and foreign policy failures in the 1930s had left it worse
off going into war than it might have otherwise been.[32]

When the battle came to French soil in May 1940, fundamental
shortcomings were exposed in France's military, but these shortcomings were not those common in popular contemporary American images of France. The Maginot Line fortifications neither made the
French overconfident nor gave them a bunker mentality. The French
were not deficient in courage after years of pacifism. Nor did the
French fail to build tanks and otherwise modernize their weaponry
and strengthen their military. The fundamental failing, as Marc Bloch
recognized in his classic account of the defeat, was one of intelligence.[33] The French high command failed to see how much new technology, notably the tank, changed warfare from what it was in World
War I.[34]

Rearmament, although clearly inadequate at the time of the 1936
Rhineland and the 1938 Sudetenland crises, was an overall success by

September 1939. In general, the French military was well funded in the interwar period. Between 1918 and 1935, France exceeded other great powers in the percentage of its GNP spent on the military. After cuts during the deflationary first years of the depression, serious rearmament began under the Popular Front, which appropriated 14 billion francs in September 1936 and nationalized armaments factories (notably tank and aircraft makers). Nationalization helped in the long run by rationalizing and modernizing production, but in the short run it slowed output. Indeed, between 1936 and 1938 tank production declined despite greatly increased funding. Only in 1939 did arms production hit its stride. The results were generally encouraging. In the battle of May–June 1940 France had slightly more tanks than the Germans, and French tanks were of higher quality. Indeed, the Germans lost the largest tank battle of the campaign, the battle of Hannut in Belgium, in which Germany's best tanks were simply outclassed. The French army was even more motorized than the German, which relied heavily on horses: hundreds of thousands of them. Finally, France had 45 percent more artillery pieces than the Germans, although it was deficient in antitank and antiaircraft guns.[35]

The only serious deficiency of French arms was its air force. Germany had twice as many fighters and over six times as many bombers as France did. Although British planes committed to the continent made up some of the difference, France had a clear—although by no means fatal—disadvantage in the skies. The shortage of military aircraft followed largely from the difficulty reorganizing the artisanal French aircraft industry for mass production. Nationalization helped achieve this, but only in 1939 did the industry begin to produce large numbers of planes. In this sector an earlier commitment to rearmament would have made a difference.[36]

The fundamental shortcoming of the French military lay in its belief that the next war would be very similar in nature to the last. France would fight a long defensive war in which it would prevail due to its superior resources: thus the importance placed on the British alliance. Defensive firepower would make the next war—like the last—one of attrition. Tanks, General Gamelin said in 1937, could be stopped by antitank guns "as the infantry had been by the machine gun." Yet,

France did not plan to simply hunker down and wait for the Germans. The Maginot Line fortifications on the French border between Switzerland and Belgium were built in order to channel the German offensive through Belgium and free up soldiers for active operations elsewhere. France's plan in the event of a German attack on neutral Belgium was to speed motorized troops into Belgium to take up advanced positions and hopefully thereby avoid fighting on French soil. While committed to mechanization, the military did not believe that a decisive breakthrough of enemy lines by motorized troops could be achieved. Consequently, France's seven motorized infantry divisions were to use their mobility solely to advance rapidly into Belgium where they would fight like conventional infantry. French tanks were seen as a support for infantry and mostly integrated into infantry divisions. When the battle began in May 1940 France had only three light armored and three heavy armored divisions, which included only one-third of its tanks. Germany, by contrast, put all of its tanks in ten panzer divisions.[37]

French military doctrine emphasized what it called *bataille conduite* or methodical battle. Battles were supposed to be tightly controlled by the generals with soldiers following timetables prepared in advance. Improvisation was discouraged. It was assumed that this, rather than unpredictable encounter battles, would make the best use of France's inexperienced citizen soldiers. Because of this doctrine and a concern about information security, the French army failed to develop flexible communications, notably radio. Communications equipment accounted for only 0.15 percent of military spending between 1923 and 1939. During the war General Gamelin communicated to his subordinates by telephone and courier. This worked fine as long as plans were followed, but if the French army had to respond to a rapidly changing situation its command and control was liable to break down. In the end, the French military's poor use of modern technology and inflexible structure would be key factors in France's defeat.[38]

Strange Defeat, 1939–1940

When war broke out in September 1939 serious divisions existed in France. Despite hopes for patriotic unity in the face of national crisis, the Sacred Union of World War I did not reemerge to overcome political differences. The Daladier government continued to govern from the Right. It kept the socialists out of the government and took advantage of the Nazi-Soviet Pact signed on August 24, 1939, to launch an anticommunist crusade. Although leading communists reaffirmed their loyalty to France on August 25, on August 26 the government issued a decree repressing the communist press and communist meetings. On September 26 the PCF itself was outlawed despite the fact that its parliamentary delegation voted unanimously for war credits and had continued to support French national defense throughout September. Even after the PCF leadership adopted a revolutionary defeatist position in October and the police began to arrest communists in large numbers, the party posed little threat to national security because rank and file communists overwhelmingly supported the war effort. No organized communist movement existed in the ranks of the army, and communists did not sabotage the factories. Still, the military feared a communist plot to seize Paris to the very end of the war. As late as June 13, 1940, General Weygand informed the cabinet that the communists were taking over the capital, and Admiral Darlan maintained that the Germans had transported PCF leader Maurice Thorez from Moscow to Paris in order to make him president of France. Both were unfounded rumors.[39]

Foreigners were also feared, especially the 400,000 who lived in the Paris region. Immediately after the war began the government transformed the internment camps—originally created in November 1938 to house refugees—into prisons for male enemy aliens, most of whom had fled Nazi Germany. Soon almost 20,000 foreigners were crowded into eighty camps. As a result of massive criticism from abroad and complaints from members of the French parliament, all but 6,428 were released by February 1940. Approximately 9,000 of them joined the French Foreign Legion to fight against the Nazis, revealing the government's failure to distinguish between friend and foe in this case. The unfounded fear of a fifth column seeking to sabotage French military efforts emerged effortlessly out of interwar anti-immigrant attitudes. It was a major factor behind the government's decision to allow the stripping of citizenship from naturalized individuals suspected of endangering national security. It continued to influence government policy even after the 1939 roundups had been discredited: another 8,000 "Greater Germans," 5,000 of whom were Jews, were interred when fighting began in May 1940. They were considered to be security risks by a government whose feelings of insecurity had become systemic.[40]

While the overwhelming majority of France's citizens, immigrants, and refugees supported war against Germany despite everything the government did, the political and military elites failed to act forcefully to defeat the enemy. The French and British did nothing to help the Poles, maintaining in a September 12, 1939, communiqué that the "war will be won on the western front." Above all, the French government wanted security, as Daladier made clear in his response to Hitler's peace proposals after the Polish campaign. In a radio address to the French nation, on October 10, 1939, Daladier revealed that he would not cease hostilities "without first having received sure guarantees of security."[41] Security was what Marshal Pétain had in mind in September 1939 when he wrote to General Gamelin, the head of the French military command: "I hope that you will not be foolish enough to take the offensive against the German army."[42] He did not have to worry, for Gamelin fully supported the Anglo-French strategy of fighting a long war of attrition. Since Allied prospects in such a war appeared to be excellent, the French were unwilling to risk a major offensive.

In retrospect, this strategy appears misguided. It put France on the defensive and deprived it of an early opportunity to defeat Germany. In the fall of 1939 the Germans deployed their best divisions on the Polish front, leaving thirty-three relatively weak ones, with virtually no tank or air support, to defend their western frontier. In contrast, the French had seventy divisions with 3,000 tanks and ample air support behind them. Furthermore, the Polish campaign was not as easy as it seemed: by the end of it the Germans had only six weeks of oil reserves and their tanks and planes were in no condition to turn around and fight in the west. The Wehrmacht's military leaders told Hitler that they could not be prepared for war against France until the spring of 1940. Yet Gamelin did nothing to take advantage of the situation, and virtually no one challenged him to pursue the offensive. It seems that Colonel Charles de Gaulle, whose ideas were rejected by the elite, was the only significant military leader to speak out against this policy. In January 1940 he wrote: "In the present conflict, as in those that have gone before it, being inert means being beaten."[43]

As a result of French and British concerns about taking the offensive, the "phony war" (*drôle de guerre* in French) ensued, lasting until the Germans attacked on May 10, 1940. The French and British governments used this period to step up military production at home and supplement it with purchases from the United States. But the Germans produced more deployable tanks and planes than the French did. They turned out over 600 tanks in the two months before fighting began in 1940, compared to about 560 for the French, and about three times more airplanes during the September 1939–May 1940 period. For whatever reason, approximately 20 percent of all French planes were not airworthy when the Germans invaded, while almost all of the German planes were in flying condition. This was true even for planes recently delivered to the French air force from the factory; they often lacked crucial pieces of equipment. By June, 60 percent of French military aircraft could not be used in fighting. If the war had lasted until July, nothing would have been left of the French air force. Waiting did not work for this aspect of the French war effort.[44]

Waiting was also detrimental to morale. In September 1939 the rank and file French soldier clearly believed that France would prevail despite Germany's larger population and greater resources. By Christmas, however, both the troops and the civilian population began to have reservations about this "phony war," and morale plummeted. It would only revive with the improvement of the weather in the spring. Daladier was sensitive to this and attempted to overcome negative attitudes by enlarging the anticommunist crusade and committing France to support the popular cause of underdog Finland in its war against the Soviet Union. In a secret session of the Chamber of Deputies in February 1940, Daladier obtained enthusiastic, unanimous support for his plan to back the Finns. But he hesitated to act, partly because of British doubts, and by the time he decided, the Finns had capitulated to the Soviets. Within a week after this, on March 19, 1940, Daladier resigned under a storm of criticism over his handling of the Finnish situation and other matters.[45]

During the winter of 1939–40, Daladier and Gamelin grasped at straws as they sought alternatives to direct confrontation with Nazi Germany. In addition to the bungled Finnish campaign they also relied heavily—too heavily—on French intelligence reports that Germany was on the verge of economic collapse due to the Anglo-French blockade and that war was so unpopular among the Germans that Hitler would be overthrown as soon as things went bad. Daladier attempted to stop the Germans from obtaining Swedish iron ore, which he assumed was so vital for the war effort that lack of it would force the Nazis to capitulate by September 1940. But the surprise German invasion of Norway and Denmark in April dashed all hopes for this scenario. Similarly, plans to divert the war to the Balkans and to deny Germany access to Soviet oil from the Caucasus—both pie-in-the-sky schemes—came to naught in this winter of endless waiting.[46]

The lack of a coherent military strategy, other than the dubious strategies of waiting and defense, was matched by similar weaknesses in politics. Having solidified his government with anticommunism and having refused to reach out to the socialists, Daladier relied on the Right's support, but it was fickle. Pierre Laval criticized him for not pursuing an unlikely Italian alliance, which he believed was essential for French victory. Marshal Pétain helped undermine the French war effort by telling the Italian ambassador in November 1939 that the "present conflict is not good for France, even if she succeeds in winning a conclusive victory." He later said the same thing to the Germans. Pierre-Étienne Flandin, with support from Laval and others on the Right, advocated French neutrality while the Germans and Soviets fought over Central Europe. Meanwhile, Daladier found it increasingly difficult to govern his unruly cabinet. Paul Reynaud, the second in command, was an especially troublesome thorn in his side. When the Daladier government collapsed in March 1940, it was replaced immediately by one with Reynaud as prime minister and Daladier as minister of war. The Reynaud government obtained power with only a one-vote margin of victory in the Chamber of Deputies, despite the fact that France was at war. Radicals, who believed Reynaud had engineered Daladier's fall, voted against it as did many on the Right upset with socialist participation in Reynaud's government.[47]

Daladier had ruled almost exclusively by decree; parliament was so divided that nothing of importance could be approved through normal democratic means. Reynaud continued this high-handed form of governance, with some new twists. For almost a month, from April 14 to May 9, Reynaud held no cabinet meetings. He communicated with Daladier in writing, never in person, even though Daladier was in charge of military policy and France was at war. In political circles Reynaud was viewed as a "relatively dangerous marginal" politician. Indeed, Reynaud, lacking a significant political base of his own, had to keep Daladier in the government in order to secure minimal radical support. On May 9, Reynaud tried to resolve the political deadlock by resigning with the intention of forming a new government without Daladier. Although the resignation was reversed the next day, France technically lacked a government when the German invasion began. In sum, the government that fought the battle of France was a politically precarious one, whose members did not speak to each other, and which acted only through decrees.[48]

Communication and intelligence were also lacking in military circles. Gamelin was notorious for keeping close counsel. From his office in Vincennes, just outside of Paris, he issued directives to the army without consulting his key officers or venturing to the front lines. His relations with his subordinates were frayed at best; many of them lacked confidence in him. In January 1940, he decided on a military strategy of forward defense in the Netherlands, against the advice of his military staff, which preferred the Escaut Plan, which would have concentrated troops around Lille where they could have stopped the German offensive. The Dyle-Breda variant, as Gamelin's strategy was called, moved motorized divisions, which had been part of the strategic reserve, forward into the Low Countries. This would lead the French military into a disastrous situation by the end of May as the reserve needed to stop the German breakthrough was inadequate and these forward troops were trapped by the German march to the English Channel.[49]

Gamelin's biggest mistake was to misjudge where the German offensive would occur. De Gaulle said of Gamelin: "He had persuaded himself that, at his level, the essential thing was to fix one's purpose, once for all, upon a well-defined plan and then not to let oneself be deflected from it by any avatar."[50] Certainly this was true of how Gamelin reacted to the intelligence information he received about a possible German advance through the Ardennes. As early as April 12, 1940, the General Staff received a highly reliable intelligence document that indicated that the Germans were concentrating on breaking through Luxembourg and crossing the Meuse around Sedan in northern France rather than on a maneuver through Belgium similar to the Schlieffen Plan of World War I. But the General Staff did not take this seriously, even though war games in 1937–38 indicated that the German army could succeed in a rapid offensive through the Ardennes. Gamelin had rejected the results by saying "That's total fiction."[51] Instead, Gamelin was convinced that the documents retrieved from a German military plane that crashed in Mechlen, Belgium, in January 1940 contained the key to a future attack. These documents outlined an offensive through the Low Countries similar to the German strategy of August 1914. Remarkably neither Gamelin nor anyone else in the military high command focused on forecasting the Germans' changing plans. It certainly did not help that they were distracted by plans for operations in Scandinavia, the Balkans, and the Caucasus and by the political crisis of April–May 1940.[52]

Gamelin never doubted that he knew precisely what the shape of the war would be on the western front. The Germans did, however. Soon after the Mechlen incident serious debates occurred within the German General Staff over whether to invade through the Belgian plains or through the Ardennes. The German military had already carried out war games on the Ardennes gambit; they revealed the possibility of victory if the offensive were fast enough, but also the distinct chance that the French could stop such a move at the Meuse River, if they recouped their forces in time. The Germans had to cross the

Meuse within five days in order to be assured of success. Hitler believed this was possible, and he ordered the Ardennes offensive to be the focus of the German invasion, with a major feint into Belgium and the Netherlands to distract the enemy. His generals were far less certain of this plan, although Colonel Ulrich Liss, who played the role of Gamelin in the war games, thought it could work. Colonel Liss was convinced that the Allies "would rush into Belgium, that the Allied high command would leave weak forces behind to cover the Ardennes, and that once they grasped what was going on, they would still be slow to redirect their efforts."[53]

Hitler and Liss turned out to be right, but only because Gamelin and the French military ignored evidence of German intentions. As early as March, members of the French parliament observed that Sedan could be a key German objective, but General Huntziger who commanded the army there responded to their fears on April 5 by writing that he saw no reason to "reinforce the Sedan sector." Later in the month French intelligence reported that German divisions were massing on the Luxembourg border and that German reconnaissance flights had concentrated their attention almost exclusively on the Luxembourg-Northern France line from the Ardennes to Calais. For lack of analysis of this raw intelligence data, no one did anything to readjust military strategy to meet this potential threat. Gamelin blithely continued planning for the war that he expected and ignored these hints about the coming German offensive.[54]

When fighting broke out on May 10, 1940, the Germans seemed to do exactly what Gamelin expected by advancing rapidly into the Low Countries. Gamelin responded with a massive French (and British) deployment of troops along the Dyle-Breda line, which meant that the best French fighting units were deployed as far away as the Netherlands in a risky forward defense operation. In France itself, the poorest equipped and trained units, some of which were Series B infantry divisions in which the soldiers were all at least thirty-five years old, were left behind to defend the sector from the Maginot Line—which terminated where France's border with Belgium began—north along the Meuse River to where it flowed into Belgium. It was sheer madness.

Gamelin left no reserves and virtually no tanks along the Sedan-Ardennes-Meuse line.[55]

While the French military concentrated exclusively on the Dyle-Breda line, the Germans moved steadily through the Ardennes. They had only four roads available to transport massive amounts of equipment and troops, but favorable weather allowed them to reach the Meuse River in good time. If the French had deployed only a handful of bombers to the area the German advance could have been stalled, as the German air force was initially engaged exclusively in the Low Countries in an effort to fool the Allies about the nature of the offensive. But this did not happen. Instead, the Germans advanced with ease, crossing the Meuse at three locations on May 13. At the crucial Sedan crossing a Series B division fell apart after suffering eight hours of continuous attack by Stuka dive bombers, which destroyed its morale. At the crossing at Houx, Belgium, the French troops fought well, but were handicapped by the fact that they reached the river at approximately the same time as the Germans commanded by General Rommel. At the third crossing, Montheremé, France, the Germans were prevented from making substantial progress until the breakthroughs at Houx and Sedan made the French position there untenable. Gamelin, who was told of the massive German advance through the Ardennes on May 12, did nothing to counter it as he was convinced that it was not the main field of operations. Only on May 14 did Gamelin realize his mistake. The three French heavy-armored divisions were ordered to counterattack, but each was delayed for one reason or another and never fully engaged the Germans. Further confusion resulted from the French belief that the breakthrough aimed at surrounding the Maginot line. No one understood that the primary German objective was to cut off French and British troops in the Low Countries, disrupt their supply lines, deprive them of escape routes, and force them to surrender. As a consequence by the end of May 15 there was little to prevent the Germans from heading to the Channel.[56]

The war looked increasingly desperate for the French. As early as May 16 rumors circulated in Paris that the government was preparing to flee the capital for the provinces. The following day thousands of refugees from Belgium and Northern France flooded the Gare de l'Est railroad station, inaugurating what would become a massive exodus of millions to the south. On May 18 Reynaud dismissed Gamelin, appointing General Weygand as head of the French Army. At the same time he brought Marshal Pétain into the cabinet and appointed Georges Mandel, Clemenceau's disciple, to the position of minister of the interior. Before the end of the month Weygand would sack fifteen generals who had been involved in the Meuse defeat, and Mandel would round up thousands of suspected fifth columnists in an effort to show that the government meant business. To hedge all possible bets, however, Reynaud took the unprecedented step of having his government attend a mass at Notre Dame on May 19 at which the assembled multitude invoked Saints Geneviève, Michel, and Jeanne d'Arc to save France. Two days later, on May 21, Reynaud again broke precedent by explaining before the Senate more or less accurately why France had suffered serious setbacks in the early days of fighting. Reynaud promised the nation that there would be no more fiascos now that General Weygand and Marshal Pétain were in charge of the military.[57]

Unfortunately for Reynaud, and for France, Weygand and Pétain were no improvement over Gamelin. Both men were tied to the past, to the defensive tactics that prevailed in French military circles during the interwar period. De Gaulle understood this clearly; on June 3 he wrote to Reynaud, protesting that they were "men of former times" and that Pétain was a defeatist. At the time, de Gaulle still believed that France could prevail against Germany, but only if the military accepted his ideas on mechanized warfare, which had proven successful in tank skirmishes with the Germans in northern France around Abbeville. This was not to be, but an attempt was made in the third and fourth weeks of May to organize an Allied attack on the German columns racing to the Channel. Indeed, a British attack with French armored support on Rommel's troops near Arras was very successful, but distrust between the Allies and a breakdown of communications in the crisis fouled up plans. In one famous incident General Weygand flew to Ypres to meet with General Gort, commander of the British Expeditionary Force, but was unable to find Gort who had not been notified of the meeting. With the collapse of the northern front on May 25, which led to the capitulation of Belgium and the Netherlands, the French and British armies were pushed back against the Channel, and all hopes of a counterattack disappeared. The British opted to evacuate their troops from the continent to fight another day in another place rather than lose them all in a futile last stand. Fortunately, the German army paused to regroup, providing enough time for the British to repatriate the vast majority of their soldiers, as well as a large number of French. In all, a total of 558,000 Allied soldiers were evacuated from Dunkirk between May 27 and June 4 when the Germans took the port. The British had originally thought that only 100,000 could be saved.[58]

Dunkirk would go down in British history as a heroic event, but to the French military leaders it was an act of betrayal. Left on their own, Weygand and Pétain grew more bitter and defeatist after Dunkirk. With little confidence in success, Weygand massed what was left of the French army along the Somme River, which was not a very formidable defensive barrier. Troops were brought in from Belfort in the east and Southern France to bolster the lines. No retreat was possible, Weygand maintained. He could not envisage how or where another defensive line could be established to stop the Germans. A loss on the Somme, Weygand claimed, would require France "to negotiate with the enemy." On June 5, 1940, the Germans attacked on two fronts, along the Somme and through Alsace. By June 6 the French were in serious trouble, lacking supplies, reserves, and munitions to confront the enemy. On the following day the French front began to disintegrate. Although French troops fought tenaciously and inflicted heavy losses on the Germans of nearly 5,000 troops a day over a seventeen-day period—almost twice the average German casualty level during fighting in May 1940—the Germans prevailed as France pleaded for a peace in the midst of this final major battle.[59]

With defeat on the Somme imminent, the French government decided to leave Paris for Tours on June 10. It communicated this act, without any explanation, through a very brief radio announcement: "The government must leave the capital due to compelling military considerations." The following day, Parisians fled the city in record numbers; by June 13 almost no one was left. Possibly as many as 8 million French took to the highways in June, fleeing the Germans, hoping to avoid the war. Chaos ensued. The *New York Times* correspondent, P. J. Philip, spent forty-eight hours traveling by car between Paris and Tours, a distance of 150 miles. When he arrived in the new capital he discovered a government that was spread along about 100 miles of the Loire River. He noted that the minister of the interior, Georges Mandel, could communicate with his subordinates in the field only via radio broadcasts at designated times of the day. The *New York Times'* expert military analyst, Hanson Baldwin, wondered how long the French government could last without the natural and industrial resources of the north. He concluded in a June 16, 1940, article that it was "extremely doubtful that the French Army can long endure" under such circumstances since it would have to be "supplied largely from outside the country."[60]

Within the government the Somme fiasco sparked a ferocious struggle over what to do next. Although French troops fared well against the Italians, who entered the war at the last minute, this minor success could not make up for massive losses in the north. Pétain and Weygand advocated capitulating to the Germans and hoping for the best. Pétain's main concern was to save the honor of the military. As early as May 26 he wrote Reynaud that "It is essential that the people's admiration for the army be maintained. The army is the material and moral bastion of the nation." Pétain rejected schemes to unite France with Great Britain or to continue fighting the Germans from the colonies. He doggedly insisted that France needed an armistice in order to survive. Weygand agreed, telling de Gaulle: "When I'm beaten here, England won't wait a week before negotiating with the Reich." De Gaulle, on the other hand, schemed to continue fighting, arguing for moving the government to Brittany, where it could easily evacuate to Great Britain if necessary, or to North Africa, where the nation's colonial resources could be exploited to carry on the war.[61]

Neither one of de Gaulle's alternatives to capitulation carried much weight. A retreat to Brittany would have cut French troops off from vital supplies needed to continue the war while the North African gambit would have required an extraordinary effort to transport 500,000 troops and obtain far more support from the French empire than it could provide. Furthermore, de Gaulle's schemes met with near total opposition in the cabinet. Pétain refused to consider leaving France, telling members of the cabinet "I shall stay among the French people to share their sorrow and afflictions. As I see it an armistice is necessary for France's future existence." The June 16 meetings of the cabinet were crucial in deciding what to do. In a desperate effort to keep France in the war, the British hastily proposed the creation of an Anglo-French union. This led to a heated debate. Pétain called the union "a marriage with a corpse!" Others proclaimed, "We do not want to be a British dominion!" and "Better to be a Nazi province. At least we know what that means." Reynaud replied, "I prefer to collaborate with my allies rather than with my enemies." The cabinet rejected the plan, and Reynaud resigned, hoping that his successor, Pétain, would fail to obtain an acceptable armistice and that he would become prime minister again at the head of a French government in exile in North Africa.[62]

On June 17, Marshal Pétain became prime minister. He immediately addressed the nation via radio, proclaiming that he had contacted the enemy to ask for the conditions of peace. He offered the nation "the gift of my person to diminish its suffering" and added his profound regret "that it is necessary to cease fighting." Immediately, troops laid down their arms. Over a million were taken prisoner by the Germans within the next few days. De Gaulle understood that any chance of continuing the war from France or North Africa was now hopeless. From London he prepared a talk for the BBC that placed blame for defeat on the French High Command; British intelligence prevented him from delivering it, as they hoped to win Pétain to Britain's cause. A few French politicians tried unsuccessfully to move the government from Bordeaux—to which it had retreated after Tours—to Morocco. They were accused of treason by the Pétain government and placed on trial for their acts. Only the French navy succeeded in avoiding the total disgrace that afflicted all other national institutions in the spring of 1940. Under Admiral Darlan's leadership the navy prevented the Germans from taking over the fleet. On June 17 Darlan ordered all navy and commercial ships out of the metropolitan France's Atlantic ports to colonial destinations. Those ships unable to leave were to be destroyed. The navy's facilities at Brest, which equaled Toulon in importance, were razed so the Germans could not use them. The French Atlantic ports were left in such disrepair that the Nazis could not rely on them for their planned invasion of England in the summer and fall of 1940. In a small but important way Darlan the Anglophobe and future collaborator helped to stop the Nazi war machine from achieving total victory in 1940.[63]

But the war was over. No one wanted to fight after the June 17 announcement of a possible armistice, even if the terms were not acceptable. And they were not. The Pétain government chose to collaborate with the Germans rather than fight on and most French initially agreed with that decision. The nation had lost almost 100,000 men; another 200,000 had been wounded. German losses were also heavy, but only about half of the French totals. The Germans took 1.8 million prisoners, most of them in the waning days of the 1940 war, between June 17 and June 22. Until Pétain called for an end to hostilities, the average French soldier fought ferociously. Once capitulation became the only possibility, however, the army gave up the ghost. Many French soldiers would spend the rest of the war in German camps, paying a far higher price for defeat than they had expected.[64]

The phony war and its aftermath of May–June 1940 did not have to end this way. France could have won. The troops were ready to fight and mostly fought well. The French military was reasonably well equipped. The Nazi's blitzkrieg tactics were no secret to the French and could have been effectively neutralized. But, the French High Command, Generals Gamelin, Weygand, and Pétain, failed miserably to connect the dots, to understand how to most effectively use modern military technology and counter German military tactics; and the French political leaders, Daladier and Reynaud in particular, were incapable of challenging these officers to fight the kind of offensive war that might have brought victory. The colossal and tragic defeat of 1940 cannot be explained by some generic concept of decadence, as many have argued. On the contrary, the failures of the French elite and French intelligence were to blame. American Ambassador Bullitt, in a July 1, 1940, telegram to Secretary of State Cordell Hull, summed up the situation: "The simple people have done well, as always. It is the elites, the upper classes, who have totally failed."[65]

2 National Revolution

With sudden defeat in June 1940, France was left with few options. Although a small minority, led by General Charles de Gaulle, chose to go into exile to continue the war from overseas, the vast majority of the French chose to remain at home and hope that the armistice pursued by Marshal Pétain would work out for the best. The armistice terms proved to be exceedingly burdensome and collaboration with the Germans, which the armistice mandated, soon became unacceptable to most of the French. Further, the Vichy regime, which emerged in the summer of 1940 as a temporary alternative to the Third Republic, pursued a radical National Revolution that the population largely rejected. To be sure, Vichy initially had substantial support from those disgusted with the Third Republic, happy to be out of the war, expecting a quick British capitulation to the Nazis, or hopeful that collaboration might bring tangible benefits or disguise a "double game," but such support was short-lived. By the late fall of 1940, most Frenchmen favored an English victory in the war, rejected the policies of the new government, and opposed collaboration with Germany. Alone among the leaders at Vichy, Marshal Pétain remained popular throughout the war, due more to the role he played at Verdun during World War I than to his political prowess in the 1940s. This chapter traces the contours of the National Revolution, its contradictions, and the reasons for its profound failure, both on its own terms and also with the French population.

The armistice inaugurated this revolutionary experiment by defining the relationship that the new order would have with Nazi Germany. By its terms, Germany occupied two-thirds of the nation, including the entire Atlantic coast, Paris, and the north. Germany essentially annexed Alsace and Lorraine while the departments of the Nord and Pas-de-Calais came under German military command in Brussels, and a large part of northeastern France was designated for German colonization. In these northern "Germanic" areas a form of "ethnic cleansing" of the French would take place during the Nazi occupation. The armistice effectively dismembered France—broke it into at least two parts—with a demarcation line between the German-occupied north and the so-called Free Zone in the south that could only be crossed with papers issued sparingly and sporadically by the Germans. This was a sort of Berlin Wall, before the fact and without the physical structure, policed with cruelty and brutality by the Nazi occupiers. In theory, the French state was considered sovereign over French territory on both sides of the demarcation line. In practice, the Germans all but controlled the north—especially the far north and the east—and had extensive influence over the south.[1]

The armistice required the French to reduce their military to 100,000 men in metropolitan France and to pay a massive indemnity to the Germans. As a result, the French army was dissolved and reconstituted as a smaller, armistice force, suitable only for domestic policing and the defense of the French empire, for which the Germans ultimately allowed a French North African army of 115,000 men. In the meantime, while France waited for a peace to be signed, well over one million French soldiers were deported to Germany as prisoners of war. Most of them would remain in German camps until 1945, despite the Vichy government's feeble and self-defeating attempts to free them. Meanwhile, the French were required to pay reparations and occupation costs that by some estimates equaled as much as one-half of the nation's revenue. The burden was so heavy that the French people were literally turned into slaves of the Third Reich, required to work for it, either directly or indirectly, for little or no recompense, and forced to consume less and less each year due to its claims on French resources. As a result, the French were compelled to adopt draconian rationing policies for basic commodities.[2]

At the time, however, very few people were aware of the armistice's terms and many of those who were depicted it as just, given the circumstances. On Tuesday, June 25, 1940, Marshal Pétain spoke to the French nation about the armistice, two days after Great Britain announced that it no longer considered France to be a sovereign state since the armistice had reduced it to servitude. Pétain reassured his countrymen that, to the contrary, the agreement with Germany was the best that France could obtain. Rather than dwelling on the armistice, he called upon the French to look to the future: "A new order begins," he claimed, as he quickly referred to the past for hope: "The earth does not lie. It remains your recourse. It is the nation." Pétain argued that France needed "an intellectual and moral revival" to overcome defeat, which he attributed to the interwar dominance of the "spirit of pleasure" over "the spirit of sacrifice."[3]

The theme of sacrifice became a trope in the post-armistice period, as though sacrifice provided some expiatory solution to the nation's problems. The Catholic Church, in particular, welcomed sacrifice, accepting defeat as a form of divine punishment for France. The Catholic hierarchy saw Pétain as a "providential man" whose idea of National Revolution coincided with its spiritual concepts. Cardinal Gerlier of Lyon spoke for many in the Church when he said, as late as 1941, "What an impressive coincidence between the teachings of the Church and the words of the Marshal." Exactly what that meant can only be understood in terms of the Church's rocky relations with the Third Republic and its high hopes for Pétain's new order in which the values of service, discipline, and the family would prevail over secularism and anti-Catholicism. Within the Church very few leaders understood the threat of Nazism to Christian values, as they emphasized the evils of communism and ignored the Nazis' paganism.[4]

In order for Pétain to inaugurate this new order, the old one had to be done away with. This meant replacing the Third Republic with a constitutional order that was more conducive to Pétain's ideas and those of his followers on the extreme Right. In July, after the armistice had been signed and France became more or less resigned to its fate within the Nazi order, Pétain and Laval acted. In the spa town of Vichy, where the government had finally settled after leaving Bordeaux, the remaining senators and deputies from the Popular Front legislature elected in 1936 met and decided the republic's fate. For the most part, they chose freely. The only pressures were political.

Pierre Laval was Pétain's bulldog at Vichy. On June 23, Laval had entered the Pétain government as deputy premier. Soon he became the architect of the Vichy regime. He used his parliamentary skills to line up votes for a change of regime. On the one hand, he reassured the nation's representatives that he would preserve republican ideals, convincing the vast majority that a vote for full powers for Pétain amounted to no more than what the legislature had granted to Daladier and Reynaud. The republic would be continued, they were led to believe. A new constitution would be drawn up in consultation with the legislature and voted upon by the nation in due course. Even a large majority of socialist legislators believed that this would be the case. On the other hand, Laval told the assembled representatives on July 6 that "parliamentary democracy has lost the war; it must disappear, ceding its place to an authoritarian, hierarchical, national and social regime."[5] But few seemed to listen to this or, more likely, the majority believed it unimportant since Pétain rather than Laval would be in control. Pétain had gained the support of politicians on both the Left and the Right: Léon Blum called him "the noblest, the most human of our military chiefs" in March 1939 and expressed no reservations about his appointment to the government in 1940. Blum, like many others, had been fooled by Pétain's stature as the "victor of Verdun."[6]

The Senate and the Chamber of Deputies, meeting in a joint emergency session, on July 9, voted 624 to 4 in favor of revising the constitution and, on July 10, voted 569 to 80 (with 17 abstaining) to give Petain the power to revise the constitution. Only the Left presented any opposition to Laval's maneuver: 91 percent of the no vote was cast by leftists, primarily socialists (communist deputies having been removed from the parliament during the phoney war). Over half of those who voted yes—321 members of the 1940 parliament—would be banned from political life after World War II, even though they pleaded that they had voted for the continuation of the republic. Léon Blum, who voted no in 1940, clearly understood what his vote meant. Writing three months after the events of July 11, Blum said that Laval's "obvious objective was to cut all the roots that bound France to its republican and revolutionary past. His 'national revolution' was to be a counterrevolution eliminating all the progress and human rights won in the last one hundred and fifty years."[7]

The *New York Times* cut through the rhetoric and obfuscation as early as July 12, 1940, when it proclaimed: "The Chamber approved a totalitarian regime on the fascist model." Given constitutional powers by the legislature, Petain proceeded on July 11 to abrogate the founding laws of the Third Republic and give himself complete power over all aspects of government from the legislature to the executive, with one exception, the ability to declare war, for which he had to obtain the approval of parliament. Clearly, the Marshal was now in a position to implement virtually anything he desired, without fear of contradiction from other governmental agencies. On July 12, therefore, he decided on the line of succession, naming Pierre Laval as his Dauphin, despite the fact that the Constitutional Law had granted full powers to the Marshal alone and not to anyone else.[8]

Pétain had accepted power in order to protect France from total ruin and to implement the National Revolution, based on the new slogan "Work, Family, Fatherland" [*Travail, Famille, Patrie*]. To achieve the first required complete collaboration with the Germans, who called all the shots regarding the armistice and the degree to which France remained a sovereign state. As we will see in greater detail in the next chapter, collaboration proved to be a disastrous failure. The National Revolution, by contrast, was a peculiar French undertaking that had little to do with the Germans, except for the fact that it could not have been implemented without their victory. Yet, it is not easy to define the National Revolution. Historians have spilled a lot of ink arguing whether it was fascist or authoritarian. Most agree that it was neither one, but some of both. It was a peculiar French development, steeped in the history of the country rather than in the mechanical reproduction of the extreme right elsewhere in Europe.

Central to this revolution was Marshal Pétain, who led it. Unlike Hitler or Mussolini or even Franco, Pétain was no militarist or political leader. If anything, he was a pacifist who shunned political parties and grand political projects. During his years in power, he refused to implement a one-party state, such as existed in the rest of fascist Europe. In fact, he maintained many of the symbolic trappings of the republic, including the celebration of the national holiday on July 14, the flying of the tricolor flag, and the national anthem, "La Marseillaise." Unlike most on the far Right, he evidently believed that Captain Dreyfus was innocent. If Vichy was the revenge of the anti-Dreyfusards, Pétain was not one of them. Nor did he engage in the imperialistic or expansionistic aspects of fascism. Indeed, lacking a real military, he had little choice in the matter. But the Marshal was far from being a liberal democrat. His politics included authoritarian and exclusionist principles that called for the elimination of democracy, the purging of the bureaucracy, and the exclusion of Jews, Masons, communists, and foreigners from the nation. Pétain understood the National Revolution to be related to the fascist experience in Italy and Germany, but "totally different from these two historic revolutions." Or, as many at Vichy believed, the revolution was a third way between Marxism and capitalism aimed at establishing a particular French sense of community.[9]

This community did not include everyone. Indeed, exclusion of Jews and other groups such as the Gypsies, Masons, and communists has to be understood as the essence of Vichy. The National Revolution was based on this negative principle, one that we will investigate in detail in chapter four. Here let us outline a few aspects of exclusion, in order to understand in general terms what Pétain sought to achieve through his National Revolution.

Vichy's exclusionary policies did not evolve out of the policies of the Third Republic, as some have maintained. They were qualitatively and quantitatively different. Immediately after assuming power, in July 1940, the new regime began stripping naturalized citizens of their citizenship. Eventually 15,000 had their citizenship rights revoked, 6,000 of whom were Jews. At the same time, the regime decreed that anyone who did not have a French father could not be employed in the public sector. By the end of the year this requirement had been extended to several professions in the private sector, including medicine, dentistry, the law, and architecture. In August, the regime lashed out at secret societies, notably the Freemasons, prohibiting them and imposing heavy fines on anyone who adhered to them. Vichy, like other authoritarian regimes, feared the supposed international secret conspiracies of the Jews and the Masons, not to mention the communists.[10]

The regime was preoccupied by the pursuit of these and other undesirables in its first months in power. The law of July 17, 1940, stripped all state officials of immunity from dismissal, giving Vichy carte blanche to fire anyone deemed untrustworthy. Gaullists and others who had left France between May 10 and June 30 were stripped of their nationality, unless they could prove that their mission had been officially sanctioned. The High Court of Justice was replaced by a Vichy-appointed Supreme Court that was instructed to try a broad spectrum of suspicious government officials, while a special court martial was created to try those designated traitors by the regime. No appeal was allowed for cases tried by the court martial, whose sentences had to be executed within twenty-four hours after a verdict. The rule of law as the republic had understood it was completely undermined by the creation of these courts.[11]

Vichy topped off its exclusionary laws by issuing a number of decrees affecting foreigners and Jews. On September 27 the regime implemented a law on the status of "foreigners in excess in the national economy." All male refugees between eighteen and fifty-five years of age who came under this vague appellation could be placed in work camps, where they would be required to labor without pay. Increasingly, as we shall see later in more detail, Vichy used camps to deal with excluded groups. In early October Vichy promulgated three exclusionary laws regarding Jews. One stripped all North African Jews of their rights of citizenship, which had been granted in 1870. Another defined who was a Jew and either excluded totally or limited access for Jews to a vast array of government and private sector jobs. And a third made it possible to intern all foreign Jews in camps. As Michael Marrus and Robert Paxton have pointed out with emphasis, the Nazis forced none of these laws upon Vichy. The National Revolution did not include Jews in its concept of community and the new order of things.[12]

Once Vichy had excluded the impure elements that were assumed to have undermined France, it sought to renew the true national community. Of course, the issue of exclusion was never settled completely. Vichy lived in a Manichean world, one in which good and evil were absolutes in constant struggle for dominance. Thus, the good could not be defined without a constant process of scapegoating the other, which undermined the good and could never be totally destroyed. The peasant village, which Vichy upheld as its ideal, was always in peril due to the existence of the urban industrial city, peopled by Jews and foreigners and those French who had lost touch with their true roots. Vichy's peasant ideal required the disciplining of the urban other.

Ideologically the National Revolution, as Pétain understood it, was an extension of the ideas of the Action française. Although Vichy's motto, "Work, Family, Fatherland," came from Colonel de La Rocque's Croix de feu, the colonel, after a brief flirtation with the new order, broke with Vichy and eventually contributed to France's liberation by providing intelligence to the British. In contrast, Charles Maurras and the Action française chose the Marshal, Vichy, and collaboration. Although Maurras played no role in the Vichy government—he spoke with Pétain on only a few occasions—his political ideas seemed to dominate it. Paul Barlatier, the editor of the premier Marseille newspaper, the *Sémaphore,* placed confidence in Vichy because the Marshal acted and governed "in a manner that is distinctly Maraussian."[13] This included not only an exclusionary attitude toward Jews, Freemasons, and communists, but also anti-German attitudes that Maurras in particular, and Pétain to a lesser degree, held dear. Collaboration and anti-communism would eventually trump the anti-German nationalism of the two men, but they would never forsake their goal of creating a French national community based on a seemingly paradoxical combination of authoritarian political order at the center and regional social and cultural autonomy. For both men, the nation represented the highest stage of political evolution. *La France seule* ("France alone"), motto of the Action française differentiated them and the National Revolution from the collaborationist political leaders and parties in Paris. Rather than adhere to the model of German Nazism, Maurras and Pétain chose what they thought was a unique French path, one that emphasized corporatist organizations, the family, and the enrooted peasant as the bases of community. The National Revolution would eliminate class struggle, alienation, even modernity in order to return to a primitive peasant and artisan community in which class cooperation prevailed. Although some technocratic modernizers initially adhered to Vichy in the hope that it would be more dynamic than the Third Republic, Vichy was above all a reactionary enterprise: an attempt to reestablish the essence of French identity, a community in which the family was strong, hierarchy prevailed, the paterfamilias dominated, and everyone knew his or her place. It sought *la France profonde,* the True France that had been lost to uprootedness, urbanization, alien forces, and the like. Pétain and Maurras not only shared this vision of a new France but also believed in each other as uniquely destined by it. Pétain referred to Maurras as the "most French of the French," and Maurras called Pétain's rise to power in 1940 a "divine surprise."[14]

Family and Gender in the National Revolution

Prioritizing the goals of the National Revolution is difficult if not impossible to do, but no one doubts that family and gender ranked high on the agendas of those who took over power in 1940. They argued that the war had been lost because France had been feminized. One of them proclaimed that the National Revolution was a reaction "to a feminized Republic."[15] The nation's virile nature had disappeared during the interwar period as women had moved out of the private, familial sphere where they belonged to the public sphere where they did not. On June 20, Marshal Pétain told the nation that France lost the war because it had "too few children, too few arms, too few allies."[16] A week later, General Weygand wrote Pétain that population decline meant that the army had to rely increasingly on colonial troops or naturalized Frenchmen. To correct this, he claimed emphatically: *"The family must be restored to a place of honor."*[17] Vichy's minister for the family concurred when he spoke of the "necessity to restore the French family, whose disintegration is the origin of our decadence and our defeat."[18] Given this environment, it is not surprising that opinion polls indicated that the French believed the decline in births and family values to be directly related to the participation of women in the workforce. Women had let France down and caused the crisis that required the military to shore up its ranks with undesirables, the outsiders that the National Revolution wanted to exclude from the French community.[19]

Natalism and racism went hand in hand, as Francine Muel-Dreyfus has shown. Extreme natalists attacked feminism as a foreign import, identifying feminists as Jews, conflating antifeminism with anti-Semitism. French women had to be protected from undesirable foreign elements in order to reproduce the French race. Not only were racial and anti-immigrant laws implemented to achieve this goal, but Vichy also acted to exclude women from the workforce. Laws promulgated in October 1940 prohibited married women from working in the public sector and gave married men with children a preference in hiring. State poster and radio propaganda campaigns deluged women with messages about the need to return home and have children for the good of France. The state offered monetary incentives to encourage women to stay home and have children. But it also reversed the 1907 law that gave women control over the income they earned, empowered husbands to prevent their wives from working, restricted severely the right to divorce, criminalized adultery, imposed prison terms on those who abandoned their children, and punished abortion with harsh criminal sentences that included the death penalty. As a result, some women left the workforce, the divorce rate plummeted, and the number of women sentenced to prison increased dramatically—1,500 men and women went to jail for abandonment in 1942, and those sent to prison for abortion—mainly women—almost quadrupled between 1938 and 1941.[20]

Of course the family had been important to lawmakers before 1940 but, as was the case with refugees, Vichy went much further than the republic in using women and the family to pursue national revival.

Thus the Vichy Constitution that was drawn up but never implemented began with several articles on the family. Article one stated: "The State recognizes that the family, constituted by marriage and legitimate filiations, is the foundation of the social edifice." Article two recognized the superiority of the family to the state in regard to the "upbringing and education of children" and the "constitution and conservation of the family patrimony." And article three granted the family the right of representation in Vichy assemblies and a vote—the family vote—in place of individual suffrage. All authority within the family resided with the male head who controlled the family vote, family finances, and the like.[21]

The reality, however, was quite different from these constitutional pipe dreams: the state, not the male head of the household, controlled the family under Vichy. Also, Vichy's familial ideal was impossible to realize while the war continued. The wives of prisoners of war, for one, could not be dealt with in terms of the traditional family, no matter how much Vichy wanted to do so. Although the government tried to make them consult with their POW husbands on all issues, they made most decisions without them, including the decision to go to work. According to one estimate, 80 percent of the wives of POWs joined the workforce during the war. Some engaged in prostitution in order to survive. A government study carried out in July 1941 found that about 60 percent of Parisian prostitutes were POW wives. As much as the state tried to provide for these women, it did not have the resources to keep them out of poverty and in the home. As a consequence women entered the workplace and began organizing groups, beyond Vichy's grasp, to help cope with the problems they faced. Autonomy, rather than dependency, was what these abandoned wives sought, out of necessity if nothing else, during the period in which Vichy was desperately trying to shore up the traditional family.[22]

The traditionalist family goals that Vichy promoted were also undermined by the demands of the economy. Between October 1940 and October 1942 the number of unemployed dropped from one million to 77,000, partly because the Germans had imprisoned over one and a half million French soldiers. The tight labor market created by this and demand for French labor in German factories, made it impossible for Vichy to enforce the numerous laws that restricted women's employment. In fact, the government did a complete about-face in September 1942 when it suspended the 1940 law that prohibited women from working in state jobs and then, in August 1943, when it passed legislation requiring all women between the ages of twenty-one and thirty-five to work. Under German pressure, Vichy also decreed, in February 1944, that all women without children, between ages eighteen and forty-five, could be conscripted to work in Germany. Although only 44,000 French women ended up working in Germany, they attest to the bankruptcy of Vichy's position on women and the family.[23] Here, as in most areas, the National Revolution was a sham, contingent upon German occupation and collaboration, incapable of establishing its own legitimate authority outside the sphere of Nazi power.

Still, on the level of symbolism, the revolution proceeded despite reality. The *Fête des mères* (Mother's Day) was elevated to a major national holiday by Marshal Pétain in May 1941. On this first Mother's Day under Vichy rule he addressed the nation, proclaiming "the family offers us the best guarantee of [national] recovery. A sterile nation is a nation whose existence is mortally affected. In order for France to live, above all it must have families." To the old Marshal, the family was a "spiritual community that saves man from egotism," and the mother was the key to its existence and perpetuation.[24] In order to reinforce the central role of the mother, Vichy granted awards to mothers of large families and required schoolchildren to write essays about the virtues of their mothers. Plays about ideal mothers were performed on Mother's Day, and the cult of the Virgin was conjured up, especially in Catholic Church services to honor mothers. The radical alterity of the mother was inscribed in these events and ceremonies. As Marshal Pétain informed all mothers on Mother's Day in 1942, through childbearing "you realize fully your destiny as a woman; you discover profound happiness by simply obeying the laws of nature." One year later the French Union for the Defense of the Race went further, linking Mother's Day to the protection of the French race. To the union, mothers who gave birth to French children had performed a sacrifice, which "multiplied shall without doubt be the salvation of our nation, which so many rootless, dishonorable scoundrels want to destroy."[25]

But Vichy did not trust mere rhetoric and symbolism to achieve its goal of the contented mother in the family. It also concentrated on reforming the nation's educational system to emphasize the virtues of the family and motherhood. Pétain's 1938 speech at Metz had established the basis for the new educational order: "The souls of young Frenchmen must be shaped by the nation, by the narration of our history, by the love of our soil and our empire."[26] This meant purging the schools of undesirable teachers, such as Freemasons and Jews, who taught false, "international" concepts, according to Vichyite educators, and purging the textbooks of the republican values of "liberty, equality, and fraternity" for those of the new order, "Work, Family, Fatherland." But more importantly, it meant scrapping the republican ideal of equal education for all. Now, peasants and workers should be educated according to their status in the hierarchy, not for the purpose of advancing beyond their position in life. A primary education that emphasized manual labor was sufficient for the lower classes. Likewise, women were not to face heady intellectual matters. Instead, they should be taught cooking, health care, gardening, and the like to prepare them for life in the family. No woman should be allowed to pursue secondary education. The baccalaureate exam for women, which the republic had created in 1924, was essentially eliminated under Vichy, which required women to take courses in family education and pursue a watered-down academic curriculum at the secondary level.[27] Women were meant to reproduce, to raise families, to cook and garden, but never to infringe on the superior male world of virility and higher learning. Under Vichy everyone was supposed to know his or her place.

Vichy's strong sense of place and hierarchy emerged out of a Catholic culture of deference that the republic had tried to crush. Vichy was the revenge of the Church, in many respects. Vichy's policies toward women were nothing more than what the Church had been preaching for at least seventy years. Catholic educational groups, such as the Association of Parents of Students of Independent Education, mimicked Vichy on the place of women in French life: "The place of women is at the center and heart of the home [*foyer*]," it proclaimed. In the 1930s, the Catholic Ligue de la femme au foyer was created for the purpose of reinvigorating traditional family values. Its concepts and slogans, developed before World War II, became the heart of Vichy's National Revolution: "To renew the nation through the family, the mother must be in the *foyer*."[28]

The Church was virtually unanimous in support of Vichy's ideology on women and the family and embraced enthusiastically the Vichy motto of "Work, Family, Fatherland." Cardinal Gerlier exclaimed, "These words are ours." The Vatican recognized Vichy almost immediately. The Assembly of Cardinals and Archbishops proclaimed that the Church venerated Pétain and demanded "that the union of all French be realized around him." The National Revolution was, to most Catholics, the salvation of France. Catholic journals, with only one or two exceptions, waxed enthusiastic about Vichy. Only a Christian revival, with a strong emphasis on the family, could restore France in their eyes. And Pétain and Vichy were the keys to the success of that restoration. After World War II the Church would experience a steep decline in France, reflecting in part the close ties it had established with Pétain and the National Revolution.[29]

Despite the strong support of the Church and the strong convictions of those at Vichy who supported a return to the family, Vichy's family policy failed to achieve its key objectives. Women did not return to the home; the traditional family was not revived; the paterfamilias did not gain absolute control over family affairs; and women were not kept out of the public sphere. Although some historians have argued that Vichy's policies on women and the family were part of a continuum that extended from the interwar period to the 1960s, the position of Vichy in this history is clearly an extreme one, which the postwar period corrected in the direction of greater autonomy for women. The National Revolution failed to stop the erosion of family values that the forces of modernity and the Republic had supposedly initiated.

Regionalism and Tradition

One of the seeming paradoxes of authoritarian Vichy was its emphasis upon local culture and tradition. Pétain led the way in this area
as well, celebrating the many diverse regions of France in his travels
throughout the south. He was especially fond of Provence and its great
Nobel Prize–winning poet, Frédéric Mistral, whose legacy he thought
heralded the National Revolution. On September 6, 1940, Mistral's
110th birthday, Pétain proclaimed, "I see in him the sublime evocation
of the new France that we want to create, as well as the traditional
France that we want to restore." Pétain praised Mistral for upholding
the values of the family and the soil, for championing the "Latin race"
and its "spiritual treasures," and for his patriotism, which embraced
both the "petite patrie" and the "grande" while "posing an invincible
resistance to anyone who tried to eliminate class, level society, and
uproot us."[30]

Celebrating the regions, local cultures, and folklore, Vichy established itself as the enemy of Jacobin centralization and the republican
tradition while maintaining the principle of the unity of the nation.
Regionalism was synonymous with traditional values, the ones that
Vichy wished to perpetuate. As a result, folklore studies flourished
under Vichy, which supported ethnological works on peasants and
local cultures. The folklorists reciprocated by creating a National Committee for Propaganda through Folklore, which published a journal,
L'Echo des provinces, which extolled the National Revolution and the
role of folklore in it. The journal was subsidized heavily by the state,
which also supported regional folklore museums, just as the Popular
Front government had done. In addition, Vichy mobilized artists to
paint idealized pictures of daily life among peasants and artisans,
which were rivaled in Vichy-sponsored art only by depictions of saints
and other Christian themes out of a lost medieval world. In some areas,
such as Provence and Languedoc, Vichy also promoted the teaching of
local languages, although never with the thought of substituting them
for French—there were limits to Vichy's regionalist tendencies. The
same could be said of the teaching of history: Vichy encouraged the
teaching of local history, but made sure that the history of France

was also taught, with certain changes to the curriculum, such as the elimination of the revolution of 1789 as a major event.[31]

Vichy's enthusiasm for local culture included a strong anti-Parisian element. Music, for example, had to be populist in nature, rooted in folklore, close to the concerns of the people rather than cosmopolitan and international (such as jazz). Folk songs, choral music, and folk dances were considered wholesome forms that could revitalize the French people. Classical music, in contrast, was acceptable only if it came close to the concerns of the people, as in the case of Gounod's *Mireille,* which was based on Mistral's famous poem, or Bizet's *L'Arlé-sienne,* which was inspired by the Provençal nationalist Alphonse Daudet's short story. Theater, too, had to adhere to a concept of didactic art. Foreign and avant-garde theater was unhealthy. Plays had to be based on local customs, local history, and the like. The Provençal pastoral fit into this category as well as Languedocien plays based on local legends. In general, tradition ruled over the culture that Vichy wished to foster. But not too much tradition. Folklorists were watched in case they went too far in identifying with local cultures and the people. Traditional festivals, which Vichy encouraged, were controlled in order to avoid popular excesses, such as Dionysian fits of passion or carnivalesque reversals of the order of things. Regulated tradition, seemingly from the bottom up but actually from the top down, was Vichy's form of "populist" culture.[32]

Vichy's vision of culture was narrowly focused on the themes of the National Revolution, namely the return to the soil, to peasant and artisan cultural values and the village. The re-creation of True France was Vichy's primary objective, not the democratization of culture, which is why Vichy and Popular Front cultural policies were fundamentally different. Take, for example, Jeune France, which the regime created in 1940 for the purpose of rejuvenating French culture. All aspects of culture, from music to the cinema, were to be included in its jurisdiction. Although the Parisian branch of Jeune France concentrated on elite culture, the rest of the movement was concerned with decentralizing culture by creating cultural centers in places such as Bordeaux, Toulouse, and Marseille. These centers concentrated primarily on producing plays, many of which did not fit into the agenda of the National Revolution. As a consequence, Jeune France soon ran into trouble with the authorities, who shut it down in March 1942. Much like Uriage, the elite school for training future leaders of Vichy that turned against the regime, Jeune France became too independent and too divorced from the Mauraussien values that Vichy wanted to inculcate in the name of "popular" culture.[33] Vichy's regionalist policies— which included culture—were, Christian Faure rightly contends, mythical in nature, existing only in the imagination, as a mental representation.[34]

The result of these policies, in contrast to the myth, was more often than not total confusion and hostility to the regime. The promises that Vichy made regarding local empowerment were hardly ever implemented. For example, the promotion of regional languages never moved beyond tokenism, for Vichy had no intention of creating a multilingual nation. More serious, the creation of regional governments raised hopes for increased local autonomy, but nothing of the sort occurred. The seven regions set up by Vichy in the south were carefully controlled from the center. Any thought of decentralization faded as Vichy eliminated elected city governments, treated autonomist movements with disdain, and even placed strict limits on the power of prefects. Corporatism did not give power to the decentralized corporations but rather centralized it in the hands of Vichy bureaucrats. The end result was disillusion and alienation from the objectives of the National Revolution by 1941, if not earlier.

Recent regional studies have revealed an almost uniform story of high hopes for regional autonomy and the goals of the National Revolution in 1940, followed rapidly by disillusionment as Vichy or the Germans failed to allow any significant decentralization of power. In the most extreme cases, Alsace and the Nord-Pas-de-Calais, the Germans in control eliminated all signs of autonomy, including the use of the French language and religious freedom in Alsace. Significant opposition to the new order emerged immediately in these areas. But even where Vichy's more benign administration prevailed, such as the Dordogne, the new order was never popular because the armistice cut the region off from its natural outlet to the Atlantic and the regime dumped 50,000 refugees on it without warning or consultation. In the Alpes-Maritimes, in contrast, Vichy was extremely popular until March 1941, when the central government purged municipal councils and replaced their members with extreme right-wing party hacks. After that, support for the British and opposition to collaboration with the Germans increased rapidly. And the same can be said for numerous other areas of France where heavy-handed government control created opposition to both Vichy and the Germans: Franche-Comté, where German meddling in the local economy led to French opposition by 1941; Brittany, where hopes for autonomy were dashed by both Vichy and the Germans, leading the Bretons to back de Gaulle and the British by early 1941; and Cévennes, where historically powerful anti-Parisian sentiments led Protestant and regionalist forces to oppose Vichy's authoritarian policies by 1941.[35]

Of course regionalism and the appeal to tradition were not life and death issues for most people. Vichy's failure to make these myths reality was not the sole or even primary factor in turning most people against the regime. Still, it is important to realize that the Maurraussien agenda of the National Revolution included significant emphasis on local freedom and regional autonomy in the context of traditional values. When local freedom and regional autonomy were not implemented but instead were transformed into further centralization of power under an authoritarian system, disillusionment quickly followed. Freedom was a deeply held value that many refused to give up.

Peasants and Workers: The Corporate State

The positive aspects of the National Revolution—if we can call them that—never bridged the gap between ideology and practice because reality always intervened to stymie ideology. The corporate state, as it related to peasants and workers, was no exception to this rule. Despite Vichy's nauseating emphasis upon the values of rural life and the peasantry, the corporate state in practice did nothing to protect those traditional values. Quite the opposite: peasants, which the new regime promised to protect, soon became the victims of a brutal policy of exploiting rural France not seen since the Revolution of 1789. The reality for workers was just as bad, in fact worse. The corporate state, for both peasants and workers, was a complete, unmitigated disaster.

Pétain believed, as did many others, that France was still a peasant nation, self-sufficient in agriculture and capable of feeding both its own citizens and the rest of Europe. In August 1940, for example, he claimed that France "will recover all her strength by renewed contact with the earth."[36] To achieve this goal, his administration created a series of new rural institutions that supposedly gave peasants control over their destiny. To revive the family farm, which Pétain believed was the "principle economic and social base of France," Vichy inaugurated programs to return peasants to the soil, providing them with free land to cultivate. But this accomplished little, as only 1,566 families took up this proposition, of which 409 quickly terminated their ties to the soil. In contrast, Vichy's policy of *remembrement,* by which small, economically marginal plots of land were exchanged to create contiguous, more economically viable operations where previously subsistence farming had been the case, succeeded in reducing the presence of the small peasant farmer and led eventually to the creation of a more capitalist form of agriculture, in direct contradiction with the stated values of the National Revolution. In April 1942, when Jacques Le Roy-Ladurie was appointed minister of agriculture, efficiency and modernization in agriculture won out over the ideal of the family farm touted by Pétain.[37]

The same process of the transvaluation of rural values occurred with the Corporation paysanne created in December 1940. The stated aim of the corporation was to overcome class struggle and increase agricultural production. At the local level, virtually every agricultural interest group was represented in this new organization, but at the regional and national levels, where policy was supposed to be made, peasants and sharecroppers had no voice. In the national commission appointed by Vichy only the major capitalist agricultural interests were represented. The national commission's propaganda supported the National Revolution's themes of the family farm, the village community, and traditional values, but as the fascist Marcel Déat pointed out, the commission actually protected the power of the rich property owners. It became increasingly apparent with time that the peasant corporation had almost no influence on agricultural policy, despite the fact that Pétain claimed in July 1941 that it must "be a durable undertaking, the foundation stone of the corporate edifice of the new France."[38] Increasingly the corporation lost control over rural France as groups such as the Communist Party capitalized on such issues as the requisitioning of food at prices below cost and German attempts to control rural areas for their own economic interests. Even the Vichy government realized that its corporate peasant policy had failed. At the end of December 1942 a government report claimed that the peasant corporation was too statist and not corporatist enough and that it lacked funding to carry out its goals. It concluded that "it appears that in place of using the corporation as a bridge between the peasants and itself, the government cut off all communication" with the peasants.[39] By early 1943 the message had reached Vichy that the peasants thought the corporation had been taken over by the state, which used it to impose excessive obligations on them. They wanted this "foundation stone of the corporate edifice" dissolved before it did more damage. By May 1943 even die-hard peasant supporters of the National Revolution had lost confidence in the system, according to government reports. Meanwhile Pétain had gone from discussing peasants as saviors of the French race in 1940 to labeling them criminals for not selling their produce at below cost in early 1942.[40]

The myth of self-sufficient peasant France ran up against the reality of German exploitation. France was not self-sufficient prior to the war but was forced to become so as the result of German policies after the armistice. The nation went from importing 15 percent of its agricultural goods prior to 1940 to almost no imports during the German occupation. At the same time France was forced to export 700 million kilograms of cereals per year to Germany. This occurred even though fertilizer usage declined 50 percent, agricultural workers decreased by 13 percent, and the amount of land cultivated dropped by 2 million hectares under German occupation. Consequently, French agricultural production dipped to about 80 percent of what it had been in the period 1935–38, and average French caloric intake fell 50 percent or more, from about 2,400 calories a day to 1,200 or fewer by 1944. Contrary to what many believed at the time, French peasants did not benefit greatly from the misery of urban dwellers: not only did agricultural production decline but the state forced peasants to sell their goods at prices below cost, as well.[41]

The working class benefited even less from the corporate state. Not only were workers conscripted to work in Germany against their will, but their salaries declined in value as prices increased 300 percent during the war. By 1942 workers were spending 60 percent or more of their income for food. The German system, to which Vichy acquiesced, provided full employment but under conditions that bordered on slavery. French workers were forced to provide goods for German consumption and the Nazi war effort. Up to one-half of French revenue went to Germany during the war as the result of skewed exchange rates, the requisitioning of French goods, and the burdensome occupation costs imposed on Vichy. To a degree unknown in other western European countries under Nazi occupation, French workers refused to become part of this German system. Very few volunteered to work in Germany, and many joined the Resistance rather than be conscripted to work there.[42]

Vichy's form of corporatism never got off the ground as far as the working class was concerned. Pétain and the National Revolution had nothing but contempt for the proletariat. Pétain believed that the "true workers" were village artisans, who, he asserted, accepted their social and economic inferiority as part of the natural order of things. In a 1942 May Day speech the Marshal totally overlooked the French proletariat, whose day this had traditionally been, to speak about the special role of the artisan in French society. He praised the artisan as the upholder of "social peace" and added: "Class struggle is impossible in the artisan's workshop." In a March 1941 speech to businessmen, workers, and their associates he specifically condemned the old working-class leaders for producing "misery, war and defeat," weakening

the nation through policies based on hatred and revolution. He returned to this theme on May Day 1941, claiming: "May first has been,
until now, a symbol of division and hatred. From now on it shall be a
symbol of union and friendship." But, he made clear, only the artisans
had achieved this working-class utopia. The others must fall in step in
order to realize the unlimited benefits of the corporate state.[43]

Pétain's ultimate objective was to organize the working class under
the aegis of the corporate state. The Charte du Travail (Labor Charter)
was his means of achieving this. On September 22, 1941, when Vichy
issued the document, Pétain embraced it as the key to ending class
struggle by bringing all groups together to share equally in the profits
of capital, "after capital investments had been remunerated." The charter would restore among workers and their bosses "the close solidarity
that existed in the past," the Marshal maintained, and would help revive the grandeur of France through the corporate state.[44]

But these were mere utopian dreams of an old man. The Labor
Charter amounted to little in the end. Its drafting and implementation
were slowed by divisions between traditionalists who shared Pétain's
vision and neosyndicalists led by Minister of Work René Belin, who
sought minimally to protect workers' interests by maintaining separate
worker and employer unions within the new corporate structure. Some
prewar labor leaders, notably from the CGT current associated with
the journal *Syndicats,* followed Belin and took up positions in the new
labor order. In some cases, pacifist, anticommunist, and antiparliamen-
tarian sentiments combined with disappointment with the failure of
Popular Front labor reforms led them to embrace the new order in the
hope that a reformist, peaceful, and necessarily authoritarian social
order would emerge from it. In other cases, cooperation was more
circumspect, based on a pragmatic *entrisme* according to which it was
important to be present where decisions were being made that im-
pacted workers. But workers overwhelmingly repudiated the Labor
Charter, seeing clearly that the outlawing of the right to strike and of
independent unions made it little more than a tool of the employers.
As a consequence, by Liberation only a fraction of the new unions
called for by the Labor Charter had been created. As one historian

observed, Vichy was a "veritable golden age for the French business class." In the name of solidarity a sham corporate state was erected that reinforced big business at the expense of virtually every other group—peasants, artisans, workers, even the middle class. The concentration of industry into larger, supposedly more efficient enterprises occurred at a rapid pace under Vichy, due more to the demands of the Germans and the economic penury of France during the war than to state planning, which was virtually nonexistent, or the work of Vichy technocrats. By 1945 laissez-faire liberalism would be superseded by a new world of state planning, in part because of Vichy's stumbling interventionist concepts, but primarily due to France's extraordinarily weak economic position after years of being exploited by the occupying German armies.[45]

The Vichy Constitution

As we have already seen, Marshal Pétain was given the authority by the politicians of the Third Republic to draw up a new constitution that would be submitted to the French people for ratification. That document was to institutionalize, once and for all time, the ideals of the corporate state that Pétain, Maurras, and others held dear. But, like almost everything related to this so-called "revolution," Vichy failed miserably in achieving its objective. The gap between ideals and reality was, once again, too difficult to bridge.

The role of Marshal Pétain in this failed attempt to create a constitution should not be underestimated. Pétain was obsessed with the issue from June 1940 until the ultimate collapse of Vichy. In announcing the terms of the armistice he made clear that "a new order" had to be established to supersede the failed Third Republic, even though nothing in the armistice required such an outcome. On July 11, 1940, he addressed the nation on the need for a new constitution, arguing that national revival depended upon it. Rather than continuing the ways of parliamentary democracy, the new order would be based on "simple rules" and would rely on elites chosen "for their abilities and their merits," the Marshal proclaimed. Both capitalism and socialism would be banned from this order, superseded by a society in which the reign of money would no longer prevail: "In the new order, which shall be based on justice, we will eliminate all dissension." Instead: "Your work shall be defended, your family shall have the respect and the protection of the nation." And everyone will be proud to be French again.[46]

Pétain returned to the theme in August 1940, in the course of responding to Gaullist attacks. He lashed out at the "gangrene" of the 1930s, which infested the French state "by interjecting laziness and incompetence into it, even sometimes systematic sabotage for the purpose of social disorder and international revolution." Pétain added: "For seventy-five years before the war broke out, the regime that dominated the French promoted a culture of discontent." Vichy, in contrast, would act only for the "public good" without the "lies and utopian dreams" of the republic. Two months later, in October, the Marshal crowed about the accomplishments of the new order, pointing to the massive legislative initiatives undertaken: "The revisions of the naturalization laws, the law on access to certain professions, the dissolution of secret societies, the search for those responsible for our disastrous defeat." Nothing, however, was done that reflected the promise to unite the nation, unless unity were defined in terms of exclusion, which dominated this list of legislative accomplishments.[47]

Pétain repeatedly defined his new constitutional order in terms of the massive failures of the Republic. In a major speech of October 10, 1940, he attacked the Third Republic once more for enslaving the French and allowing only special interests—especially the unions—to dominate. He went on to claim that he would build his new order on the ruins of the republic, interjecting for the first time the connection between it and Nazi Germany: the new order would entail new foreign alliances, including collaboration with Germany under a just peace. On the domestic front the new regime would be based on "a social hierarchy" in which the "false idea of natural equality" would be replaced by the concept of "equality of chances." Although liberty would exist in this regime, it would be tempered by a strong dose of order, especially in regard to the economy, which "must be organized and controlled" as individual interest must bow to "national interest." All classes, Pétain concluded, would be part of a "true national fraternity" as a result of this new constitutional order.[48]

By July 1941, when Pétain addressed the Constitutional Commission of twenty that had been selected to draft a new constitution, the broad outlines of his concept of governance were widely known. He told the "founding fathers" that the idea of the "sovereign people" was dead; it had led to "total irresponsibility." In its place he provided a new definition of "people": "A people is a hierarchy of families, of professions, of communes, of administrative responsibilities, of spiritual groups." Rather than governing, "a people" is led by elites, from the lowest government official all the way to Pétain at the top. But the essential key to constitution-making, he argued, was the National Revolution, which "signifies the will to be rejuvenated" that comes from the "being" of the French people. Circular logic? Tautologies? Certainly. But none of this bothered the Marshal, who argued that the constitution had to have the "virtue of education" in it. "In this respect," he continued, "the constitution crowns the work of the school." By this he meant that the constitution must reveal the patrie in all of its glory and "teach . . . respect of religion and moral beliefs, especially those professed in France since the origins of its national existence." The new order would be patriotic, hierarchical, authoritarian, and elitist, "organically uniting French society." Like Edmond Burke in his critique of the French Revolution, the Marshal conceived of his constitution in terms of the "sixty generations that have preceded us on our soil, for which you are the responsible heirs."[49]

This was virtually worthless advice. No modern state could be based on such vagaries as fundamental constitutional principles. No wonder that the twenty "sages" found it almost impossible to draw up a constitution. Even if a document had been created and submitted to the people, it would have had no chance of gaining their approval. As much as the republic was despised, no one wanted a mystical, organic union based on order and hierarchy, with elites in total control and civil society relegated to the role of Spanish peasants under Franco. Yet, Pétain continued to address the subject as though his vision were possible. In a speech on the constitution of October 14, 1941, Pétain attacked specifically the evils of individualism, which had created a "false conception of liberty" that subordinated duty to rights and institutions to individuals. The result was "the disappearance of discipline, the neglect of hierarchy, the collapse of authority." The new constitution, he argued emphatically, would correct all of this, bolstering the state, shoring up the authority of its head.[50] The evils of individualism and class conflict continued to obsess Pétain, who insisted in his New Year's talk, for example, that the National Revolution would bring an end to them, but only if the people fully embraced its ideals.[51]

Although a constitution was drawn up for Vichy, one that incorporated most of Pétain's concerns, it was never implemented, in part because Pétain insisted that it be delayed until France was liberated from German occupation and Paris was once again its capital. The primary author of this document was the minister of justice from 1941 to 1943, Joseph Barthélemy, a devout Catholic who had been a prominent liberal republican in the interwar period. Barthélemy had reservations about Pétain's right to rule, for he believed that the Third Republic's legislature had only given him the power to "make a constitution" and then resign. For the most part, Barthélemy agreed with the idea that community took precedence over individual rights. His Catholic education also convinced him that Vichy was not a totalitarian state but rather "constrained by the higher rules of morality and law, superior creations that impose themselves upon it."[52] Thus, acting as a sort of modern-day Thomas Aquinas or Bishop Bossuet, Barthélemy set to work on a document that would be based on law, as he conceived it, beginning with the principle that the nation was a community of "traditions, memories, hopes, customs, attachment to the same soil, and aspirations." Race, or any other biological concept of the nation and citizenship, was not included in this definition, making it very difficult to square with the anti-Semitic laws passed by Vichy under the Marshal's leadership. Nor did Barthélemy opt for the Nazi concept of the unity of state and nation, which would have made this constitution a totalitarian one. On the contrary, in the first drafts of the constitution, the family emerged as the primary institution upon which all else was to be based, with the father in control and all other members subordinate to him. Women were clearly relegated to the role of housewives, with the duty to reproduce as well as to educate and discipline their children for the good of the community. But here, as elsewhere, concerns about the authority of the state trumped the corporatist mentality that the National Revolution projected. The reality that prevailed in the final draft gave the state control over the family, which obtained no real rights in the new order. Vichy did not trust the family to be the primary institution, just as it did not trust regionalism or peasant and working-class corporatism. In all three cases the constitution undermined what authority these entities were supposed to possess under the ideals of the National Revolution.[53]

What the constitution makers did trust, in the final analysis, were two seemingly contradictory concepts: the state and the individual. Article forty-six of this document contained the shocking revelation that individual effort was the key to all economic success. The state could protect the general welfare only to the extent that it did not clash with individual initiative. In other words, the Vichy regime deferred to the intellectual heritage of the past to strongly back what many considered to be a discredited neoliberal concept. But the impact of individualism was immediately countered by the overwhelming power that the constitution gave to the head of state, who was made into a sort of French Caesar, according to Michèle Cointet-Labrousse. Pétain and his successors were given virtually unlimited legislative and executive powers. Only the moral law—Barthélemy's ultimate guide—and the Constitutional Court could restrict their actions.[54]

In the end, nothing came of this effort to write the constitution that would entrench the National Revolution in the hearts and minds of the French. No one really wanted it anyway, except for Pétain, Maurras, and a few other nostalgic extremists. It did not resolve any of the outstanding issues that the Third Republic had supposedly failed to grapple with; on the contrary, it seemed to embrace the very individualism that the National Revolution found so repugnant in the culture of the republic. Not surprisingly, in late 1943, when Vichy's demise was clearly visible on the horizon, some Vichy politicians sought to save their skins by adopting a constitution similar to that of the Third Republic. Yet, for a variety of reasons including Pétain's refusal to allow authority to emanate *"d'en bas"* (from below), this attempt at implementing a republican constitution came to naught.[55]

France was governed under Vichy not by corporate entities, which had no real power, or by the family, which had even less, but by traditional institutions that it inherited from the Republic. This did not include parliamentary government, although Vichy created a simulacrum of it when it set up its handpicked, carefully vetted National Council, which was heavily weighted toward the Right. It proved to be completely worthless at the job of providing information from constituencies to the national government for use in making policy. For that purpose, and for most aspects of governance, Vichy relied heavily on the prefects, the officials that headed the eighty-odd departments into which France had been divided since the 1790s. In a superficial sense, this marked a return to the reliance on prefects to govern the nation in the nineteenth-century regimes preceding the creation of the Third Republic in the 1870s. The prefects represented everything that Vichy stood for: the State, authority, order, and hierarchy. Marcel Peyrouton, Vichy's first minister of the interior, understood this when he called upon them to help the State overcome "twenty years of errors and follies," as he put it in an October 1940 circular. Through decrees issued by Peyrouton, elected departmental and municipal bodies were eliminated, and the prefects were made the "only representatives of the State" in the departments. They could rule on virtually anything without having to compromise with elected officials or their constituents. But, this did not make their lives easier. For one thing, Vichy did not trust the prefects; it circumscribed their powers by creating seven super regional prefects in the Free Zone, as well as by establishing Commissaires du pouvoir who investigated abuses of power and corruption within the departments. Furthermore, every prefect was subject to the authority of Vichy's quasi-military forces, first the Légion française des combattants and then the Milice, which had total support

from the State even though the French almost unanimously condemned them as sadistic, Nazi-inspired organizations. In reality, therefore, the prefectoral corps suffered from enormous uncertainty under
Vichy. Prefects discovered that they could be purged at any moment,
that they had lost touch with the local community as the result of
excessive centralization of power, that they were caught between the
conflicting forces of the Resistance and the Germans, and that no one
at the local level wanted to do their dirty work after 1942, if not before.
In the Occupied Zone the prefects had additional problems. Vichy instructed them to obey the Germans, but this proved impossible, since
German orders often conflicted violently with the wishes of the inhabitants of their departments. Not surprisingly, turnover was very high in
the prefectoral corps, and the Germans deported a total of seventy-one
members of it, over half of whom died in the camps. As the experts on
the subject of the prefects concluded, the Vichy model of government
rested on "a misunderstanding of local political and administrative re-
alities."[56] Like everybody else Vichy touched, the prefects soon yearned
for the good old days of the Third Republic over the chaos, stupidity,
and brutality of the National Revolution.

In trying to govern France, even the rump France that was called
the Free Zone, Vichy faced a serious dilemma: How can a modern
society, rooted in democratic values, be governed by a highly centralized state that rejects, even deplores, any form of consultation with its
citizens? Of course the National Revolution, in theory, did not reject
such consultation; the corporate state provided a forum for legally constituted groups to speak out. But, as we have seen, this was a sham;
the State's agenda was never determined, or even greatly influenced,
by any corporate body. An official political party would have offered
the possibility of tapping public opinion, which even an authoritarian
state needs to do in order to govern. However, Vichy failed to create a
single-party state, due primarily to the inability of large sectors of the
Right to agree on what such a party should be, or whether it should
even exist. Fascists and other extremists in Paris could not agree with
Catholics and advocates of the National Revolution in Vichy. Laval and
Pétain were deeply suspicious of the Parisians, who were too close to

Nazi ideas for their comfort. And the Parisians responded with suspicions of their own: the Vichy crowd, they believed, was too soft, not fascist enough, too nostalgic and archaic in their political ideas. Instead, Vichy decided to forget the idea of a one-party state, which did not appeal greatly to Pétain in any case, and base its power on the military and the police. In other words, rather than tapping public opinion for constructive purposes, Vichy decided to use coercion and militarism to keep the populace quiescent. It is the same old story of statism winning out over the ideals of the National Revolution, whatever they might be worth. And of course, like everything else, it did not work.

The bureaucracy mushroomed as a result of this statist solution to governance; the size of the civil service increased by 26 percent under Vichy. Bureaucrats had to enforce new regulations that required everyone to have an identity card. They had to keep track of changes of address and keep watch over foreigners. Even the installation of a telephone or the purchase of a bicycle came under the State's watchful eye. Proper papers were needed for all of these, plus much more. The result was a massive paper explosion. Everyone was considered potentially guilty under the system until their papers proved that they were innocent. The bureaucracy's ultimate aim was to have a file on everyone living in France. The Service de démographie set up under Vichy created 20 million dossiers that identified everyone with a number; after the war, it was transformed into the more benign national social security system. Special police forces were created to enforce surveillance laws. The most notorious of these was the Police aux questions juives (PQJ), which enforced the anti-Semitic laws, but Vichy also created the first national police force. The end result of these intrusive police state activities was a system of bureaucratic paperwork that equaled or surpassed what existed in European fascist states.[57]

Pétain was clearly aware of this vast extension of state power, but he was primarily interested in restoring the power of the military, making it into the main pillar of sovereignty. Thus, he appointed more officers to key cabinet posts than any other head of state since 1832. The state of siege that the republic had inaugurated in 1939 was maintained in force during the life of Vichy. It allowed Pétain to give military courts extensive jurisdiction. But Pétain pinned his greatest hopes—or so it appears from his grandiloquent speeches—on the Légion française des combattants, which he created at the end of August 1940 by forcing the merger of the existing veterans' organizations into one vast organization whose purpose was to unite the nation behind the Marshal and the National Revolution. Its simplistic slogans, such as "Think and act French," "With the Legion, for France," and "Neither right nor left, straight ahead with the Marshal," appealed to the hundreds of thousands who joined it. On one occasion, in February 1942, he praised them for working hard to establish "the primacy of the spirit of sacrifice over the spirit of pleasure, the fecundity of the family over the sterility of the foyer, and social evangelism over bourgeois egoism." Duty was the key to the life of the legionnaire. He was to obey at all times, in order to "guarantee the unity of the nation." No "partisan discussions" were permitted among legionnaires; they had to provide their leader, the Marshal, with "unconditional support," serving the "public good by blindly following their leader" and promoting his doctrines—that is, the doctrines of the National Revolution— among the French people.[58]

In fact, the Legion was a totally Pétainist organization. All members had to take an oath to Pétain based on fealty they owed him for his actions in World War I. They also had to follow narrowly the ideological and political agenda laid down by the Marshal. Their final objective was to make all of the French into true believers in the National Revolution. To achieve this all political parties, even fascist ones, had to be eliminated, for parties divided the nation and undermined the attempts to unite the French behind their leader. Although parties were not eliminated, in late 1941 the Legion tried to unite the nation by reaching beyond the ranks of the veterans and accepting anyone who chose to be a so-called Volunteer of the National Revolution, whether he had served in the military or not. This resulted in the Legion mushrooming to almost a million members, all of whom were sworn to spread the ideals of the National Revolution as interpreted by Marshal Pétain.[59]

Although the Legion was supposed to substitute for a national political party, it fared poorly in its role as a conduit for public opinion. Nor was it well liked by the French; prefects warned Vichy that the legionnaires alienated local citizens by their actions. By 1943, the Legion was in a state of decline; collaboration with the Germans was not popular with the rank and file, who concluded that Vichy had abandoned the principles of the National Revolution. During the year, possibly 10 percent of the Legion joined the fascist Milice, while a larger percentage went over to the Resistance and a significant number quit the organization. In the summer of 1943 the former head of the Legion, François Valentin, even called on its members to join the Resistance in order to achieve the goals of the National Revolution. The Legion never accomplished what Pétain wanted: it failed to rally the public behind Vichy, it did not carry out the National Revolution, and it rejected Pétainist collaboration. Characteristic of the "spiritual" nature of the Vichy regime, the Legion was probably most successful in carrying out elaborate ritualistic ceremonies, similar in spirit to Robespierre's revolutionary festivals. In 1941 this involved the carrying of the sacred flame from the Tomb of the Unknown Soldier in Paris to Vichy, where the Marshal presided over a ceremony that led eventually to the spread of the flame to every corner of the south and the Empire. One year later the legionnaires carried sacred soil from every part of France to a giant cenotaph that commemorated twenty centuries of the existence of the peasant nation. And then, in 1943, the sacred flame ceremony was repeated only this time without the empire as its last destination: at Marseille and Toulon torches were thrown into the sea in defiance of the Allied takeover of North Africa, revealing the limits of spiritual renewal and the Legion.[60]

Inevitably, it seems, the military state that Pétain believed was the answer to France's decline was based on nothing less than brute force. To supplement the Legion, Pétain acquiesced in the creation of the Service d'ordre légionnaire (SOL), an elite quasi-fascistic group of around 10,000 veterans set up in 1941 under the leadership of Joseph Darnand. Eventually, this evolved into the fascistic Milice in early 1943. At the founding ceremony for the Milice, on January 30, 1943, its head, Darnand, stated that its goal was "to install in France a national socialist authoritarian regime, permitting France to be integrated into the Europe of tomorrow." Pierre Laval, the second in command to the Marshal, responded by saying, "I approve without reservation Darnand's declaration." By law, the Milice was empowered "to take an active role in the political, social, economic, intellectual, and moral rejuvenation of France." Pétain accepted all of this, without reservation. Although he supposedly complained about the Milice in private, he said nothing negative about this group of thugs in public. In the final analysis, the Marshal agreed with the main principles of the Milice: anti-Semitism, anticommunism, anti-Gaullism, and authoritarian government. In April 1943 he defended vigorously the role of the Milice in "the establishment of the new regime." He granted this new organization control over "all avant-garde missions, notably those relative to the maintenance of order, to the protection of sensitive parts of the nation, to the struggle against communism." Alongside the Legion, the Milice was "to win over the hearts of the people" through its example.[61]

To the bitter end, Pétain hoped that the Legion would achieve the unity of France. But this meant including only those who were "animated by the same patriotism" as the legionnaires were, he told the remaining handful of faithful members in August 1944! By then the total failure of Pétain and Vichy to construct a working, effective form of government should have been evident to everyone. But Pétain still believed tenaciously, against all the facts, in the ideal of the National Revolution, as the Nazis took him from France to Sigmaringen, Germany.[62]

3   Collaboration

With the signing of the armistice agreement in June 1940, the French state accepted collaboration with the Nazi occupying power. Henceforth the new order was contingent upon a German victory in World War II. During the history of Vichy, no leader who reached the top disagreed with this position. Only Marshal Weygand, who came close to being named Pétain's right-hand man, dissented from it. The others, Laval, Flandin, Darlan, and Pétain, accepted subservience to Germany as the price of losing the war. They only disagreed over the extent and degree to which France should collaborate.

On a different level, that of civil society, collaboration was a fact of life after June 1940, and not something that was necessarily accepted or embraced. The French had no choice but to live cheek by jowl with the Germans. This was especially true in the Occupied Zone, which comprised two-thirds of France. In the southern Free Zone, occupation was not directly experienced before the German invasion of it in November 1942. But throughout France the economic impact of collaboration was felt very early. By the fall of 1940 food supplies were low, and rationing had to be implemented. Although the south was slower to reject collaboration, by 1941 the French overwhelmingly opposed the German presence and hoped that the English would win the war. The disconnect between French citizens and their government increased over time as Vichy pursued greater collaboration with the Nazis. Although public opinion was well known to Pétain and other government officials, Vichy did very little to appease the growing anticollaborationist sentiment. Once again, authoritarian principles of governance trumped listening to the people.

In this chapter, we will investigate collaboration from two perspectives. The first, and most important, is state collaboration, which became the central driving force of Vichy policy. The second is non-state collaboration. In some cases it was ideological and in other cases opportunistic in motivation. Finally, there is accommodation with the occupying Germans, something that few could avoid if they wished to live a relatively normal life after the defeat.

State Collaboration

State collaboration began in June 1940 with the signing of the armistice. Yet, no one in the French government openly discussed the matter at first. When Pétain appealed to the legislature for full powers in July, he referred vaguely to the need to integrate France into "the continental system of production and exchange." Toward the end of the month the new minister of the interior, the neo-socialist Adrian Marquet, proclaimed: "A new deal will be born in Europe. France must participate in it."[1] But no one concluded that this meant collaborating with the Germans to the exclusion of the British.

Pétain approached collaboration from a purely pragmatic perspective: the Germans had won the war and France could gain a privileged economic place in the new world order only if it collaborated. Pierre Laval agreed with Pétain, but he was far more zealous in pursuing close relations with Germany. During July and August 1940, Laval went to Paris on three occasions to negotiate an agreement with the Germans. Even though Laval expressed pro-German sentiments, condemned de Gaulle, and called for the defeat of Great Britain in front of Nazi diplomats and generals, telling German Ambassador Otto Abetz on one occasion that he wanted France to "make her modest contribution to the final overthrow of Britain," he did not convince the Germans of the benefits of total collaboration. The Germans did not want French military aid, which was Laval's main offer in return for a privileged position in the Nazi pantheon of nations, and had already received in the armistice everything they wanted from France. Still, Pétain continued to believe that Laval could work out a deal with the Nazis. He did not know that Hitler had no intention of granting concessions to France, which he wanted to destroy after the war had been won.[2]

As Philippe Burrin has pointed out, Vichy's leaders did not understand Nazism, which they thought was a militaristic reincarnation of traditional Pan-Germanism. The Nazis had only contempt for France, both on racial grounds and because of its apparent lack of military prowess. Otto Abetz, the Nazi front man in Paris, seemed to be a typical Francophile German who offered the "hope of possible *entente* with the Reich." In reality, he was a staunch nationalist who aimed at total and permanent occupation of France and its dismemberment through the encouragement of separatist sentiments in Brittany, Flanders, Burgundy, and Lorraine.[3]

Vichy, however, needed collaboration to survive; without close ties with Germany, Vichy's brand of authoritarianism would crumble before the appeals of the Gaullist Resistance. As early as August 1940, Pétain revealed his acute awareness of this. He responded to Gaullist attacks on his government by addressing the French nation on the problems created by defeat. He promised, first of all, to feed the nation, but not without rationing and a massive effort to revive agriculture, which he claimed had been devastated by the war and years of neglect. He also promised to repatriate French prisoners of war, presumably by working with the Germans, although he did not say how it would be done. But above all he blamed the Third Republic for the situation in which France found itself, implying that a return to democratic government, which de Gaulle supported, was not the answer to the nation's problems. Instead, Pétain made collaboration central to solving the national crisis by striking a deal with Germany that would integrate France into the continental system and provide economic benefits for the nation. On October 10, 1940, he spoke openly on radio about this taboo subject, claiming that France was open to "collaboration in all fields and with all her neighbors," but especially with the Germans. The National Revolution, he implied, could not succeed without collaboration with Germany.[4]

Pétain returned to the subject of collaboration at the end of the month, after he had met with Hitler at Montoire on October 24. The Montoire meeting had not been successful; Hitler offered no concessions in return for collaboration. Nevertheless, Pétain and Laval came out forcefully, in public, behind a policy of state collaboration with Germany. The communiqué issued by Pétain's office stated that "the two interlocutors came to agreement on the principle of collaboration," but mentioned no details on what collaboration entailed. Pétain, in an October 30 radio address, claimed that he accepted the principle of collaboration between France and Germany, adding: "This policy is mine. The Ministers are responsible to me alone. History will judge me alone." At the same time, Laval claimed that the fate of France depended on the success of collaboration, which he believed would work to the benefit of everyone involved.[5]

Although some hoped that Petain might get concessions from the Germans or was playing a double game with them, these statements shocked the French people, most of whom rejected state collaboration. P. J. Philip, writing for the *New York Times,* commented in late October 1940 that the French overwhelmingly supported the British in the war. Vichy had lost favor by its attacks on Great Britain, he observed, even though many supported Vichy's National Revolution. He concluded: "The great majority of the French people are on the side of General de Gaulle and the British." Philip's conclusion was corroborated by numerous witnesses from occupied France, including a pro-Franco reporter for the Madrid paper, *Arriba,* who claimed that "a Frenchman growls when he sees Pétain shaking hands with Hitler," adding: "Almost the whole of French public opinion . . . is on tiptoes for the London radio, and repeats its statements and falsehoods." Virtually everyone who fled France for New York in the fall of 1940 reported something similar to the *New York Times.* Leon Feuchtwanger, who arrived in New York in late November, claimed that 99 percent of the French opposed Vichy. Clearly, this was an exaggeration, but Vichy officials in charge of opening the mail, listening to telephone conversations, and the like reached conclusions that approximated Feuchtwanger's claim: the vast majority of the French rejected the Montoire meeting between Hitler and Pétain, despised collaboration with Germany, and sympathized with the British, they stated, despite lingering concerns about Britain's role in the defeat of France and its destruction of the French fleet at Mers-el-Kébir in July 1940 to prevent it from falling into German hands.[6]

Pétain was aware of these pro-British sentiments. After October 30 he rarely spoke in public about collaboration, and then only briefly or cryptically. The unpopular Montoire meeting was followed in November 1940 by the Nazi expulsion of tens of thousands of French speakers from Lorraine in an effort to make the region permanently German. The Nazis sent them to southern France where the local population soon expressed its resentment that Vichy had been complicit in their expulsion. The Lorraine refugees were a visible, tangible example of what collaboration meant. But this did not undermine Pétain's popularity. The French assumed that he was opposed to collaboration, despite his public utterances. Letters poured in to Vichy, imploring Pétain to beware of collaborators, to get rid of Laval, to support the British, and the like. The hero of Verdun was not tarnished with the brush of collaboration, but Pierre Laval became fixed in the public eye as a devious Germanophile, someone who could not be trusted to lead the nation. Pétain's popularity soared by the end of the year, reaching its highest point in the winter of 1940–41, after the December 13, 1940, dismissal of Laval. Wherever he went during the fall of 1940, large, enthusiastic crowds greeted him, bursting out singing "La Marseillaise" and treating the Marshal as though he were the savior of France. In Lyon, where he appeared shortly after the Lorrainers had been expelled from their homes, he won over the crowd by responding to one Lorrainer's "hope for better days" by stating, simply, "We must ever hope for better days." In late 1940, the French believed that Pétain was the man of destiny who would bring "better days."[7]

The dismissal of Laval, which Pétain announced with the reassuring conclusion that "I remain at the helm, the National Revolution continues," brought great hopes that "better days" were near. But what followed was a crisis of the policy of collaboration, as the Germans concluded that Laval's dismissal represented a repudiation of it. So did the French public. Rumors spread rapidly that Laval had intended to overthrow Pétain and declare war on Great Britain. Nothing could have been further from the truth. Laval had most likely been dis-

missed because he failed to translate the Montoire meeting into con-
crete results. Furthermore, Pétain had reiterated his support for
collaboration on December 14 and appointed a successor to Laval who
was sympathetic to Nazi Germany, Pierre-Étienne Flandin. Flandin
had written Hitler in the fall of 1938 to congratulate him on the success of the Munich agreement. In 1939 he had come out against war
with Germany, and in 1940 he had favored Vichy's anti-Semitic and
anti-Masonic legislation. But, for reasons that are obscure, Washington
and London thought Flandin was closer to their point of view than
Laval had been, while Germany expressed total opposition to the new
man.[8]

If anything, the dismissal of Laval and the German reaction to it
led Pétain to reinforce his power and to strengthen the bonds of collaboration. In January 1941, he created the National Council, which was a
rubber-stamp, quasi-legislative body totally under the Marshal's control, established for the purpose of providing the regime legitimacy
until the much-awaited constitution was promulgated. Pétain appointed the members of the council, which possessed only powers that
he delegated to it. In addition, at the end of January the Marshal issued
Constitutional Act No. 7, which granted him total power over all judicial proceedings, including the Riom trial of former Third Republic
officials—Léon Blum, Georges Mandel, and others. Henceforth, Pétain's sovereign authority included legislative, executive, and judicial
matters. In essence, he was the state. At the same time, during January,
Pétain sought to patch up relations with Laval and the Germans by
offering to restore the former deputy premier to the cabinet. Although
this did not happen, in February 1941 the Marshal chose Admiral Darlan to head the government. Darlan was more anti-British than Laval
had been. He hoped to use his new position, combined with his control
over the French Navy, to make France into a major power in the Nazi's
new European order, which he believed was inevitable. Although he
was not an anti-Semite, he embraced anti-Semitic and other exclusionary policies, while reinforcing the technocratic, modernizing forces in
Vichy. To him, collaboration was the only path to take, since a British

victory in the war would strip France of its empire and navy, leaving the nation a "second-class Dominion, a continental Ireland."[9]

One of Darlan's first acts was to appoint Paul Marion as minister of information, in charge of Vichy's propaganda. Up until this point, Vichy had no effective propaganda system, even though Laval had ordered, in November 1940, that the news media support the policy of collaboration. Marion was an ex-communist who had rallied with great enthusiasm to the fascist right in the 1930s, joining ranks with Jacques Doriot in 1936. He was totally acceptable to the Nazis; Abetz found him to be very pro-German. He also appealed to the Parisian collaborationists; Marcel Déat called him "very collaborationist and very anti-English" when the two met in late February 1941. Indeed, Marion was a true believer in both the National Revolution and collaboration, although he thought that the latter could succeed only if France were totally transformed. A new spirit and a new man were needed to achieve this, but they could not be created unless a single party and total state control over information were established. To this end, Marion ruthlessly pursued opponents of the National Revolution and promoted collaboration in news media, which he controlled through censorship, subsidies, and the allocation of paper supplies. In addition, he began to create a corps of propagandists at the departmental level and attempted to unite the nation's youth movements under Vichy's control. But Marion ran into extensive opposition to his policies within Vichy. The traditionalists wanted propaganda aimed at promoting the National Revolution as Pétain had defined it and mostly opposed creating a single party or a united youth movement. This was especially true of the Church, which feared that Marion's measures would undermine its powers. Even the Germans became disillusioned with Marion since his propaganda machine did not prevent the French from becoming more anti-German and pro-British in 1941. By the end of the year, Marion's vast scheme to promote collaboration and the National Revolution had failed. When Pierre Laval returned to power in 1942, he ousted Marion and abandoned the ambitious program of a single party, united youth movement, and strict press controls, pursuing in-

stead a Third Republic system of propaganda through notables such
as the clergy and local elites. Vichy would never develop fully the kind
of totalitarian propaganda apparatus that Marion dreamed of and the
Nazis deployed throughout the war.[10]

The Darlan government's primary focus, however, was on reaching
an agreement with the Germans so as to fulfill Pétain's instruction "to
bring into operation the collaboration." An opportunity emerged with
a rise in German interest in the Mediterranean in the spring of 1941,
following Rommel's February arrival in North Africa and an April
Iraqi revolt against the British, upon which the Germans hoped to
capitalize. To entice the Germans, Darlan acceded to their request for
the use of Syrian airbases and other support in Syria in return for
purely verbal promises of concessions on occupation costs and POW
releases. The result was the Protocols of Paris agreed to in late May
1941, which formalized the agreement over Syria in part one and provided for future German use of French bases in Tunisia and Senegal in
exchange for unspecified German concessions in parts two and three.[11]

Beyond part one, the Protocols were never implemented, most fundamentally because French demands for concessions far exceeded
what Hitler was willing to grant, especially after German attention
shifted from the Mediterranean to the war against the Soviet Union in
June 1941.[12] Opposition to the Protocols by General Weygand led the
French to demand extensive concessions from the Germans in early
June, including not only an end to the payment of occupation costs,
but also economic aid from Germany, at a time when the Germans
were taking as much out of the French economy as they could. The
Germans rejected this and a subsequent attempt in July to fundamentally transform the Franco-German relationship established by the armistice. For German Foreign Minister Ribbentrop the latter effort
amounted to "a naïve French blackmail attempt." Undeterred by Germany's rebuff, Darlan attempted on several more occasions to reopen
negotiations for a Franco-German agreement, only to be told that the
Germans were too busy or that a final Franco-German treaty would
have to wait until total victory had been achieved. Even Pétain entered
into the fray, although without success. On December 1, 1941, he told

Goering that Germany could not rule Europe without France as a partner: "You cannot make peace without France," he said. "By refusing to make peace on the basis of collaboration, you risk losing the peace." In January 1942 Pétain and Darlan unexpectedly received word from Abetz that Hitler would offer a favorable peace treaty if France were to enter the war on Germany's side. Pétain and Darlan were open to exploring the possibility but nothing more came of it as Hitler—whose willingness to make a deal had been exaggerated by Abetz—turned his back on it. In the meantime, Syria had been lost to the Gaullists during 1941, and Vichy had become more isolated. Darlan fell from power in April 1942 without achieving his mission of total collaboration.[13]

Although military collaboration with Germany never worked out, in the narrow sense of the term, economic collaboration increased under Darlan. Early results include the ceding of major copper interests to Germany in April 1941 and a joint Franco-German aluminum venture agreed to in May 1941. In January 1942, the German chief economic delegate to the Armistice Commission proclaimed that France contributed more to German armaments than any other European nation. "German orders in France are the dominant factor in the French economy," he claimed. Every major French firm collaborated to some extent economically, although very few did so out of sympathy with the Nazi cause. Renault was the major exception; after the war, it would be one of the few enterprises nationalized for collaborating with the enemy. In a few cases, such as that of the Michelin tire factory, collaboration was carried out under duress, not willingly. In most situations, however, firms went along reluctantly with the Nazis: Wendel, Peugeot, Rhône-Poulenc, and Pechiney fit roughly into this broad category of reluctant collaborators. Yet the Nazis were never short of companions for their Paris roundtable lunches at which French heads of banks, chemical companies, automobile firms, and other enterprises discussed economic collaboration with their German counterparts once every three weeks.[14]

Darlan played a significant role in developing economic collaboration. He brought into office technocrats who tried to make the French economy more efficient and centralized. Either consciously or inadvertently, they also contributed to economic collaboration with Germany. Some of them, such as Pierre Pucheu at the interior ministry and Yves Bouthillier at finances, openly advocated integrating Vichy into the new order by modernizing the French economy. Their collaborationist plans stoked the rumor of a massive conspiracy—the so-called synarchy—to concentrate the economy in the hands of a small elite. By the summer of 1941 the rumor had become rampant, leading Pétain to call vainly for decentralization of power.[15]

More important than the so-called synarchy were the Comités d'organisation, which were inaugurated in 1940 to consolidate firms into larger, more competitive units and bring together industrialists and state officials to nationally manage the economy. These newly created units cooperated closely—often to their detriment—with their German counterparts in a European economy that the Nazis increasingly cartelized. Thus, to take one example, Vichy and the Germans consolidated the French dyestuffs industry into one organization, Francolor, which was brought under German control in November 1941, effectively squeezing the French out of this sector, but accomplishing the goals of efficiency, centralization, and modernization—not to mention economic collaboration. Although the French technocrats did not necessarily welcome this outcome, it was a common result of Franco-German cooperation. French banks were also consolidated into larger units, with enormous benefits for the Nazis, who obtained easy access to cheap credit. The same was true of the requisitioning of raw materials, which came increasingly under the direct control of the state to the detriment of farmers and consumers but to the benefit of the German occupiers. In fact, one can safely conclude that these attempts to plan the French economy were more often than not nothing more than blatant collaboration with the enemy, whether French technocrats knew so or not. As Henry Rousso has noted: "The leitmotif of the majority of Vichy technocrats was, in effect, the need to consolidate businesses, to eliminate the least profitable, to achieve economies of scale." But this was contradicted totally by the disadvantages of collaboration, which most of these highly educated leaders did not comprehend until the end of 1941. Until then they believed that they were increasing their market share in Germany by exporting military goods and raw materials. The fact that they received little in return was not taken into consideration until it was too late. Still, many sectors of the French economy benefited from collaboration. These included autos, airplanes, steel, cement—in fact, most industries associated with the German war effort. In addition, those in charge of the economy were convinced that after the war France would be in a privileged economic position in the new Europe as a result of extensive collaboration. To achieve that end, they expanded the state debt four times in four years, providing the German war effort ample support.[16]

In the spring of 1942, Darlan fell from grace after numerous failed efforts to sign an agreement with the Germans. By then, he had become disillusioned with the Nazi cause, convinced that the Germans would lose the war to the Americans. Alone among the Vichy elite, Darlan took a geopolitical view of the war, similar to de Gaulle's, although not as prescient as that great leader's analysis. His successor, Pierre Laval, had no such qualms. Returned to power in April 1942 as head of government, Laval pursued collaboration with vengeance. He had convinced Pétain to reappoint him by arguing that the Marshal had lost popular support because of Darlan's weak government. In the words of Admiral Leahy, the United States representative at Vichy, Laval promised Pétain that he would prepare the nation for "the inevitable German victory" by establishing "close collaboration with Germany on every matter." On April 20, 1942, he informed the nation that it was involved in a life or death struggle led by Germany against bolshevism: "No threat will prevent me from pursuing agreement and reconciliation with Germany," he added. A week later Laval informed Admiral Leahy, in private, that "a German victory . . . is preferable to a British and Soviet victory." On June 22, in an infamous radio broadcast, he told the entire nation virtually the same thing: "I desire the victory of Germany, for without it bolshevism would tomorrow install itself everywhere."[17]

The French universally condemned Laval's statement; they did not want a German victory or closer collaboration. Still Laval persisted. The most notorious of his policies was the so-called *relève,* which was implemented in the summer of 1942. For public consumption, the *re-lève* was advertised as an agreement with Germany to repatriate French prisoners of war. For every Frenchman who went to work in Germany, Laval hoped, one French prisoner would be returned. He also argued that the arrangement would aid the Germans in defeating the archenemies of western civilization, the Bolsheviks, as French workers would relieve Germans from factory work in order to fight on the eastern front. But the reality turned out to be quite different: for every three skilled workers sent to Germany only one French POW was liberated, and since very few who departed happened to be skilled, few prisoners returned home during the war—only 90,000 by one estimate. Furthermore, very few French workers were attracted by this opportunity, despite misleading propaganda about it. Laval promised 350,000 workers would depart in the summer of 1942, but no more than 40,000 had left by the end of July and only 240,000 by the end of the year. This led the Germans to threaten to requisition labor, which Laval preempted by having Vichy do it beginning in September 1942. Eventually, in February 1943, the *relève* was replaced by the Service du travail obligatoire (STO) which amounted to a form of conscription of French workers that allowed for very few exceptions. As most historians have argued, the STO led to the creation of the Resistance movement known as the Maquis, as thousands of young Frenchmen fled from the cities to the countryside in order to avoid going to work in Germany. In short, this aspect of collaboration fed the fires of the Resistance and failed to achieve the objectives that Laval and the Germans had established for it.[18]

Laval also pursued collaboration with the Germans on police matters, continuing the efforts of Darlan who had created Special Sections or Courts to try dissidents such as communists and members of the Resistance—terrorists in the eyes of Vichy and the Nazis—without due legal process. Laval appointed as chief of police René Bousquet, a civil servant intent on collaborating closely with the Germans. Bousquet informed his Nazi counterpart, Oberg, that the French police were committed to act with Germany "against terrorism, anarchism and communism, the common enemies of our two countries."[19] He could have added the Jews to this list, since the French police under Bousquet carried out extensive roundups of Jews during the summer of 1942. In the midst of these roundups, which we will investigate in detail in the next chapter, Bousquet and Oberg agreed to cooperate fully on all police matters. To Bousquet and Vichy this agreement was important because it appeared to give the French sovereign control over their territory. Neither seemed to mind that it required doing the Nazi's dirty work, thereby freeing German soldiers to fight the allied forces.[20]

Pétain and Laval remained enthusiastic about collaboration throughout 1942, despite the German invasion of southern France in November. They both applauded the Nazi defeat of the Allied landing attempt at the channel port of Dieppe during August and assured the Germans that all of France supported their efforts. This was clearly not the case. Although Pétain remained popular, his government's policies were not. Laval, in particular, lost support, as a German army report of October 24, 1942, revealed: "The enactment of the compulsory labour law and the anti-Jewish campaign, which is incomprehensible to the French mind . . . seem to be the major causes of the fall in Laval's prestige."[21] Still, Laval persisted in collaborating, even after the Allied invasion of France's North Africa empire on November 8 and the German takeover of hitherto unoccupied southern France a few days later. When General Weygand informed him that his policy was opposed by 95 percent of the French, Laval snorted back that the figure was closer to 98 percent. Although Pétain protested the German takeover of Vichy, he did so only to appease French public opinion. Both Pétain and Laval opposed the Allied invasion of North Africa, called upon Admiral Darlan—who was in North Africa at the time—to resist it, and rejected Darlan's cease-fire agreement with the Allies, ordering him not to take "any action in any circumstances against the Axis forces." If anything, Laval became more collaborationist as the result of the events of November, during which he increased his governmental power, gaining the right to promulgate decrees. On November 20 he gave a carefully drafted radio talk on why France continued to collaborate, arguing that if the Americans won the war, "We would have to submit to the domination of communists and Jews. We do not want universal bolshevism to come in the wake of its Anglo-Saxon accom-plices and extinguish the light of French civilization for ever."[22]

Instead, Laval and Pétain chose German dominance. The November German invasion of the Free Zone meant the end of whatever sover-eignty Vichy possessed. Hitler, who mistrusted the French, immedi-ately dissolved the minuscule armistice army, leaving Vichy with no effective armed force. The French military elite, which universally de-spised the Germans, turned sour on collaboration and became disillu-sioned with Pétain and Vichy, although very few joined the Resistance as a result. Laval, however, believed that Germany would allow France to restore its military, but his appeals to Hitler on the matter went nowhere. Pétain, forever the stoic martyr, argued that adversity was the key to greatness, warning the nation that "communist barbarism, if it triumphed, would destroy forever our civilization and national independence." In short, the only choice was collaboration—no matter what the cost—as far as these two men were concerned.[23]

The public face of collaboration changed after 1942. Pictures of workers marching off to Germany or of POWs coming home to he-roes' welcomes disappeared from the newsreels, replaced by shots of the French Anti-Bolshevik Legion (the LVF) whose volunteer members fought against the Soviet Union on the eastern front beginning in 1941. Anticommunism was used in propaganda to justify collabora-tion. By the summer of 1943, anticommunist meetings, anniversary celebrations of the German invasion of Russia, and commemorations of the founding of the LVF monopolized the news. In one clip of an anticommunist meeting, held in the Salle Wagram in Paris, Monsei-gneur Mayol de Lupé appeared in a Nazi uniform to speak in favor of the LVF, warning the faithful against the dangers of "the Anglo-Judeo Masonic" ideology! In another, the news included images of a mass for the members of the LVF. By the end of the year, crazed fascists dominated the collaborationist message in the news. Images of a De-cember anticommunist rally at the Vélodrome d'Hiver included the head of the fascist Milice, Joseph Darnand, who proclaimed: "As for us, we prefer to die rather than to submit to the victory of Israel." This was the type of collaboration that Laval and Pétain increasingly accepted and engaged in.[24]

At the end of October 1943, Pétain attempted to break out of the straitjacket that he had created for himself. He confronted Laval on his unpopularity and the sorry state of the nation, asking him to resign. But the Marshal's scheme to get rid of Laval and one-up de Gaulle by recalling the Third Republic's legislature came to a dead end when the Germans delivered an ultimatum to him at the end of November. It required Pétain to submit all new laws to the Germans for approval, allow Laval to control the cabinet's composition, purge anti-Germans in the French administration, and appoint only collaborationists to government posts. In effect, the old man was now required, once more, to write his obituary if he accepted the German conditions. After some hesitation, he capitulated. Within a month, the Vichy government was under the control of the Parisian thugs who were "more Catholic than the Pope" in their adoration of Nazism. Authoritarian Vichy gave way to the fascists, men such as Darnand, Déat, and Henriot. Although Laval opposed them, mainly because they undermined his power, he could not stop them from taking over as the Nazis insisted that they be included in the government. Collaboration was now more than ever a one-way street; any hint of power sharing between Vichy and Germany had totally disappeared.[25]

As Michèle Cointet has argued, in 1944 Vichy became *"l'État milicien."* Darnand and the Milice took over, under the auspices of the Nazi SS, which Darnand had sworn to support in August 1943. He had created the Milice, with the blessing of both Pétain and Laval, out of the members of the extremist Service d'ordre légionnaire (SOL), which he had helped found in January 1942 to provide paramilitary support to the National Revolution. Darnand neatly summed up the purposes of the SOL, which became those of the Milice, in a speech in Nice in February 1942: "Against Gaullist dissidence, for French unity, / Against Bolshevism, for nationalism, / Against the leprosy of the Jews, for French purity, / Against pagan Freemasons, for Christian civilization. . . ."[26] The Milice was Vichy's effort to take on the growing Resistance and thereby satisfy the Germans. With it, the thugs came to power

With Nazi backing, Darnand and the Milice—some 15,000 strong—created a police state, establishing a system of courts martial in January 1944 to circumvent the normal channels of justice. The miliciens sat as judges on these courts, guaranteeing that justice would be quick—from trial to execution in twenty-four hours, with no right to appeal. Laval defended these tribunals, claiming that state lawyers had given him sound advice about their legality. Laval and Darnand both believed that the Bolshevik threat justified total collaboration with Germany in order to defend Western civilization. The Milice's tactics were brutal, but they were necessary in the eyes of the collaborators. The Milice drew up a list of suspects, mostly Gaullists and communists, and pursued them through endless identity checks in the streets and occasional random roundups. It hunted down Jews and encouraged the French to inform on suspicious neighbors. These actions were legal under the new law of December 1943. Because there was no check on the Milice's actions, it ran wild, torturing, pillaging, stealing money, and pilfering food supplies from civilians in the name of "law and order" and the defense of Western values.[27]

Until August 1944, Marshal Pétain accepted this new form of collaboration without protest and with some enthusiasm. He repeatedly warned the nation that the Liberation of France was a sham, being carried out by terrorists who called themselves patriots. Their victory, he argued on April 28, 1944, would lead to the triumph of communism and the destruction of French civilization. Not until the Allies approached Paris in August 1944 did Pétain turn on his collaborationist supporters by attacking the Milice for being an extremist organization, but even then he tempered his remarks by praising its record in combating terrorism. Indeed, Pétain had said nothing when the Milice tortured and massacred members of the Resistance in the spring. Laval had even praised its actions, although he was disturbed when miliciens executed his Jewish political colleague Georges Mandel, who had been Clemenceau's right-hand man during World War I.[28]

From August 1944, the doomed fate of Pétain, Laval, and collaboration was realized. The Germans presented the Marshal and the Vichy government with an ultimatum on August 19: either go to Germany willingly or be forced to do so. Pétain responded with a protest to Hitler, but this accomplished nothing. Against his will, Pétain was escorted to Germany, where his government remained until the war's conclusion in 1945. Collaboration now assumed totally fascist stripes, as the Parisian fascist leaders—Darnand, Doriot, Déat, and Brinon—took over. Although the fiction was maintained that Pétain exercised control over this rump government and remained "in sole possession of French legitimacy," continuing the policy of collaboration with the Germans, by late 1944 the Marshal was focused on preparing for his postwar trial in the hope of clearing his name. Meanwhile, the motley fascist crew assembled in Germany planned to invade France to liberate it from Gaullists and communists, using the Milice, the remains of the LVF and other paramilitary forces, as well as the French POWs and workers in Germany. They soon discovered that the POWs and workers had no desire to engage in civil war and collaboration. The fascists could count on only a few thousand loyal anticommunist and anti-Gaullist troops to achieve their goals. With the defeat of Germany in May 1945—but not until then—the collaborationist cause ended.[29]

Non-State Collaboration

When the war ended in 1945 the myth began that everyone in France, with the exception of a handful of traitors, resisted the Germans. Today we know from numerous historical monographs that this was not the case. French exceptionalism turned out to be a Resistance myth. Some people collaborated; some resisted; and most ended up between the two extremes. Philippe Burrin's *France under the Germans* has provided us with a detailed statistical profile on who collaborated. According to Burrin, the typical member of a collaborationist organization in the early years of Vichy was male (85 percent), urban, and middle and upper middle class (71.4 percent versus only 27.5 percent workers and peasants, who comprised 63 percent of the workforce). Over time, however, membership shifted to the lower middle class and the working class, away from the elite. In the process, political ties changed too: in 1941, one-third of collaborationists had previously been involved in politics, primarily on the far Right (two-thirds, versus 22 percent on the Left and 8 percent on the moderate Right), but by 1944 only 7 percent had previous political involvement. The first members of collaborationist organizations rallied to the cause out of conviction—four-fifths in 1941—but among those who joined in 1944 only 41 percent were true believers. By then the vast majority of new collaborators were pragmatists: they cited self-interest or pressure from superiors or family members as the reason they adhered to collaborationist groups. Furthermore, a large minority of them deserted the cause after a few months. Collaboration was not something they believed in strongly. In all, some 250,000 joined collaborationist organizations, including the Milice, and probably about two million "leaned towards collaboration," or around 5 percent of the population. Of these, about 20,000 fought for the Germans during the war, half for economic reasons, half for ideological ones. In short, collaboration was a minority phenomenon, just as membership in a Resistance organization was.[30]

On one level, however, the argument can be made that all French collaborated with the Germans in some form or another. In order to get by, to obtain necessary documents and food, some contact or accommodation with the Germans was necessary. In addition, tens of thousands of French worked for the Germans, in armament industries or for the Todt organization in charge of building the Atlantic Wall. Their livelihoods were interconnected with the German war effort. Any peasant who produced for the market was also implicated in collaboration, since German requisitioning of French agricultural products helped the Nazi war effort. In fact, there was almost nothing one could do to avoid collaboration, if we accept this line of argument. Collaboration was part of daily life for all French, from longshoremen to cabaret performers.[31]

But some forms of collaboration deserve more attention than the everyday ones that no one could avoid. For example, on an intimate level, sexual relations between Germans and the French were, for the most part, freely chosen. As many as 70,000 children were born as the result of liaisons between German men and French women during the war. Although some of these liaisons were purely mercenary, in the form of prostitution, most were not: at the end of the war up to 20,000 of these collaborators would be punished for their acts. Far more common, however, were the everyday letters of denunciation that French men and women sent to the authorities or collaborationist publications. These numbered in the millions; in Paris alone the Germans received three million letters that informed on the activities of French citizens and foreigners. Jews were the focus of many of these letters. One letter from a World War I doctors' association with 1,500 members complained about the large number of foreign Jews who practiced medicine in France despite laws prohibiting this. Some members of the Milice wrote scores, even hundreds, of letters denouncing their fellow citizens, relaying to the Germans bits and pieces of conversations they had heard in cafes and on the streets.[32]

For the most part, however, collaboration has to be seen in terms of institutions and structures. Individuals definitely collaborated, but they usually did so within the confines of some broader entity, which helped determine their degree of collaboration. For example, collaboration can be viewed in terms of regions. Certain regions seemed to be more susceptible to the appeal of collaboration than others. The west of France, along the Loire valley, is a case in point. The Vendée had a long history of opposition to Paris and to the Left. Notables dominated the politics of the area, and they tended to opt for the Right, if not the far right, promoting the Church and traditional, hierarchical social values. The appeal of Pétain and the National Revolution was strong here. This seemingly made the west ripe for collaboration, especially outside of urban centers such as Nantes, but many small towns and rural areas opposed the Germans once food requisitioning began. Collaboration soon ran into strong local grassroots opposition that political leaders in the area could not ignore. On the other hand, the nearby area of Brittany had an entirely different reaction to collaboration, despite a similar historical experience. Autonomist and separatist movements were strong in Brittany, although separatists were only a small minority. In the case of the latter, the Germans seemed to support their goal of an independent Brittany. Nothing came of this, however, nor did autonomists obtain anything of note from either the Germans or Vichy. In fact, Vichy proved to be as intent on centralizing power as the Jacobin Republic had been. Soon disillusioned with the new order, the Breton autonomists joined the pro-British and Gaullist forces that had emerged in maritime Brittany shortly after the defeat of 1940 and had provided probably a third of the Gaullist military in the early years of the Resistance. By 1941, if we can believe police reports, the Bretons were solidly in the camp of the Gaullist Resistance. Only a handful of pro-Nazi separatists and peasants attracted to the corporate state remained loyal to Vichy and collaboration.[33]

A similar anti-German and anti-Vichy mentality existed in the far north of France, where memories of German atrocities during World War I were strong and pro-British sentiment deeply entrenched from years of cross-channel relations. In both the Pas-de-Calais and the Nord, departments that the Germans detached from France and governed from Brussels, collaboration attracted only a small minority, although the Flemish independence movement initially provided some support for it. As in Brittany, however, the Germans did not support the separatists, and their enthusiasm for collaboration faded. In contrast, Alsace proved to be more receptive to the Nazis, even though Nazi policies stripped the Alsatian Church of its rights, imposed heavy penalties for speaking French, and conscripted German-speaking Alsatians into the German army. Although most of the 160,000 conscripts served reluctantly, a significant minority served willingly, with patriotic zeal for the German cause; 2,100 volunteered for the German Army and Waffen-SS before conscription was introduced. They and some of the conscripts fought tenaciously on the Eastern front. Some, notably Alsatian SS troops party to the infamous Oradour massacre in June 1944, even participated in operations against French citizens. After the war, thirteen of the Alsatian SS at Oradour were found guilty of war crimes and one—who, unlike the others, had volunteered for the SS—of treason.[34]

In the south of France, the so-called Free Zone, pro-Vichy and pro-Pétain sentiments were stronger than in the north. Yet this did not impact the degree of collaborationist sentiments. If anything, the south was more opposed to collaboration than the north. In the Gard, whose capital was Nîmes, collaborationist movements had no more than a few hundred members; a strong Protestant tradition mitigated against it and reinforced resistance. The same seems to be true of the Dordogne, where anti-Vichy sentiments emerged early and collaboration had little support. We can even add to this list the city of Clermont-Ferrand, whose collaborationist credentials were seemingly established in the classic French documentary, *The Sorrow and the Pity*. Yet, John Sweets's monograph on the city persuasively concludes that collaborationist movements were extremely weak there. Sweets warns us: "If one were forced to choose a myth, the Gaullist myth of a 'nation of resisters' would be far more accurate than the new myth of a 'nation of collaborators.'"[35]

Other parts of the south were not as free from collaboration. Lyon, the undisputed center of the Resistance, should be placed in a special category, but Marseille and the area around Nice in the Alpes-Maritimes look like centers of collaboration. In Marseille, the popularity of the Corsican politician, Simon Sabiani, played a significant role in legitimizing collaborationist organizations. As local head of Jacques Doriot's fascist Parti populaire français (PPF), Sabiani used his talents as a city boss to herd supporters into pro-German groups such as the Milice and the Todt organization. But most of those who followed Sabiani were desperate for jobs; they collaborated out of need, not ideology. And, despite Sabiani's appeal as a quasi-fascist political leader—a sort of Marseille Mussolini—the number of collaborators remained very small, if we use Burrin's method of determining who they were. Only 1 to 2 percent of the city's population of 700,000 participated in a collaborationist organization. For Nice, on the other hand, we have less specific information, but it was the home of the head of the Milice, Joseph Darnand, who began organizing his collaborationist movement in the fertile soil of the Alpes-Maritime during the early years of the war. Paul Marion and Jacques Doriot, two notorious collaborationists, were very popular in the region, drawing large crowds when they spoke. But, in May 1941 the postal censors who read people's mail reported that in the Alpes-Maritimes the majority opposed collaboration with the Germans and Anglophile sentiments were solid, including the hope for an English victory.[36]

If the evidence for collaboration is generally weak in the provinces, in Paris it is strong. Every important collaborationist in the nation ended up eventually in Paris, where the Germans established a receptive environment for them. Simone de Beauvoir heard constant praise of their kindness and general acceptance of their presence in the summer of 1940. The Germans were on their best behavior in Paris, trying to win over the French. At first this meant plenty of food, but by the winter of 1940–41 scarcity became common, changing the meaning of collaboration for many. Occupation inevitably meant control by the occupying power, with the French granted power and access to resources only if they contributed something of value to the Germans. The Parisian municipal government met on only a few occasions under the Germans, who preferred that the prefect of the Seine and the prefect of police exercise power in place of elected officials. The Germans also controlled what Parisians read. The "liste Otto" prohibited the publication or sale of works by prominent Jews, leftists and anti-Nazis. Newspapers were censored; only collaborationist papers could be published. Radio Paris and the cinema were both strictly regulated. The radio became a tool for German propaganda that virtually no one believed. American and British films were banished from the screen to the dismay of everyone; German films, such as the rabid anti-Semitic *The Jew Süss,* were promoted along with French collaborationist ones. The Nazis pillaged works of art—at least 20,000 were confiscated—and took over control of Jewish property.[37]

Yet, Parisians participated in Nazi activities and even collaborated with their German occupiers. Although the 1941 anti-Semitic exhibit, The Jew and France, was seen by only 200,000, many of whom were Germans, Nazi-censored films had larger audiences than the prewar cinema: gross receipts doubled between 1938 and 1942, as Parisians went to the cinema for countless reasons, many of which had nothing to do with collaboration, including keeping warm in a city without heating fuel. The theater flourished, even though Jews were excluded from it and censorship restricted what could be played. Prominent French playwrights such as Montherlant, Anouilh, Cocteau, and Giraudoux presented their works before audiences that were often one-third or more German. Artists, such as Derain, Van Dongen, and Dunoyer de Segonzac, participated willingly in Nazi-sponsored artistic events, including a trip to Berlin organized by Goebbels. And some

Parisians eagerly helped the Nazis confiscate Jewish property through the so-called Aryanization policy.[38]

On a day-to-day level, Parisians collaborated just as provincials did wherever they faced a continuing German presence. Workers in the large Parisian suburban factories engaged in automobile or airplane production, had to work for the Germans or suffer the consequences of unemployment, including possible conscription to work in Germany under slavelike conditions. Small shopkeepers, such as bakers, artisans, and café owners, faced a similar situation: they either had to serve Germans or endure the cost. The haute couture industry is a case in point that may allow us to understand the dilemmas that Parisians faced in confronting the Germans. In 1940, the Nazis took control of the French textile industry, and notably the production of wool, needed to clothe their troops. In the process, they also attempted to take over the haute couture industry, transferring it from Paris to Berlin. Nothing came of this, primarily because the industry's leaders convinced the Germans to keep it in Paris where the industry's specialized workers were concentrated. The industry survived the war relatively intact, although in seeking to please the Nazis it eventually participated in their anti-Semitic culture: many haute couture houses shunned former Jewish customers and placed notices in newspapers to inform people that their business was not run by Jews. As much as possible, however, these houses tried to keep their Jewish artisans employed. They even successfully obtained the release of Jewish furriers from the Drancy camp in March 1943.[39]

The most vocal collaboration in Paris did not come from workers or industrialists, however, but rather from intellectuals who had been debating fascism for twenty years or more prior to the German victory of June 1940. This was the so-called war of the writers, as Gisèle Shapiro has called it. It pitted two generations against one another: those over fifty were overwhelmingly on the side of collaboration, while those under fifty generally joined the Resistance camp. The collaborators tended to come from the old notables who had lost out under the Third Republic. They also tended to be less well educated than the resisters. And they rallied around a traditional notion of France as the defender of the values of classical civilization and the Church. By 1940, however, many who became collaborators had accepted Nazi pagan values over classicism. Henry de Montherlant, in his 1940 work entitled *The June Solstice,* viewed the Nazi victory as inevitable, part of the alternation of the seasons, a pagan triumph of the sun over bourgeois, Christian morality. His views were supported and expanded on by the racist, pro-Hitler intellectuals of the time, led by such brilliant anti-Semitic writers as Drieu la Rochelle and Céline. During the war these writers dominated the Parisian press and intellectual scene. Extreme right newspapers such as *Je suis partout* flourished, printing anti-Semitic articles by such talented writers as Robert Brasillach. In a September 1942 contribution to the paper, Brasillach wrote, "We must separate from the Jews *en bloc* and not keep any little ones." Later, in November 1944, after he had learned about the horrors of the Holocaust, he proclaimed, "I am an anti-Semite, history has taught me the horrors of the Jewish dictatorship." But, to his Parisian intellectual opponents, Brasillach's worst crimes were to call for the deaths of his enemies, from members of the Resistance to Gaullists. After the war he would be tried, convicted, and executed for these extremist pronouncements.[40]

Brasillach was an extreme example of this type of intellectual collaboration. More common were writers such as Jean Cocteau and Jean Giono, who expressed some sympathy for Nazism and Hitler but had reservations about the German cause that increased as the war progressed. On the other hand, Drieu la Rochelle provides us with the case of an intellectual who embraced collaboration completely but remained close to many members of the intellectual Resistance. In 1940 Drieu and Otto Abetz approached the publisher Gaston Gallimard about reviving the noted avant-garde journal of French literature, the *Nouvelle Revue française* (*NRF*). During the interwar period Drieu had shunned the *NRF* because it was, in his opinion, the hotbed of Jews, communists, surrealists, and other leftists. Now he became editor of it and reached out to try to include in the journal such notable writers as André Gide, André Malraux, and Jean Paulhan (its prewar editor). While Gide contributed to the first issues but then turned against

Drieu, Malraux refused to publish in *NRF* or anywhere else during the occupation. Paulhan would not write for the *NRF*, but he gave his approval to Drieu's revival of the journal and encouraged others to write for it. Both Gallimard and Paulhan benefited directly from their association with Drieu. Gallimard was able to continue his publishing house, publishing his authors even though many were antifascist, while Paulhan maintained a literary Resistance from his office in the same building where Drieu published the *NRF*. Drieu even helped Paulhan get out of jail when he was arrested for Resistance activities. These ties—and many others—with Resistance leaders of the French "republic of letters" did not prevent Drieu from expressing rabid pro-Nazi views, but they reveal a blurred line between collaboration and Resistance that existed in many such relationships during the course of the war.[41]

Gaston Gallimard did not exactly collaborate, although he facilitated the publication of the *NRF* under fascist editorial direction. Others in the publishing world were not as subtle or discreet. Bernard Grasset, the publisher of Proust and Malraux, created a series entitled "In Search of France," to which such noted fascists as Jacques Doriot and Drieu la Rochelle contributed books. Robert Denoël received German subsidies and published books such as *How to Recognize a Jew*. But he also published books by communists such as Elsa Triolet and Louis Aragon. Although Denoël and Grasset went further than most, it seems that virtually no prominent Parisian publisher escaped the Nazi effort to control publishing. All agreed to print some piece of Nazi drivel.[42]

The line between intellectual collaboration and Resistance was never as clear-cut as the postwar myth of "The Resistance" would have us believe. Simone de Beauvoir, for example, flirted with collaboration by doing a cultural program on Vichy radio, although she studiously avoided Radio Paris, which the Nazis controlled. More importantly, in order to keep her job as a teacher, she signed an oath that she was neither a Jew nor a Freemason. Jean-Paul Sartre criticized her for this, but his actions were no better: he accepted a post at the Lycée Condorcet in the fall of 1941, even though the post had come open due to the dismissal of a Jewish professor. And both Sartre and Camus engaged

in minor forms of collaboration by publishing in collaborationist journals and having their plays and books performed and published with
the approval of the German occupiers.[43] Clearly, collaboration in some
form or another was hard to avoid, even by the "just." More to the
point, however, are the outright forms of collaboration that intellectuals such as Charles Maurras engaged in during the war. Although
Maurras began as an opponent of Nazi Germany, he soon changed his
mind. In "the war of the writers," Maurras concluded that collaboration
was the only path to take in order to eliminate the decadent, individualistic, amoral attitudes of the literary crowd assembled around the
interwar *NRF*. He defended Pétain's Montoire meeting with Hitler in
1940, arguing that the French had to rally behind the Marshal on collaboration. After 1942, when Vichy had become a satellite of Nazi Germany, he decided that only a German victory over communism could
prevent "the re-emergence of Masons, Jews, and all the political personnel eliminated in 1940." As for the Resistance: "if the death penalty is
not sufficient to put a stop to the Gaullists, members of their families
should be seized as hostages and executed." Like Drieu and Brasillach,
Maurras became increasingly extremist, anticommunist, and anti-Semitic, as the war went on, siding completely with the Nazi cause as the
only solution to French decadence.[44]

In his trial after the war Maurras would make what many thought
was a perceptive observation when he said, "It is the revenge of Dreyfus!" The image of the supporters of the persecuted Jewish Captain
Dreyfus rising up and slaying anti-Semites like Maurras seemed to
capture the spirit of the Liberation. Yet, nothing could be further from
the truth. The Dreyfusards who were still alive in 1940 were more
likely to be collaborators and anti-Semites than members of the Resistance. Many Dreyfusards who had become pacifists in the interwar
period blamed the Jews for starting World War II: they believed that
belligerent Jews, concerned narrowly about the fate of their compatriots, had forced France to confront Hitler in 1939. These Dreyfusard
pacifist followers of Aristide Briand, the great French advocate of European union and reconciliation with Germany, became leading advocates of collaboration with belligerent Nazi Germany during the

occupation. As Sartre pointed out in his essay on collaborators, the pacifists thought an alliance with the German warrior state could achieve the goal of a Europe united in peace.[45]

While intellectuals might differ and argue over collaboration, pursuing somewhat ambiguous paths in some cases, the leaders of collaborationist political parties were clear in their political commitments. Most left Vichy in the summer of 1940, disgusted by the government's failure to implement the National Revolution, as they understood it, and its unwillingness to declare war on Britain and create a fascist state. In Paris, with the support of the Nazis, they hoped to establish a true fascist form of collaboration by creating a single party, a united youth movement, and other trappings of the totalitarian state. The extreme fractionalization of the collaborationist cause and the petty personal squabbles that divided Parisian party leaders—each one convinced that he alone could unite the faithful—undermined their efforts. Their failure was an outcome that the Nazis more or less preferred because they did not want a powerful French fascist party capable of challenging their control.

In 1940, at least a dozen collaborationist parties existed in Paris, each one enjoying some German financial support. Most of them, however, were small, insignificant, extremist groups with only a few hundred members. The most important of them, in terms of membership, was Jacques Doriot's PPF, which at its peak had approximately 50,000 followers. Founded in 1936, in reaction to the Popular Front, the PPF was primarily an anticommunist party that attracted workers and the lower middle class to its ranks. Doriot was a man of the people who collaborated with Germany in order to build a new Europe free from Bolshevism and the influence of Jews and Freemasons. He despised Pierre Laval, whom he thought of as a failed leader of the Third Republic fainthearted in his support of Germany and the National Revolution. Nevertheless, when Laval returned to power in 1942, Doriot expected to be appointed to his government, as a check on Laval's supposedly moderate policies, but the Nazis were more interested in cooperating with Laval and Pétain to win the war and consequently backed Laval completely at Doriot's expense. Earlier, in 1941, Doriot had taken the lead among the Parisian collaborationists by volunteering for combat on the eastern front, an act of ideological commitment unmatched by any other political leader during the war. This cost him dearly in terms of the Parisian political game: he lost control of the PPF while he was out of the country and incurred the suspicion of the Nazis who feared that he was trying to build a paramilitary base. Despite Doriot's many attempts to unite with other collaborationist leaders, he failed to do so except for a brief period of time when he was in exile in Germany at the end of the war. His mysterious death—when his car was strafed by an airplane of unknown nationality—in January 1945, shortly after being chosen to lead the powerless Vichy government-in-exile, brought an end to that.[46]

As the war went on, Doriot's PPF lost membership, declining to no more than 20,000 in late 1942. The urban centers of Paris, Marseille, and Nice were its strongholds, but they faded in importance after Doriot strongly supported the *relève* and the STO, which the French working class vigorously opposed. Clearly, Doriot's form of collaboration was not embraced by the French: the notion of sacrificing indefinitely, ad infinitum, for the German cause turned off even his most ardent supporters. Still, the anticommunism of ex-communists remained a potent force among the rank and file members of the PPF: in November 1942, almost one-fourth of the party's delegates to the national congress were former communists. But not even this base could save the party from further decline in 1943 and oblivion in the last year of the war.[47]

Doriot's most serious rival in Parisian collaborationist politics was another veteran of the interwar period, Marcel Déat. Both men were refugees from the Left: Doriot had been expelled from the Communist Party in the thirties, while Déat had been thrown out of the Socialist Party (SFIO). After his expulsion from the SFIO, Déat had created the Union socialiste républicaine in 1935. Influenced by the Belgian socialist De Man, it rejected class struggle in favor of a national revolution in which all social classes would participate and in which state planning would play a major role. Like Doriot, Déat opposed communism and parliamentary democracy, favoring a corporatist state and one party rule. He was extremely critical of Vichy for failing to carry out the National Revolution and for not collaborating closely enough with Germany. But he differed with Doriot regarding Laval: when Pétain dismissed Laval in December 1940, Déat rallied to his defense. This paid off in February 1941 when Laval supported Déat's creation of the Rassemblement national populaire (RNP), a national socialist party, which intended to unite all fascists. It brought together everyone from extreme rightist thugs in the Cagoule to veterans, trade unionists, and pacifists, but it never accomplished its aim of representing all Parisian and French supporters of collaboration and National Socialism. The RNP failed to gain Doriot's support, increasingly supported extremist Nazi views on race that were unpopular in France, and developed a cult of Déat as leader that alienated many on the Right, especially those who thought that they should be the leader. Soon the groups that it had united either broke away or were expelled by the ambitious Déat, and the dream of a single party suffered another serious defeat.[48]

The RNP may have reached a total of 30,000 members at its peak, but that peak occurred early and included many who joined only for opportunistic reasons, to help repatriate POW relatives for example, rather than out of conviction. The failure of Déat to get along with his main partner, the anti-Semitic thug Deloncle, meant an early decline of the party. In September 1941 Déat, believing that Deloncle had plotted to assassinate him, expelled him and his followers from its ranks. When Laval returned to power in 1942, Déat expected to be appointed to office in the new government. Instead, Laval, who believed that Déat was too ambitious and extremist, deliberately shunned him. Only after Déat had lost virtually all of his followers as the result of his support for the highly unpopular *relève* and STO did he rise to power in Vichy, due to his loyalty to the Nazis who imposed him on a reluctant Pétain and Laval in 1944. As minister of labor and national solidarity, Déat was called upon by the Nazis to provide more French workers for German industry. He also intrigued unsuccessfully in June and July to get Vichy to declare war on the Allies. Like Doriot and the other collaborationist Parisian leaders, Déat would end up in Germany in late 1944, squabbling over who should lead the Vichy government-in-exile.

Beyond Doriot and Déat, the ultracollaborationists in Paris had very little power and influence. Deloncle was probably the most significant of the lot. He had become an extremist hit man after the February 6, 1934, riots, obtaining funds from fascist Italy to eliminate exiled enemies of Mussolini. After the defeat of France he organized the Mouvement social révolutionnaire, which was nothing more than an anti-Semitic, antiresistance vigilante group. With support from the Germans it killed Jews and blew up a synagogue. In May 1942, however, Deloncle's subordinate, Georges Soulès, who had Laval's backing, overthrew him. Soulès did not deviate significantly from Deloncle's position. Although he scrapped vigilante tactics, he dedicated the movement to extreme forms of collaboration, including the elimination of the Jews from Europe. His followers were few, but they were true National Socialists. In contrast, Bucard, the head of the Francistes, was the Parisian leader closest to Vichy and its dream of becoming a leading state in a German-dominated Europe. His movement was fascist to the core and backed by Vichy. Completing the list were a number of anticommunist leftists who had utter contempt for the liberal state and parliamentary government, but believed that Franco-German reconciliation was possible. These included socialist pacifists of the Paul Faure variety as well as former communists such as Marcel Gitton, who founded the Parti ouvrier et paysan français in 1941.

The collaborationist camp in France was extraordinarily diverse, more than in any other country in Nazi Europe. Its recruits originated from across the political spectrum, although few came from the Radical Party and the Christian Democrats. The collaborationists believed that they were working for the national interest, struggling against such enemies as Jews and communists, striving for peace and contributing to the creation of the new Europe. This last objective appealed in particular to notables on both the Left and Right. They believed that Germany had begun the unification of Europe and that they should help forward the cause. Flandin, for example, argued for European economic integration under German leadership. Alfred Fabre-Luce pointed out that Germany was reversing the decline of Europe, from which France could benefit by participating. The liberal notable Jacques Chardonne claimed "we must learn from our conquerors" and accepted the challenge to remake France in light of the Nazi model. Thousands—maybe as many as 43,000—joined Groupe Collaboration, an organization that encouraged cultural exchanges between France and Germany. Its leader was Alphonse de Chateaubriant, an enthusiastic pro-Nazi intellectual, who thought that National Socialism embodied true Christian values. In 1940, Otto Abetz chose Chateaubriant to be the editor of *La Gerbe*, a weekly that published essays by leading French pro-Nazi intellectuals.[49]

The Parisian collaborationists were a noisy, motley crew, whose monopoly over paper, printing presses, and the radio made them seem far more powerful and important than they were. Most people bought and read the collaborationist press for the advertisements, not for the news, which was totally unreliable. From all indications, with the exception of a handful of programs, almost no one listened to Nazi-controlled Radio Paris. The vast majority preferred the BBC because its programs were entertaining and informative—subtle rather than blatant propaganda. For the most part, it seems, the French people never accepted collaboration. Among the populations under Nazi occupation, they were the least inclined to join collaborationist groups, according to Philippe Burrin.[50] Compared to the French people, the record of the Vichy state and many other French institutions is disappointing.

The French Catholic Church is an important case in point. As a general rule, the Catholic hierarchy collaborated with the Germans throughout most of the war, while the laity rallied to the Allied cause and, in limited numbers, to the Resistance. The Church viewed the rise of Pétain to power as a miracle, uniting Church and State in the pursuit of the same values (Work, Family, and Fatherland) and in opposition to the same enemies (notably communism). Only on the issue of anti-Semitism did they differ, and not always, as we shall see in the next chapter. The Church saw in Vichy's National Revolution the possibility of spiritual renewal and the reversal of years of adversarial relations with the republican state. It had little knowledge of Nazism and even less concern about the pitfalls of collaboration. Unlike the French Protestants, who mistrusted the State and had close ties with Swiss and German counterparts who depicted Nazism as a totalitarian menace to Christianity, the French Catholic hierarchy had a history of privilege and obedience to secular authority, disrupted by the French Revolution but now restored by the events of 1940. Until late in the war, the Church counseled the faithful to obey the State, regardless of the circumstances. To the very end of hostilities, the hierarchy condemned the Resistance and refused to allow priests to say mass for its members. By contrast, the Protestant elite, led by Pastor Boegner, moved rapidly toward resistance to the Germans, although many accepted Vichy as legitimate—at least in the beginning.[51]

The Catholic hierarchy's failure to recognize the evils of collaboration was due to a great extent to the failure of the papacy to draw attention to them. Although Pius XI had condemned Nazism in the 1930s, the French Church paid more attention to his 1937 encyclical on communism, in which he claimed: "Communism is intrinsically perverted and in no domain can anyone who wishes to save Christian civilization allow any collaboration with it." By contrast, Pius XII, Pope during the war, made no public comments on Nazism. The French Church's Assembly of Cardinals and Archbishops strongly endorsed Vichy on July 24, 1941: "We desire that . . . sincere and total loyalty be observed towards the established authority. We revere [vénérons] the head of State and we demand that all French unite immediately behind him." It is hard to imagine stronger support than that expressed by the word Vénérer (from the Latin venerari), which is used almost exclusively in speaking of the veneration of saints.[52]

Although the Church hierarchy continued to venerate the Marshal until it was forced to recognize de Gaulle, this did not mean that it accepted everything that came out of Vichy. But as far as collaboration went, the Church had no major complaints until 1943, when Vichy adopted the STO. Radio Vatican, whose views were often critical of Vichy and the Nazis, but whose influence on the French Catholic hierarchy was minimal, came out forcefully against the STO as early as February 16, 1943: "The Church does not accept regimes built on forced labor or on collective or individual deportations of people." Rather than follow this advice, the French Church initially expressed only sympathy for those conscripted, advising them "to obey and leave." Only one or two bishops were courageous enough to tell the faithful otherwise. Cardinal Liénart of Lille was one: he proclaimed on March 21 that Christians did not have to obey the STO, because they were being coerced against their will to go to Germany. That position was eventually endorsed, cautiously, by the hierarchy, which was deeply concerned that total freedom of conscience might supersede obedience to authority in the minds of the faithful. To ensure that this would not happen, in October 1943 the Assembly of Cardinals and Archbishops condemned those who opposed "the authority and the legitimacy of the regime." This condemnation included those who joined the Maquis, the rural Resistance to which many workers escaped in order to avoid the STO. Not until the Pope personally called on the French Church, on June 13, 1944 (a week after D-Day), to aid the Maquis spiritually, did the hierarchy change its attitude and cease excommunicating priests who performed mass and other religious services for these rebels. Still, some members of the hierarchy remained close to Vichy and collaboration at this late date: on June 16, 1944 the Bishop of Bordeaux claimed that the real danger was bolshevism, not Nazism, and that all Christians should remain obedient to Vichy as the only legitimate government of France.[53]

Yet, the number of bishops, archbishops, and cardinals who collaborated enthusiastically with the Nazis was never large. Cardinal Baudrillart, who died in 1942, was one of these: he feared the Communist menace, despised the British for harboring de Gaulle, and embraced Hitler in 1940. Others, such as the Archbishop of Paris, Cardinal Suhard, openly celebrated the founding of the collaborationist LVF in 1941. But most of those in the hierarchy who collaborated did not go beyond supporting the STO. This was true of Bishop Dutoit of Arras, who spent his last years hiding from the Nazis in Lille, as well as the

Bishop of Mende, who was arrested in 1944, the Archbishop of Aix, the Archbishop of Reims, and the Bishops of Auch, Montpellier, Orléans, and Nancy.[54]

If almost all French had little choice but to collaborate in some form or another, some collaborated more than others. They tended to be Parisians—mainly intellectuals—and those who held positions of power. Clearly, state collaboration was far more prevalent and important than the day-to-day collaboration of the average French man or woman who often had to cooperate with the enemy in order to survive or help a close friend or relative caught up in the Vichy-Nazi network of camps, forced labor, and the like. Gritting one's teeth, smiling against one's will, and accepting close relationships with those who occupied the country were part of the grim reality of the time.[55] But, beyond opportunistic collaboration and accomodation with the Germans, very few collaborated out of conviction. Philippe Burrin counts only 100,000 collaborationist party members in the period 1940–42, a tiny percentage of the total population of 40 million. Yet, at the highest levels of the state, collaboration was far more common. Over 10 percent of the members of the Third Republic's last parliament collaborated with the Germans, and as many as one-third were either Vichyites or collaborators between 1940 and 1942. Seventy-seven of them accepted appointment to Vichy's National Council, a pseudo-parliamentary body intended to give the regime a patina of legitimacy. In contrast, only twelve parliamentarians joined de Gaulle in London between 1940 and 1942.[56]

At the very top these important political figures collaborated in order to save France from a worse fate, or so they argued after the war was over. They did so out of conviction. Most of them were virulent anticommunists, anti-Semites, and Europeanists. They confused the German conquest of Europe for European unification. They believed that Nazi victory was inevitable and that France had to get on board the Nazi monolith before it was too late. Even when defeat was inevitable, many remained convinced that they were right and the Resistance was wrong. Their prejudices were insurmountable obstacles to understanding reality. They believed against all evidence that France bene-fited from collaboration with the Nazis. As Robert Paxton has argued convincingly, France gained very little, if anything, from collaboration; Germany was the only beneficiary in this marriage of inconvenience.[57]

When all is said and done, the French record on collaboration was no worse than that of other western European nations. The conquered Dutch and the Danes, for example, did no better than the French. Al-most all Dutch bureaucrats—98 percent of them—signed the "Aryan declaration" form that the Nazis required of them, and hundreds of thousands of Dutch—800,000 in all—joined the collaborationist Neth-erlands Union party, which aimed at negotiating a place for the Nether-lands in Nazi-dominated Europe. In Denmark, the government openly collaborated with the Nazis, authorizing the sending of a Danish free corps to fight the Soviet Union in 1941. Until mid-1943, the Danes supported collaboration, from which they—unlike the French—initially gained material benefits, with considerable enthusiasm. Only after the Nazis placed pressure on Denmark did the population and the government turn against them. In other words, in similar situa-tions the Dutch and the Danes acted on the basis of their perceived self-interest in order to obtain or maintain a privileged status in the new order of things. If anything, the French were quicker to perceive that collaboration would not work, rejecting it far before either the Danes or the Dutch did. What made collaboration in France especially unique in comparison with either Denmark or the Netherlands was the Vichy government: Vichy stood by the Nazis to the bitter end, regard-less of the consequences.[58]

4

From its first acts until its ignominious end in 1944, the Vichy regime excluded groups of people from social, cultural, economic, and political life in France. The essence of the new order resided in the dichotomy of inclusion/exclusion as True France attempted to expel the other from its utopian dream of "Work, Family, Fatherland." Jews, communists, Freemasons, and Gypsies were among those who suffered most from these policies. We are much more aware of this today than people were during the war. French men and women struggling to survive from day to day had little time to be concerned over the plight of others. Even such an astute observer of daily life as François Mitterrand failed to comprehend the significance of Vichy's anti-Semitic legislation.[1] In 1994 he claimed that he was so absorbed in his work at the time that he did not notice the fate of the Jews, even though several of his close friends were Jewish. Great newspapers such as the *New York Times* also paid scant attention to these matters. In July and August 1942, when thousands of Jews were rounded up in France, the *Times* published only two relatively minor dispatches on the fate of the Jews in France. It focused overwhelmingly on military matters, reporting on the failed August raid on the French port of Dieppe in scores of prominently displayed articles over several weeks.

Human rights, genocide, and crimes against humanity were not prominent concepts in 1940. Prejudice dominated the world to a degree foreign to us today. The United States not only excluded non-European immigrants, it prohibited them from becoming citizens until the 1950s. When American statesmen were asked during the war to allow more Jews to enter the country, they refused to consider the proposal, arguing that the American public opposed it. As is evident from Studs Terkels's interviews with Americans who experienced the war years, prejudices against blacks, Jews, and other so-called undesirables were widespread in the United States. Few Americans shrank from calling blacks "niggers" or Jews "Yids." Such openly and vehemently expressed sentiments were commonplace both in the military and on the home front, creating an atmosphere of fear among those subjected to them, since almost no one was willing to stand up for the rights of minorities. One consequence of prejudice was the internment of Japanese Americans during World War II.[2]

The French were neither better nor worse than the Americans, only different. As we have already seen, during the 1930s French laws gradually restricted foreigners from engaging in certain professions and placed limits on immigration. When war broke out in 1939, the Republic incarcerated refugees and others who seemed to threaten national security. Foreigners in general, whether they were Germans, Jews, or Spaniards, came under suspicion of forming fifth columns and were often put in special camps for the duration of hostilities. Communists, Gypsies, and other questionable French citizens were also restricted or confined. But the Republic did not exclude these groups totally, as Vichy would later do. Democracy in republican France always held out the possibility that onerous laws might be modified or even reversed.[3]

With France's defeat in June 1940, the new Vichy regime proceeded to institutionalize a policy of exclusion, with little prodding from the Germans. Marshal Pétain led the way with speeches on the need to return to the earth, to adopt spiritual values in place of the materialist, hedonistic pursuits of the interwar period. These were code words for the exclusion of Jews and others from the national family: in March 1941 the Marshal told Grand Rabbi Schwartz that Jews were not French because they played no role in the nation's rural life.[4] But Pétain never came out openly against the Jews, although his advisers considered having him do so in October 1940; they concluded that the French would turn against him if he publicly supported the newly enacted anti-Semitic laws. As a result, in listing his government's accomplishments in his October 9, 1940, speech, the Marshal made only vague references to these laws that few would understand. "The revision of naturalizations, the law on access to certain professions, the dissolution of secret societies, the search for those responsible for our disaster . . ." were some of the allusions to policies directed against the Jews and other undesirables.[5]

By the time Pétain delivered his October radio address, the main lines of Vichy's exclusionary legislation had been established. As we saw in chapter two, these included the removal of Freemasons, Jews, and other enemies of the new order from public life. July 1940 legislation stripped more than 15,000 naturalized citizens, of whom over 6,000 were Jews, of their citizenship. At the same time, the law proclaimed that no one could be employed by the French government, at any level, who was not a French citizen born of a French father. Later in the year this law would be extended to veterinarians, doctors, dentists, pharmacists, lawyers, and architects. Although exceptions were made for those who had served in the French military, the law effectively excluded all naturalized citizens and foreigners, as well as many who were French citizens at birth, from these areas of public and professional employment.[6]

Secret societies, especially the republican Freemasons, were also the object of Vichy's exclusionary legislation. The law of August 13, 1940, outlawed all secret associations and sequestered their properties. Protecting or perpetuating secret societies became a crime. Public officials had to take a written oath renouncing secret societies and proclaiming that they did not belong to one. To insure that the Freemasons could not circumvent the law, the government explicitly singled them out in an August 19, 1940, decree that dissolved their organizations in metropolitan France, Algeria, and the colonies.[7]

But the Jews were the ones who suffered most from the new order of exclusion and scapegoating because of Nazi policies and deep-seated anti-Semitic attitudes within the Vichy regime and among its supporters. Jewish immigrants suffered from the law of July 1940, which revoked the citizenship of many naturalized Jews, and a law of October 4, 1940, which authorized the internment of foreign Jews in camps. Jews were also confronted with anti-Semitic legislation that applied to all of them, regardless of citizenship status. The Germans controlled the Jews in the Occupied Zone through orders issued in late September 1940, which required Jews to register with the local authorities and to identify their businesses publicly with signs that stated "Jewish enterprise." Soon after this, on October 3, 1940, Vichy issued its own Jewish law, in which a Jew was defined as anyone with three Jewish grandparents or, if married to a Jew, with two Jewish grandparents. Under the law, Jews were excluded from all major governmental offices and most minor ones. In the latter case, Jews who had served in either the First World War or the 1939–40 conflict or who had received the military Legion of Honor were allowed to maintain their government posts, but not if they were teachers. No Jew was allowed to teach in the French school system. Nor could any Jew hold a position in the communications industry. In regard to the liberal professions—law and medicine, for example—a *numerus clausus* was promised to limit the number of Jews in them.[8]

These laws dealt a devastating blow to the Jewish community in France. But they also caused enormous confusion. It was difficult to determine precisely who was a Jew. No census had ever identified Jews, nor had the French government recognized Jews as a separate race, as the Germans did. To rectify this confusion and further exclude Jews, the government issued a new Jewish law on June 2, 1941, which established two definitions of who was a Jew. In one, a Jew was defined as per the October 3, 1940, law but with the added proviso that this definition applied whether one adhered to the Jewish faith or not. The second definition stated that anyone who currently practiced the Jewish religion or who did so on June 25, 1940, and had two grandparents who were Jewish was considered a Jew, but anyone with two Jewish grandparents who could prove that he or she adhered to another religion on or before June 25, 1940, was not Jewish under the law. The 1941 law also eliminated most of the exceptions for Jews who had served the French state, substituting a vague reference to exceptions based on "exceptional services" for the clauses in the 1940 law that recognized service in war and receipt of the military Legion of Honor. The new law also added a virtually meaningless clause that exempted

Jews whose families had been present on French soil for five generations and had provided "exceptional services" to the State. On a more
ominous note, the law threatened Jews with exclusion from all professions (and was followed up by decrees implementing the *numerus clausus* promised in 1940), further prohibited Jewish employment in
sensitive private sector jobs, imposed heavy penalties on anyone who
tried to circumvent the new Jewish law, allowed the administrative
internment of French Jews, and required all Jews to submit to a census
within a month.[9]

The 1941 statute only made the law more difficult to interpret by
confusing religion and race to the point where neither one was clear
from a legal standpoint. Since Jewish communities did not have records on who belonged to the faith it was impossible to prove who
was a Jew on the basis of lineage. Creative genealogists could easily
provide evidence of almost anything one wanted. This led Vichy to
change the rules of the game and require proof that one's grandparents
belonged to one of the accepted faiths according to the 1905 law on
the matter. If such proof was not available, Vichy assumed that one
was a Jew. But in the courts, some judges refused to accept Vichy's
position and placed the burden of proof on the government to show
that an individual was Jewish. As a result, many lawyers succeeded in
establishing that their clients were not Jewish since the state seldom
had enough evidence to support its case. Not until 1944, however, did
the nation's highest judicial body, the Conseil d'Etat, finally decide that
the legal presumption was that a defendant's grandparents could not
be considered Jewish unless the state could prove that they were.[10]

Unfortunately, not many Jews challenged Vichy on legal grounds,
either because they lacked the resources or, more often, because they
were proud of their heritage and refused to deny it. Most of them
accepted the Jewish census and endured the brutality of the government's anti-Semitic policies. During 1941, those policies became more
stringent and totally excluded the vast majority of Jews from national
life. The law of June 21, 1941, created a *numerus clausus* for higher
education that limited Jews to 3 percent of all university students. On
July 22, 1941, the government passed a law that intended "to eliminate

all Jewish influence in the national economy." It stripped Jews of their property through a process of "Aryanization," which created non-Jewish administrators over everything that Jews owned. Here Vichy followed the German lead, for the Nazis had already established a policy of Aryanization in the Occupied Zone and Vichy wanted its own Aryanization policy to make sure that Aryanized properties remained in French hands. To prevent Jews from circumventing Aryanization by transferring property or changing their names, Vichy passed several other laws that forbade them from acquiring commercial and private property and that restricted their right to change their names or to use pseudonyms.[11]

None of these actions caused non-Jews to stand up in large numbers for the rights of their fellow citizens. Anti-Semitic attitudes were relatively strong in France; the public viewed Jews as excessively powerful and rich. As late as 1946, an opinion poll revealed that about 40 percent of the French thought Jewish citizens were not truly French.[12] As a consequence, the sequestration of Jewish property did not arouse great concern among non-Jews; in fact, a number of ambitious French entrepreneurs hoped to benefit from it. Yet, the process of Aryanization was not very efficient in France, perhaps due to the slow, methodical ways of the legal system. As late as 1944 only 17,000 properties out of a possible 45,000 had been either "aryanized or sold off," according to one scholar. Although their rights were limited, French Jews had recourse to the courts where some sued successfully for neglect of their property. But these were the exceptions to a general rule of expropriation and pillage of Jewish properties. Those appointed by Vichy's office for Jewish affairs to administer confiscated property were mostly virulent anti-Semites who took their 10 percent fee, or more, from the accounts they controlled. In addition, the Germans periodically levied fines on the French Jewish community, collecting them from these funds. Meanwhile, the Jewish victims of Aryanization were restricted to withdrawing small sums from their accounts to pay for essentials.[13]

Lack of concern for the fate of the French Jews was common during the war. No one in France took up the cause of the nation's 100,000 Algerian Jews who were stripped of their citizenship in October 1940.

The children among them were even expelled from the French schools. A young, bewildered Jacques Derrida, the future deconstructionist philosopher, was one of them. He would never forget this traumatic event, which would play a major role in the development of his philosophical concepts. Nor did many French become concerned about the fate of Jewish lawyers who lost their positions in the legal system. The Paris bar, for example, refused to take an oath to Pétain, defended its autonomy fiercely, and defended lawyers who aided Gaullists or communists, but it stood by when 250 Jewish lawyers were excluded from practicing law by Vichy's *numerus clausus*.[14]

Lawyers were no exception; virtually every profession acquiesced or rejoiced when Jews were excluded from it. Finding its exclusionary anti-Semitic policies uncontested by the nation's elite, Vichy policy became increasingly harsh and cooperative with the Germans. In 1941, Admiral Darlan acquiesced to German demands for a French Commissariat-General for Jewish Affairs (CGQJ), appointing a virulent anti-Semite, Xavier Vallat, to that post. This gave the Germans the means to organize anti-Semitic operations throughout France. Later in the year, in November, the Nazis successfully pressured Darlan to set up a French version of the Judenrat, the Union générale des Israélites de France (UGIF), headed by prominent French Jews and financed by dues levied on all Jews. Although the UGIF would also make positive contributions to the Jewish community during the war, the Nazis used it effectively to control French Jews and levy heavy fines on them, beginning in December 1941 with a fine of 1 billion francs. At the same time the liberal minister of justice, Joseph Barthélemy, created the Special Section courts to try enemies of the regime from Jews to communists and drafted a new constitution that excluded Jews from the French community, claiming that Jews comprised "a race that conducts itself as a distinct community that resists assimilation."[15]

Those in charge of Vichy did virtually nothing to protect the Jews. They were either anti-Semitic or opportunists who sacrificed the Jews to achieve other objectives. Admiral Darlan and Pierre Laval wanted to protect French Jews against German policies, but they were quite willing to round up foreign Jews and subject French Jews to the harsh legal regimen that Vichy imposed on them. Both men were opportunists on the Jewish question; they went along with anti-Semitic policies as long as they did not give rise to a popular backlash. When popular resistance to these policies emerged in 1942, they tried to back away from the more extreme ones, but discovered that this was virtually impossible to do. In early 1942, for example, Darlan became nervous about stripping Jews of their property and deporting them: "The Jews are winding up as martyrs," he complained. But Darlan, as second in command at Vichy, was ultimately responsible for these policies implemented by Vallat, as well as for the actions of his minister of the interior, Pierre Pucheu, who established a separate Police for Jewish Affairs (PQJ) in late 1941 to pursue Jews throughout France. Like Laval, Darlan willingly collaborated with the Germans in persecuting Jews and other matters in order to restore sovereignty over occupied territories, only to discover that sovereignty was elusive and collaboration was unproductive.[16]

Darlan's fear that "the Jews are winding up as martyrs" was very real. France had not experienced the long period of racial reeducation during the 1930s that had convinced the vast majority of Germans that the Jews were to blame for their fate. Anti-Semitism was strong in France, as it was throughout Europe, but its advocates had not convinced the French to call for the elimination of the Jews from the nation, as the Nazis had succeeded in doing in Germany.[17] Of course, there were attempts to convert the French to such a position. In September 1941 an exhibit entitled The Jew and France opened in Paris. It proved to be a major disappointment for the Nazis, as only 200,000 visited it, including a large number of German soldiers. Many of the French who saw it were sympathetic to the Jews and remained so after seeing it. The Nazi Propaganda-Abteilung concluded that the French were not necessarily philosemitic, but that they did not approve of attacks on the Jews.[18]

In the spring and summer of 1942 the Jewish question came to a head as the Nazis moved from a policy of expulsion of the Jews to one of elimination. Before this switch occurred, the Nazi occupying force had used a variety of tactics against the Jews. They had dumped 8,000

German Jews on Vichy in 1940 in an effort to cleanse the Fatherland of them; most of them ended up in internment camps in southern France like that in Gurs, which was notorious for its unhealthy conditions. The Nazis also rounded up foreign Jews in Paris on a number of occasions beginning in May 1941. In October 1941 they supported a mini-Kristalnacht in Paris by providing explosives to a group of Cagoulards who bombed seven synagogues. Shortly after this, as we have seen, the Nazis forced Vichy to create the UGIF, which they used to extract money from the French Jewish community.[19]

Persecution was radicalized and systematized during 1942. In March, the Nazis dispatched the first trainload of Jews to the Auschwitz extermination camp: 1,148 Jewish men selected from camps around Paris. In June 1942 the Germans required Jews in the Occupied Zone to wear the yellow star on their outer garments. In Paris this was unpopular among many non-Jews, who viewed it as debasing and humiliating. Some gentiles wore the Star of David as a sign of sympathy with the Jews and were promptly arrested. Others gave up their seats on the metro to Jews, leading the Germans to require Jews to travel in the last train car. Police reports revealed that Parisians overwhelmingly opposed these measures. Such blatant public discrimination offended Parisians' sense of equality in a way that earlier anti-Semitic policies did not. Gentile Parisians may not have liked Jews, but they did not want them to be debased and humiliated.[20]

As we now know, in late 1941 and early 1942 the Nazis changed their policies on the Jews from exclusion and expulsion to elimination, the "Final Solution of the Jewish Question." In the late spring and early summer of 1942 the Nazis worked out an arrangement with Vichy on rounding up Jews for deportation to the east for the ostensible purpose of working in German war factories. René Bousquet, as head of the Vichy police, was called upon to provide police support in rounding up Jews. Bousquet offered total cooperation if he could retain control over the police. He refused, however, to round up French Jews. Pierre Laval, speaking for Vichy, backed up this position. Eventually an agreement was reached by which the French police would arrest foreign Jews only, with no German involvement in the process. Laval and

Bousquet had protected French sovereignty from German police activities on national territory at the expense of these defenseless immigrants. On July 3, 1942, Laval informed the Council of Ministers that he was happy to round up foreign Jews, especially the ones that Germany had dumped on French soil in 1940.[21]

The Germans wanted 100,000 Jews from France before the end of 1942 and limited their request to able-bodied men and women between the ages of sixteen and forty in order to fool the French into believing that deported Jews would work for German industry. At the last minute, however, Laval insisted that children be included, in order to increase numbers and because he believed—wrongly; it turned out—that the French would accept roundups if families were kept intact.

The roundup of Jews in Paris during July and August 1942 cannot be described without sorrow and pain for these innocent victims who were sent off to almost certain death by the French police who arrested them. Fortunately, however, the roundups were not totally successful. The police were supposed to round up over 27,000 foreign Jews in July, but they detained only 12,884. Only 3,031 of these were men, while 5,802 were women. Clearly, in light of previous roundups in 1941, which had been aimed solely at Jewish men, families had prepared for the July police raids by hiding their adult males, not suspecting that women and children would be included in them. We know, from countless records, that many Jews were warned about the July roundups. The UGIF learned about them beforehand and quickly told the foreign Jewish community that it was in danger. Government officials were also informed in advance, and some leaked what they knew to their friends or neighbors. Annie Kriegel, who later became a prominent historian of French communism, found out about the roundup from workers at the Parisian prefecture. She hid in a house in the Marais district, where a sympathetic French woman took in about fifty Jews that night. Others were warned by the police to leave before the roundups began. Tragically, some Jews either did not believe the warnings or did not think that they would be victims of the police raids. One Parisian doctor claimed, after being warned: "But I am a doctor.

They won't arrest a doctor." In one typical case, which occurred in August in Toulouse, a Jewish family debated what to do after a neighbor who worked at the prefecture burst in to tell them to leave immediately. The head of the family did not believe him, but his wife insisted on leaving since she trusted the informer, who had been kind to her. They left in fifteen minutes, barely ahead of the police, but their relatives in the neighboring apartment building hesitated and were arrested.[22]

After the first roundup in July, a further roundup in August included the unoccupied southern zone. Like the July roundup, the August one did not succeed as well as planned. For one thing, the thousands of foreign Jews that the Germans and Vichy believed they could gather from southern camps did not materialize. At the main camp for Jews at Gurs, there were in July only 2,600 of an expected 20,000 Jews. In effect, Vichy, after interning foreign Jews and others through 1941, followed an aggressive policy of clearing the camps of inmates at the end of 1941 and early 1942. As Denis Peschanski has pointed out, the camps were not permanent facilities, intended to house people for long periods of time; in fact, the French camps, unlike the German ones, were makeshift constructs in which inmates were encouraged to leave as soon as they could. As a consequence, by May 1942, credible independent reports counted in the camps of the Unoccupied Zone only 11,211 inmates, down from a high of 54,800 in November 1940.[23]

When the roundups ended in the south, Vichy and the Germans had gathered up 7,100 Jews, far fewer than what they had expected. By the end of 1942, the Germans had deported 42,500 Jews from all parts of France to extermination camps in the east. They had fallen far short of their quota of 100,000. In 1943 and 1944, the number of French and foreign Jews who were sent to Auschwitz from Drancy and other transit camps did not equal the total for 1942. Out of approximately 330,000 Jews living in France in 1939, a little less than one-fourth were rounded up and sent to the eastern camps. Only a handful of the deported would return to France after the war. The vast majority of them were exterminated in Auschwitz, some in other camps—a total of around 75,000.

These are some of the bald figures, but they must be put in context. Michael Marrus and Robert Paxton argue that without the support of the French state the Germans would not have been able to round up so many Jews during the course of the war. They make this claim even though France's record of saving Jews from extermination was one of the best of all European nations, far better, for example, than the Netherlands. But they have some key evidence to support their position: if the pace of roundups of 1942 had persisted in 1943 and 1944, France's record would have been among the worst in western Europe. This is the issue: What happened to slow the pace of Jew hunting after the summer of 1942? Was Vichy the hero or the villain in this situation? Can we praise the French people for their bravery in saving Jews or condemn them for their blatant anti-Semitism? Did Jews save themselves from Nazi destruction or should we point our finger at complacent French Jews for neglecting the fate of their foreign-born brothers and sisters? For the most part, these questions can only be answered by looking more closely at the complex relationships that existed between and among Jews and gentiles in 1940s France. From them, one conclusion emerges clearly: Vichy was not the hero. Its policies often put Jews in harm's way.

The French reaction to the roundup of Jews during the summer of 1942 was almost universally negative, even though virtually no one knew exactly what the fate of the Jews would be. Almost everyone criticized the deportation of women and children—especially children. Laval was off the mark when he urged the Germans to take children on the grounds that the French would not accept the breaking up of families. Most likely, however, the French would have rejected any formula arrived at by Laval and the Germans. In the summer and fall of 1942 government surveys of public opinion, based on millions of opened letters and thousands of tapped telephone conversations, indicated enormous sympathy for Jews from a French public that had not objected to the earlier anti-Semitic laws. The prefect for the Marseille-

Aix area wrote: "Delivery of foreign Israelites to the Germans is considered by many as a 'national disgrace.'" He added that most French believed that Jews should have less economic power, but they did not think that this gave the authorities the right to deport them. From Toulouse came a more graphic protest from the prefect: "The spectacle of a train composed of boxcars in which women fainted from the heat and from the odors of straw soaked with urine strongly and unfavorably impressed the French non-Jewish population which went to see them."[24] Parisians expressed similar sentiments about the roundups, leading one German official in Paris to warn his superiors that the French were turned off by the detention of children and were, in general, sympathetic with the Jews. The Paris prefecture of police similarly concluded on July 17, 1942, that the roundups had "rather profoundly troubled public opinion."[25] Only two government-appointed prefects in the Unoccupied Zone reported to Vichy that public opinion in their departments backed the government's policies on the Jews. Five said feelings were mixed, while twenty-four stated that the public in their departments opposed it, a conclusion that would have not pleased their superiors. Perhaps the prefect of the department of Loir-et-Cher best expressed the conflicted mentality of many French toward the Jews in his August 8, 1942, report to Vichy: "Clearly the Jews do not benefit from any great sympathy. But the procedures used against them are judged to be inhumane and unacceptable. They have unquestionably provoked profound hatred against the occupying power."[26]

The rounding up and deportation of Jews marked a significant turning point for public opinion, on all levels, which condemned the regime for its complicity in these actions. Elite leaders of public opinion in France and among French exiles in London immediately attacked the Vichy regime for its anti-Semitic actions. On August 8, 1942, on the popular BBC program *Les Français parlent aux Français*, André Labarthe condemned the roundups vehemently and called upon the French to oppose them and the policies of Pierre Laval: "What is going on in France? Has it become the land of the pogrom, of humiliation? Are Jews being martyred, their families destroyed, arrested, deported, crushed? Are innocents being stomped on?"[27] Although Labarthe was no Gaullist, he was merely following the path that Charles de Gaulle had outlined as early as November 1940 when he soundly condemned Vichy's anti-Semitic laws, claiming that a victory for the Free French would once again make France "a protagonist of freedom and justice for all men, irrespective of race or religion."[28]

The Gaullist position was seconded by some leaders of the Protestant and Catholic churches in France. Unlike de Gaulle, these men had more or less accepted Vichy as a legitimate government and, in most cases, would continue to treat it as such after the events of the summer of 1942. Timidity, acceptance of the powers that be, and even respect for the objectives of Vichy prevailed among them. This was particularly the case with the Catholic hierarchy, which believed that Catholicism had much to gain by embracing the new order. Protestants, on the other hand, were far more skeptical of government, especially of Vichy's fundamentalist Catholic position. Memories of persecution by the state made most Protestants reluctant to support any regime as authoritarian as Vichy. The Swiss theologian Karl Barth played a major role in convincing French Protestant leaders of the evils of Nazism. Pastor Boegner, the head of the Protestant Federation and the key spokesperson for French Protestantism, adhered closely to Barth's ideas. While Boegner accepted Vichy's legitimacy, he protested early on against Vichy's anti-Semitic policies: on July 26, 1940, he came out against the armistice clause that required the return of German refugees, many of whom were Jews, and in March 1941 he objected to Vichy's Statute on the Jews, writing to the Chief Rabbi about the "countless trials and injustices" that the Jewish community had experienced. But Boegner failed to transcend completely the period's anti-Semitism: He softened his 1941 condemnation of Vichy by stating that he understood the serious difficulties created "by the recent massive immigration of foreigners, Jews, and others, and by hasty and unjustified naturalizations."[29]

When Vichy issued its Second Jewish Law in the summer of 1941, Pastor Boegner and Protestant ministers throughout France attacked it with such force that Pétain asked the Vatican to express its opinion on the law. Rome equivocated, but seemed to support Vichy with some reservations. The French Catholic Church did the same. Cardinal Gerlier of Lyon, the head of the Church in the Unoccupied Zone, criticized some parts of the Jewish Laws but his public statements were cryptic rather than clear and forceful. However, Gerlier was never an anti-Semite: not only was he a close friend of the president of the Central Jewish Consistory but also he approved the clandestine circulation of a text that hailed the Jews as the forerunners of Christianity—not the killers of Christ. Still, Gerlier did not speak out clearly on the Jewish question until the events of the summer of 1942 made his ambiguous position untenable.[30]

The first religious leader to denounce publicly Vichy's roundup of Jews was a Catholic prelate, Archbishop Saliège of Toulouse. During mass on August 23, 1942, he proclaimed that Jews were "part of the human race" and should be treated with dignity and not as animals or subhumans. The Bishop of Montauban followed up on this, proclaiming on August 28, 1942, "that all men, Aryans or non-Aryans, are brothers because created by the same God." He condemned the roundups as "a violation of the most sacred rights of the person and of the family."[31] These and other protests from the pulpit, combined with a number of private objections to the roundups by leading French clerics, including Cardinal Gerlier, made their mark on Vichy by late August or early September 1942. Shortly after this, the French Protestant clergy also attacked Vichy, reading from the pulpit a letter from Pastor Boegner that condemned Vichy's policies on the Jews. At the September 1942 annual meeting of the French Reformed Religion in the Cévennes Mountains north of Nîmes, these clergymen also decided to inaugurate a network to hide Jews.[32]

Vichy reacted to these signs of disaffection with a two-pronged policy. On September 2, 1942, Laval told the Germans that he faced serious opposition to the roundups and could not allow them to continue at the same pace. He told Oberg, the Parisian-based head of the SS and German police, that Cardinal Gerlier had protested to him personally, in the name of the Catholic Church. Although Laval assured Oberg that he agreed with Nazi anti-Semitic policies, he wanted to back off from pursuing the Jews in order to mollify public opinion. In the fall of 1942 the roundups slowed to a trickle, although it seems that not until mid-1943 did Laval try to stop them totally in order to revive Vichy's flagging support among the French. In the meantime, Vichy also tried to silence the Church by publishing articles on matters such as Thomas Aquinas's anti-Semitic statements and by promising to subsidize Catholic educational institutions. In private, however, Cardinal Gerlier of Lyon and Cardinal Suhard of Paris continued to protest Vichy's Jewish policies, although they never considered breaking off ties with the regime.[33]

For pragmatic and opportunistic reasons, therefore, Laval and the Vichy regime tried to stop or at least slow the roundup of Jews in France. By the late summer or early fall of 1942 Laval knew that deported Jews were being sent to extermination camps, but this did not influence his policy. Public opinion, on the other hand, did have some influence. Vichy wanted the Germans to be discrete in regard to Jewish affairs in order to calm opinion, but it never asked for a complete end to roundups and deportations. In early 1943, for example, Vichy gave in to German demands to round up more foreign Jews, while stipulating that French Jews could not be included. Laval hoped that this arrangement would assuage public opinion, but the results were not good for either Vichy or the Nazis: only a few thousand Jews were rounded up, mainly by the SS rather than by the French police, and many of them were French. In June 1943, in order to appease the Germans once more, Laval considered reversing the naturalization of 16,000 Jews, thereby making them eligible for deportation. He changed his mind at the last minute for purely pragmatic reasons: in trouble over his policy of forcing French laborers to work in Germany, Laval assumed that this measure would further undermine his government in its struggle to contain the Resistance. Due primarily to Vichy's amoral pragmatism, only 17,000 Jews were deported from France in 1943, considerably fewer than the 42,000 sent to the extermination camps in 1942, although possibly more than would have been the case if the French government had opposed German demands. But the Nazis did not give up easily: in 1944 they imposed on Vichy a group of fascist ministers that gave carte blanche to the Milice, which rounded up Jews—both foreign and French—in large numbers, almost 7,000 in the first four months of the year. Laval might not have been directly responsible for these roundups, but his pragmatic, collaborationist policies had led to—even encouraged—the creation of the Milice and the rise of the fascists to power.[34]

Vichy's policies failed to protect the Jews, even the French Jews whom Laval and company claimed to have saved from the Nazis. Almost one-third (24,500) of the Jews deported were French. The point is that Jews were saved despite, rather than because of, Vichy. They were saved because of the actions of individuals, many of whom had strong religious convictions. The Church, as an institution, was not a major force in protecting Jews; its policies were often misguided or wrong on such issues as the anti-Semitic laws and the legitimacy of the Vichy regime. In general, institutions failed to help the Jews and other excluded individuals. For the most part, Jews in France had to rely on individuals and communities who helped the excluded without any thought of recompense or even thanks, as an act of kindness toward others in need.

While only a handful in the Catholic hierarchy stood up for the Jews, many among the rank and file did. The Jesuit theologian Pierre Chaillet and the members of the Lyon-based Témoignage chrétien (TC) movement stand out in the effort to guide the Church toward a new understanding of relations between Catholics and Jews, Catholics and Protestants, and Catholics and unbelievers, establishing in the process the intellectual basis for what later became Vatican II. Influenced greatly by Jacques Maritain's 1936 work, *Integral Humanism,* Chaillet and his supporters adopted the revolutionary notion that conscience was primary to all Catholics. Regarding Jews, these thinkers followed closely the 1937 papal encyclical, *Mit brennender Sorge,* which condemned Nazism as a racist, pagan movement that the Church had to reject or lose its soul. A November 1941 article in the movement's clandestine journal recalled Pope Pius XI's 1938 statement that all Christians are spiritual descendants of Abraham: "We are spiritually Semites." In June 1942, TC published 20,000 copies of a thirty-two-page brochure entitled "Anti-Semitism," which argued that Hitler intended to eliminate the Jews from Germany and Europe and pointed out that Vichy had implemented policies that deprived Jews of their rights and property, even imprisoning them in camps. These were gross injustices that violated the Christian and French revolutionary notions of the rights of man, the brochure stated. For Christians, in particular, the repudiation of Judaism could not go unchallenged, since the Christian faith had Jewish foundations and Jewish ancestors. As Abbot Charles Journet put it: "Anti-Semitism is more than anti-Semitism, it is anti-Christianism."[35]

Father Chaillet and his fellow Jesuits in TC continued their attacks on Vichy and Nazism until the end of the war, condemning Vichy for its role in the roundups and divulging that, contrary to its statements, Vichy allowed the Germans to deport French as well as foreign Jews. In early 1943, Father Chaillet reported in TC that Nazi firing squads and gas had killed hundreds of thousands of Jews—700,000 at least—in Poland and Eastern Europe. He concluded: "there can be no doubt whatsoever concerning Hitler's plan to exterminate completely all Jews on European soil." TC rejected the Church's equivocal position on whether Nazism or communism was the greater evil, arguing in an August 1943 article that German neopaganism was a far greater threat to Christian civilization than Russian communism. If the Germans won, the article maintained, the "historical existence of France and its spiritual tradition" would be eliminated.[36]

While Father Chaillet and his followers focused on publishing clandestine reports about Nazi and Vichy policy regarding Jews, they also helped Jews, especially children, escape detention and deportation. But other Catholic clerics and laymen put more energy into direct action than Chaillet and TC did. In Marseille, for example, several Dominican monks and nuns hid Jews from the authorities. The Capuchin Father Benoît may have personally helped as many as 4,000 Jews escape detention and certain death. He provided them with shelter in the homes of Marseille citizens—primarily, but not exclusively, Catholics—and obtained counterfeit papers for them. Armed with their new identities and provided with an extensive support network that stretched across southern France, Jews left the country for Spain or Switzerland or traveled to safer parts of the French interior, such as the Protestant redoubts in the Cévennes mountains or Chambon-sur-Lignon. Later, when Father Benoît was forced to flee Marseille for Nice, he used his connections on the Côte-d'Azur to continue his activities until the Nazis took over the area in 1943 and Father Benoît's superiors forced him to take refuge in Rome.[37]

The clerical elite was often indifferent or hostile to the Jews, while those lower in the hierarchy, like Father Benoît, were often sympathetic to their plight. In Marseille and neighboring Aix-en-Provence, for example, Church leaders had little interest in the fate of the Jews, although in Nice Bishop Rémond actively supported them. The Germans concluded that the parish priests were more solidly opposed to roundups than the hierarchy was. Although it is hard to quantify what these priests did, a considerable amount of circumstantial evidence indicates that Jews were protected by rank-and-file members of holy orders. Many Jewish children were saved by clerics who took them in and gave them Christian identities. Despite parental fears that their children would be converted to Christianity, this happened only occasionally. Ruth Kapp Hartz, known as Renée at the time, provides one example of how Catholics treated these children. In danger of arrest by the Nazis, she was whisked off to a convent in 1943. She soon discovered that many other Jewish children were hidden there, most of whom were French, not German as she was. They all learned Catholic prayers, went to mass regularly, and assumed the identity of Catholic orphans. At no point, however, did the nuns try to convert her or the other Jewish children to Christianity. In fact, the mother superior refused to let them take confession or communion, fending off all attempts to promote their spiritual development with assertions that they were not yet ready for it. After the war the children were returned to what remained of their families with their Jewish identities intact.[38]

Protestants were disproportionately active in hiding Jews during the war. In the Cévennes mountains, where memories of persecution at the hands of Louis XIV's armies lingered, the Protestant community opened its homes to Jews fleeing persecution. The region's Protestant ministers were acutely aware of the fate of Europe's Jews and had created a journal in the early 1930s that criticized Nazi and Christian anti-Semitism. They rejected all attempts to blame the Jews for the death of Christ and embraced Judaism as part of the Christian dispensation. In 1940, the leaders of this movement organized a symposium in the Cévenol city of Ganges to attack Vichy's anti-Semitic laws from the perspective of their philosemitic reading of the Bible. Beginning in September 1942, after they became aware of the seriousness of the persecution, virtually all Cévenol Protestant ministers began protecting Jews from roundups, leading Jews throughout France to seek refuge in the Cévennes. The vast majority of them were hidden safely in out-of-the-way Cévenol villages until the end of the war. Only in a handful of cases did disgruntled inhabitants of the region inform the authorities about suspicious outsiders in their midst. By providing Jews with identities as rural Protestants—obtaining fake baptismal certificates for them and integrating them into communal activities such as church services—the citizens of the Cévennes helped save at least 1,200 Jews from arrest and deportation.[39]

Closely associated with the Cévennes Protestants in the effort to shelter Jews was the town of Chambon-sur-Lignon, located in the department of Haute-Loire, on the northern edge of the Massif Central. Chambon had connections with all of the major centers of Resistance in southern France. Jews from Marseille, Nîmes, Toulouse, the Cévennes, and many other areas of the south found their way to Chambon, where they were sheltered and, often, taken to refuge in Switzerland. Like the Cévennes, Chambon was a Protestant stronghold, whose ministers and inhabitants welcomed the Jews and were adamantly opposed to Vichy and the anti-Jewish laws. Vichy and the Germans could not penetrate the wall of silence that existed in Chambon, even though its leaders were harassed and even imprisoned on occasion. Perhaps as many as 5,000 Jews were saved by this tiny community of no more than 3,500 inhabitants.[40]

In some cases Vichy itself aided the cause of protecting the Jews, although usually inadvertently or for its own exclusionary reasons and prior to the concerted German policy of rounding up as many Jews as possible. In 1940 and 1941, for example, the regime encouraged the Jews to emigrate. The camps in which Jews were held in the south were relatively open; inmates could come and go without much trouble, especially if they had money. This meant that Jews who could obtain the proper papers from Vichy and the foreign consulates in Marseille could escape to the United States or elsewhere. By 1942, however, this became less possible as the Germans began demanding Jews. At the same time, Vichy created or allowed organizations to oversee conditions in the camps. One of these, the so-called Nîmes Committee, which was made up of a number of refugee and charitable groups, played a major role in emptying the camps of Jews prior to the 1942 roundups. With the acquiescence of Vichy, the committee liberated virtually all children under fourteen from the camps by May of 1942, saving most of the Jews among them from being transported to Auschwitz later in the year.[41]

Jews were not passive in the story of their salvation from the extermination camps. Although they could not easily act on their own—for obvious reasons related to the oppressive Vichy and Nazi regimes—they often worked with Catholics and Protestants to protect themselves. For example, Georges Garel, a Jewish engineer from Lyon, worked with Archbishop Saliège of Toulouse and the local branch of the Oeuvre de secours aux enfants (OSE) to hide almost 1,500 Jewish children in Christian institutions. Nationally, the OSE helped save between 7,500 and 9,000 Jewish children during the war, hiding them in the homes of Jews and gentiles and spiriting them off to Spain and Switzerland via Resistance networks. Its efforts were reinforced by the Jewish Scouts, which sheltered Jewish children in its rural retreats. When the Scouts were forced to go underground in 1943, they called on Catholics and Protestants to take in some 250 children. Other Jewish groups, such as the Mouvement des jeunesses sionistes, provided Jews with false papers. Thousands were aided by this organization. Even seemingly collaborationist organizations such as the UGIF, which the Nazis forced Vichy to create for the purpose of controlling the French Jewish community, engaged in acts of resistance to the anti-

Semitic order, using its offices to help Jews escape roundups, at great risk to the leaders of the organization.[42]

When the war ended, possibly 30,000 Jews had survived as the result of rescue operations. Another 50,000 escaped the Holocaust by leaving France. This meant that the vast majority of Jews—about 150,000—survived within France without any significant help from others. Some survivors were embittered by their experience during the war. Gilbert Michlin is one example of this. He accused the French of being as anti-Semitic as the Germans, as his impoverished, foreign-born family received no help from the French, was rounded up by French police and sent to the death camps. He alone survived because of his skills as a mechanic. Michlin's family suffered from all of the disadvantages and prejudices that strangers encountered in 1930s and '40s Paris. Even Renée, the little Jewish girl who was protected by the nuns, had her doubts about Parisians after the war was over: her family returned to Paris in 1945, where they encountered virulent anti-Semitism. Her schoolmates called Renée a "dirty Jew," and the family discovered that their neighbors had denounced Jews to the Germans during the war.[43]

Clearly there is no neat moral tale to tell about the exclusion of Jews in wartime France. There were heroes and villains, rescuers and denouncers. The million or so letters denouncing Jews that poured into Vichy and German government offices indicate that a significant anti-Semitic element existed in France at the grassroots level. For example, a Catholic militant lawyer from Avignon who was a member of the Action française wrote to Xavier Vallat, Vichy's head of Jewish Affairs, to warn him about the Jewish presence in the former papal city. Jews were using all kinds of trickery, he claimed, to obtain certificates of patriotism, good moral behavior, and service to the Church. He called on Vallat to appoint individuals loyal to the National Revolution to investigate these matters in each department. In another letter, from the department of Tarn, a writer accused the local Jews of gluttony, sexual misconduct with their Christian maids, and involvement in a communist organization. He called on the authorities to lock up all

Jews before they succeeded in starving the area's good French citizens. But few could top the writer who complained that a Jew had borrowed his name, leading him to fear that in the future his family would have Jewish physical features because of this interloper.[44]

Yet, these distorted views of reality did not dominate French public opinion. If they had, the number of Jews incarcerated would have been far higher. Without doubt, the French were most successful in saving Jewish children from the camps. When the war ended less than 13 percent of all Jewish children had been deported from France, which was significantly below the 20 percent registered in Belgium, whose record was better than most on this score. The French also did much better at saving French Jews than they did at saving foreign Jews. According to one estimate, only 9 percent of French Jews died in the wartime camps as opposed to 45 percent of foreign Jews present in France in 1940. Whether this accomplishment should be celebrated or not is debatable. Clearly foreign Jews were far more vulnerable than their French counterparts: they often did not speak French, lacked French friends or acquaintances, had little support from a French Jewish community that was more concerned about the fate of its own kind, and lived in major urban centers, without significant resources to pay for visas, false documents, and the like that were essential for survival. And finally, they were actively pursued by Vichy and were often rounded up early in the war and placed in French camps where they became easy prey for anti-Semitic government officials. In contrast, most French Jews had sufficient support to evade the roundups, which did not specifically target them until late in the war. In short, French Jews did not experience the Holocaust in the same way or to the same extent that their foreign-born brethren did.[45]

In 1945, when the excluded came home to France, there were very few Jews in their ranks. Only 3 percent of Jews who had been deported returned alive. Returning in much greater numbers were individuals deported for resistance activities and prisoners of war. They were the focus of national attention in 1945, not the returning Jews. Today, of course, the Jews are the main focus of attention in historical monographs and efforts at remembering, while resisters and prisoners receive less notice. Yet neither one of these scenarios should be viewed as perverse or a distortion of historical reality. In 1945, French Jews did not think of themselves as a special case. They did not question the priorities that prevailed at the time. As far as most of them were concerned they were French first and Jews second. Raymond Aron, for example, said virtually nothing about Jews in his wartime articles in the London journal, *La France libre.* He did not want to feed enemy propaganda by concentrating on the issue. The same attitude existed within the internal Resistance: Jewish members of the Resistance fought for France, not for Jews, even to the point that they refused to discuss anti-Semitism among themselves. Marc Bloch, the famous medieval historian, consciously joined the Resistance as a French patriot and not as a Jew. Even predominantly Jewish units of the Resistance had no particular Jewish character to them. Often these were communist units comprised primarily of party members who were communists first and Jews second. This was true even of the special Jewish unit of the communist Resistance, the Manouchian brigade. As one historian of the period has argued, most Jewish communists probably accepted the communist daily *L'Humanité*'s analysis of Vichy's anti-Semitic laws: expropriating the property of rich Jews was no substitute for a communist revolution that would end capitalism. Communism and patriotism trumped the Jewish question in their eyes. Still, this does not mean that the Resistance neglected the fate of the Jews. De Gaulle condemned Vichy's anti-Semitic laws in November 1940, and as early as July 1940, he welcomed Jewish participation in the Resistance. Every major Resistance movement in France, with the possible exception of the Organisation civile et militaire, condemned anti-Semitism at some time during the war. The Resistance journal *Franc-Tireur,* for example, condemned the Nazi myth of a Jewish conspiracy in its first issue of December 1941.[46]

More needs to be said, however, about why the fate of the Jews was not a serious concern among the French from the end of World War II until at least the late 1960s, when the Holocaust became more central to historical understanding of these dark years. According to Annette Wieviorka, a complex web of factors made the Jewish question relatively unimportant in France—even among French Jews—in the immediate aftermath of the war. As indicated above, when the war ended the Jews comprised only a small portion of those who returned from the Nazi camps. Although almost 76,000 Jews were deported, only 2,500 returned alive. In comparison, out of 63,000 non-Jewish deportees, 37,000 returned to France. In addition, approximately 900,000 prisoners of war and 700,000 workers came back to France from Germany at approximately the same time. In the confusion and turmoil of these massive repatriations at the war's end, the small number of returning Jews received little attention. They were only one small part of the German internment system in the eyes of contemporaries. Furthermore, very few people were aware at the time that Jews had been sent to extermination camps while most other deportees were not. In fact, the French and most Europeans were unaware that the Germans had created different types of camps, specializing in very specific activities. Instead, almost everyone believed that prisoners were dumped in one kind of camp, under one broad designation. This conception of the German system lasted a long time; it had a major influence on how the camps were depicted in Alain Resnais's classic 1956 film about them, *Nuit et brouillard*.

French Jews did not help clarify these matters in the postwar period. Jews who returned from the camps were often not listened to, even by other Jews, when they told horrific stories of mass extermination. Simone Veil, who would later become a prominent political figure under the Fifth Republic, stated that no one in her family wanted to hear her tales about Auschwitz, except those who had also been there. Most returning Jewish deportees remained silent in the face of this kind of reception. Still, a few wrote and published memoirs about their ordeals, although most of these were read as part of Resistance, not Holocaust, literature. The point is, most French Jews viewed their war experiences through the eyes of the French historical tradition—the Republic, the Revolution and the Rights of Man—more than their Jewishness. Unlike Polish Jews, for example, French Jews had no separate cultural tradition based on a language different from French, as Yiddish was different from Polish, or on a tight-knit community such as the ghetto or the shtetl. Zionism was virtually nonexistent in France, even after World War II, although it was a powerful force in Eastern Europe. The suffering that French Jews experienced during the war did not discredit the Republic or the Revolution in their eyes; instead, they blamed Vichy and the Nazis for their plight. In short, French Jews generally did not think that their France—as differentiated from the "other" France of Vichy—had participated in the Holocaust.

Vichy was an exceptional regime in the eyes of the overwhelming majority of French Jews. To combat Vichy and the Nazis, French Jews joined communist and republican Resistance groups, worked closely with French Christians, and fought for the same ideals of liberty, equality, and fraternity that other opponents of collaboration did. They could do so because they and their fellow resisters adhered to the concept that Judaism was a religion that accepted the republican secular tradition. They did not think of Jews as a race or part of a culture based on alterity ("otherness") or difference. French Jews had no idea of multiculturalism; they were largely assimilated into French culture. For all of these reasons, and others, they generally did not feel threatened or different after the war ended—unlike Polish Jews who felt totally deserted by everyone in a world that wanted to destroy them. Very few French Jews left France for Israel in the postwar period. They saw no reason to go, for France was their nation too.[47]

While Jews suffered from exclusion more than others during the war, the communists succeeded in gaining the most publicity as martyrs of Nazi persecution. After the war the communists were popularly known as *le parti des fusillés,* so-called because supposedly the Nazis shot 75,000 party members in cold blood. Today, we know that this is pure fiction. At most, fewer than 30,000 French of all political stripes were shot by the Germans. Yet, there is no doubt that the communists suffered from exclusion by both Vichy and the Nazis. In fact, because of the Nazi-Soviet Pact, communists were hounded and imprisoned at the end of the Third Republic, as their party was outlawed and its representatives excluded from parliament. Beginning in March 1940 a special police brigade was created for Paris and the department of the Seine to arrest and detain communists. About one hundred were apprehended before the defeat of France in June. Vichy merely continued the Republic's policy, stepping up police activities, arresting 2,560 communists and placing another 1,660 under administrative internment in the department of the Seine between July 1940 and March 1942. The Communist Party was virtually wiped out by Vichy in its Paris region stronghold. Only after the German invasion of the Soviet Union in June 1941 helped revive the party, did it become the leading force in the internal French Resistance. Still, thousands of communists were arrested, placed in camps, and deported to Germany during the course of the war: during 1942 and 1943 Vichy arrested some 8,000 communists; for the entire war the number was over 10,000. The Nazis, in reprisal for assassinations of Germans by the Resistance, executed many of these political prisoners, whom Vichy dutifully handed over to the occupying power. Often fifty or more communists were shot by firing squads for the death of a single German. Despite these horrific acts, it is safe to conclude that the communists suffered far less from exclusion than Jews, who were also subject to reprisal executions. Communists were considered political, not racial, enemies by the Nazis and therefore, unlike the Jews, never slated for systematic extermination regardless of their actions.[48]

Homosexuals and Gypsies are usually prominently mentioned in the long list of persecuted outcasts under German occupation and Vichy rule. Yet they were not singled out in France to the extent that they were elsewhere in Europe. In the case of homosexuals the only known instances in which they were rounded up and deported to camps in the east occurred in German-occupied and controlled areas such as Alsace, where the Vichy authorities had no jurisdiction during the war. Under German law homosexuality had been severely punished since at least 1870, but French law did not penalize homosexuality from 1791 until 1942 when Vichy made homosexual acts between adults and minors a crime. Consenting adults, however, remained exempt from punishment. Roger Stéphane, who was a homosexual, a Jew, and a member of the Resistance, claimed that the French police were interested only in his involvement in the Resistance, although they were aware of his other identifying traits. Admiral Darlan, who wanted to outlaw homosexuality in order to remove it from the navy, could not get Marshal Pétain's support for it. Therefore, the police spent no time arresting homosexuals in French-controlled territory, and they deported no one for being a homosexual.[49]

Regarding the Gypsies, however, the evidence is more complex. Prejudices against Gypsies in France were probably greater than those against the Jews. Beginning in 1939, prefects throughout France began issuing orders to prohibit the movement of "nomads," as they called the Gypsies. On April 6, 1940, a decree issued by the minister of the interior prevented nomads from moving around in France as long as the war lasted and required them to report to the local authorities in order to be assigned a place of residence. The state justified these actions by claiming that nomads were potential spies. Yet, nomads were not placed in camps at this point. When the Germans occupied the north, nomads were prohibited from living or traveling in the twenty-one Atlantic coast departments, but with the exception of a camp created in the Côte d'Or, Vichy did not incarcerate them, although the Germans did, including hobos and traveling salesmen in the mix, and charged the expenses to the French government. In the spring of 1942, a model camp—better than most—for Gypsies was set up in the south, in the Camargue region of the delta of the Rhone River, an area well known to Gypsies who congregated annually in the town of Saintes-Maries-de-la-Mer to celebrate their heritage. In contrast with other camps in the south the Camargue camp placed people in homes modeled on the local architectural style. And the camp, if it can be called such, came under the jurisdiction of the Service social des étrangers rather than the Inspection générale des camps.[50]

This did not mean that all nomads enjoyed favorable handling by the authorities. For one, two-thirds of the 3,000 nomads put in camps ended up in German ones. Still, even the Germans were not greatly concerned about Gypsies in France as they released many of them during the course of the war: at the Montreuil-Bellay camp in the west of France, for example, 800 were discharged between 1941 and 1943. Moreover, few French Gypsies lost their lives in the extermination camps of the east: the Auschwitz records indicate that 145 were killed there. For the most part, both the Germans and the French were primarily interested in isolating the Gypsies for security reasons. The French, in fact, were so concerned about their actions that they did not release most Gypsies from the camps until 1946, after everyone else but war criminals had been let go.[51]

The release of the Gypsies from French camps marked the end of a dark period in French history that began with the incarceration policies of the Third Republic and lasted until the Fourth Republic came into existence. Truly this period could be called "The Age of the Camps," in France and in Europe in general. France, along with such discredited regimes as Nazi Germany and the Soviet Union, set up and maintained an extensive network of camps from the late 1930s until the mid 1940s. As many as 600,000 people spent some time in French camps during these years. Of them, a little less than one-fourth ended up in Nazi camps. The majority of these—Jews mainly, but also communists, Gypsies, Freemasons, and members of the Resistance—did not return alive. Vichy authorities willingly participated in the incarceration and deportation of these human beings, without concern about their ultimate fate, despite the fact that many of them knew— Laval and Pétain among them—about the Final Solution as early as the late summer of 1942. Under these circumstances it seems morally malevolent to make the argument that the French camps were fundamentally different from the German ones. As Zev Sternhell has argued incessantly, contextualizing French fascism and excusing its excesses by pointing out how much worse the Germans were is an unacceptable form of historical relativism and apologetics. But the fact remains that the French camps were different, even though they ended up facilitating the Nazi extermination of the Jews. For one, very few inmates died in the camps, despite horrible conditions: while millions died in German and Soviet camps, only 3,000 lost their lives in French camps. For another, they were not set up according to any carceral plan, as the others were: they were makeshift operations, often intended to be used temporarily to solve a refugee problem or a problem of public order or, under Vichy, to exclude groups of people. Furthermore, the inmates

in these camps, more often than not, could come and go without re-
striction. This was especially true of the Spanish political refugees in
the late 1930s, who were placed in the camps as a temporary housing
and security measure, but it was also true under Vichy, at least during
1940 and 1941, when inmates ebbed and flowed in the camps. The
overwhelming majority of the 600,000 individuals who spent time in
the camps left after a few months. And finally, camp personnel often
sympathized with the inmates and either looked the other way or provided them with opportunities to escape. There was no monolithic,
totalitarian system in the camps, no kapos, and very few ideologically
inspired guards. In short, like everything else about France in the dark
years, the carceral system was a bundle of contradictions, exceptions,
and brutalities. Yet, in the end, to return to Sternhell's warning about
historical relativism, no matter how much the system lacked the sadistic efficiency of the German camps it was part of the vast web of collaboration between Nazi Germany and Vichy France that led to the
extermination of tens of thousands of excluded people who were under
the care and responsibility of the French State.[52]

One final, controversial comment needs to be made about the
relative position of the French among western European nations in
regard to the exclusion of the Jews. Were the French better or worse
than other European countries in saving (or not saving) Jews? One
might begin to answer the question by comparing France to the Netherlands, a country in which anti-Semitism was supposedly nonexistent and the Jews were exterminated in large numbers: over 80
percent of all Jews in the Netherlands lost their lives during the war.
In the past, historians and others exonerated the Dutch for this terrible outcome, arguing that they could have done little or nothing to
prevent it, given the highly urban, compact geography of the country
and the lack of neutral neighbors such as Switzerland and Spain
where Dutch Jews could have found refuge. But recently evidence
has emerged to contradict the accepted story. The Dutch managed to
hide hundreds of thousands of workers from German labor conscription, but did very little to help the nation's approximately 160,000
Jews. There were plenty of places for the Jews to hide, but with a few

notable exceptions, like Anne Frank, the Dutch were unwilling to take them in. Nor did they provide Jews with papers that could have helped them leave the country or obtain another identity, even though the Dutch were masters at counterfeiting government documents in large numbers for Dutch workers. Furthermore, anti-Semitic rural orthodox Calvinist communities hid the largest number of Jews—one-fourth of those who survived—not the secular, urban population. And, the Dutch state, whose leaders fled to London rather than remain behind as Vichy did, failed totally in preventing the Germans from rounding up the Jews. In fact, the bureaucracy that was left in place to carry on day-to-day activities as normally as possible, collaborated with the Nazis at a level that went far beyond what Vichy did. Today, Dutch historians argue that if the Queen had stayed in the Netherlands, many more Jews might have been saved. Which leaves us in a quandary regarding the French experience, where anti-Semitism clearly flourished and the government collaborated, but also where more than 75 percent of all Jews were able to escape their Nazi antagonists and avoid being sent to Auschwitz. Why? What did the French do that the Dutch did not? Could it be that the existence of a functioning French government contributed to saving Jews, not because of ethical concerns or philosemitic policies—since neither existed in the heart of darkness that was Vichy—but for purely pragmatic reasons, namely to appease the disgruntled French population which totally opposed the roundups of Jews? And might it not also be the case that a nation with a revolutionary historical heritage that values the rights of all people, regardless of race or religion or other distinguishing characteristics, is better equipped to engage in the kindness of strangers than a nation like the Netherlands, where no such universal concept of humanity existed? As Bob Moore and other Dutch historians have hinted, the major difference between France and the Netherlands was the French Revolution: Dutch political culture was one based on hierarchy, subservience, and loyalty to one's ethnic or religious group, while French republican political culture rested upon the universal Rights of Man and included the notion of rebellion against unjust authority, both born in the French Revolution. To quote Professor Moore: "At a communal and individual level, there is no doubt that the traditions of deference to authority and a collective unwillingness to take risks meant that the majority of Dutch men and women were unlikely to become willingly involved in helping Jews."[53]

5

Resistance

For approximately three decades after the Liberation the official story of World War II in France was one of Resistance. The sixty children's books on the war published by 1948 emphasized the heroism of the Resistance while hardly mentioning the role of the Allies in liberating the nation and entirely avoiding discussing the camps or the fate of the Jews. In these books all of France, including children, takes part in expelling the Germans. De Gaulle assumes the heroic role that Pétain had played in Vichy literature, while Joan of Arc takes on the clothing of the Republic and the Resistance. *The Marvelous Adventures of General de Gaulle as Told to the French Children* became the model for this new type of hagiography, which was based on the general's concept of himself as France's providential leader. De Gaulle, in turn, established the parameters for this mythical concept of the Resistance in his August 1944 address from the balcony of the Paris City Hall: "Paris! Paris outraged! Paris broken! But Paris liberated! Liberated by itself, liberated by its people with the support and the help of the whole of France, of France that is fighting, of France alone." Only as an afterthought did he mention the Allies.[1]

In the early 1970s, notably following the publication of Robert Paxton's groundbreaking work on Vichy and the release of Marcel Ophuls's powerful documentary, *The Sorrow and the Pity,* the myth of a nation of resisters led by De Gaulle was exploded. As greater attention was given to the camps, the fate of the Jews, collaboration, the National Revolution, and French fascism, a new understanding of them and appreciation of their importance emerged, reducing the Resistance to a less significant, even divisive element in the story. Yet, in recent years, the Resistance has experienced a minor revival as historians have discovered its diversity, resilience, and magnitude. Not all French resisted, but neither did they all collaborate as some revisionism suggested. The history of the Resistance deserves a place, once more, at the center of the story of France during the war, although a center that has been enriched and qualified by scholarship on the dark side of the war years.

The narrative of the Resistance is a complex one, not the simple heroic account that General de Gaulle provided in his memoirs. If one is to believe the general, the Resistance began with his famous BBC speech of June 18, 1940, in which he appealed to the French people to continue their struggle against the Germans rather than capitulate. But almost no one in France heard this message, and if they did they probably discounted it, since de Gaulle had no authority upon which to base his appeal. In the weeks and months that followed, very few prominent French politicians, businessmen, or military figures rallied to his side. Most members of the national elite were suspicious of him and many were hostile to his cause. At the time, given France's desperate circumstances, it seemed better to follow the Marshal and sue for peace, hoping that French sovereignty would be preserved and reforms undertaken to revive the nation. Very few political figures understood, as de Gaulle did, that France's defeat was only the first skirmish in a war that would engulf the entire world before it was over.[2]

But de Gaulle did possess certain advantages in 1940 that allowed him to emerge eventually as the dominant figure in the external and, eventually, the internal Resistance. Most importantly, he had the support of British Prime Minister Winston Churchill, who recognized him as a soul brother, someone determined to fight the war to the bitter end. Although Churchill's relations with de Gaulle were turbulent, leading him at times to threaten to sever ties with the general, they survived the war intact, to the benefit of both of them and their causes. In the summer of 1940, Churchill's government gave de Gaulle's Free French movement the recognition it needed to begin to form a quasi-government-in-exile, intent upon uniting the French behind a military movement that would eventually retake control of France. If Churchill had not encountered de Gaulle during the last days of the Third Republic, the external Resistance would certainly have taken a different path. As it was, the relatively obscure de Gaulle, who had only become a general in the heat of battle in 1940 and who had been catapulted into politics at the last minute as under-secretary for national defense in the final government of the Third Republic, emerged as the only viable and willing candidate to lead the Free French.

De Gaulle also benefited from his clear, distinct message about the reasons for the French defeat. He blamed it squarely on the highest ranks of the military. As a leading advocate of tank warfare and offensive tactics during the 1930s, de Gaulle went against the prevailing wisdom of General Gamelin and others, including Marshal Pétain, that the best strategy was a defensive one in which tanks played only a minor, supporting role. He was a maverick who refused to accept the wisdom of his superiors and the hierarchical structure of the military. Instead, he spoke out loud and clear about the shortcomings of French strategy, to the point of insubordination. As a result, he was not well-liked by either his superiors or his peers, virtually none of which joined him in the summer of 1940. But, in the long run his unpopularity among officers helped more than hindered the Free French movement: as the only general who did not blame the Republic for defeat, he offered the prospect of a revival of French democracy and was consequently able to gain the support of France's leading political and trade union leaders. In this light, de Gaulle's June 18, 1940, message over the BBC represented an act of military insubordination and democratic Resistance virtually unknown in French military circles. He accused Marshal Pétain of failing to prepare the nation for war in 1940 and of submitting to the enemy. Only victory in battle and the revival of liberty in France, de Gaulle claimed, would overcome this dark heritage.[3]

At first, however, de Gaulle made little progress toward consolidating an external Resistance movement. Not only did very few French join his cause in the summer of 1940, but also the British had doubts about his leadership abilities. Among the French, de Gaulle made headway primarily among northerners, especially Bretons who comprised over two-thirds of the fighting men in his military by September 1940. Marginal types, such as members of the Foreign Legion, joined de Gaulle, but only one general rallied to his cause in 1940, General Catroux in Indochina. He had similar problems with political figures: only two Third Republic politicians joined him in the first months; most prominent French exiles went to the United States because they believed England would be defeated and they had no faith in de Gaulle. Compared to the Czechs, Dutch, Poles, and Norwegians in England, Free French forces were tiny by the end of 1940, numbering only a few thousand.[4] Yet, de Gaulle's decision to continue the war alongside Great Britain sat well with French opinion despite the July 3, 1940, British destruction of the French fleet at Mers-el-Kébir in Algeria to prevent it from falling into enemy hands. Pétain publicly accused the British of treachery, attempting to rally the deep-seated forces of French Anglophobia in response to the attack, in which over a thousand French sailors were killed. De Gaulle, in contrast, and despite his well-known interwar Anglophobia, supported the British on the BBC. Despite fears that the French would agree with Pétain on the issue, public opinion overwhelmingly sided with de Gaulle. Under the circumstances of German occupation, Anglophobia did not play well in France, where the only hope for defeating the Nazi enemy seemed to be British victory. The French people, for the most part, had chosen to side with the British as early as July 1940.[5]

De Gaulle's primary objective after the armistice was to gain control over the French Empire in order to legitimate his claim to represent France. Churchill supported him in this, believing that Britain would benefit from friendly Free French territories. In August 1940, Cameroon and most of French Equatorial Africa rallied to de Gaulle. In an effort to consolidate his African holdings, in early September de Gaulle, with British military support, attempted to take Dakar. He failed, creating some consternation about his ability to displace Vichy. Still, by the end of the year he had rallied all of French Equatorial Africa, set up a Free French radio station in Brazzaville, and gained the support of colonial outposts in Asia and the Pacific, including French Polynesia, French India, and New Caledonia. De Gaulle could no longer be considered a leader without land or followers, even though many of the latter were captive colonial peoples. Seizing the day, he traveled to French Equatorial Africa in the fall of 1940, where he delivered the Brazzaville manifesto on October 27. In it, he announced the creation of a Council for the Defense of the Empire, which was one of the first institutions created for the purpose of reviving the Republic, and he pledged "to account for his actions to the representatives of the French people as soon as it is possible to appoint them freely."[6] At the same time that de Gaulle was making these important commitments to the revival of democracy and the Republic, Pétain was meeting Hitler at Montoire. The contrast between the two could not have been more graphic.

Despite these successes in 1940, de Gaulle failed to gain the international recognition that he believed the Free French deserved. The United States, under Franklin D. Roosevelt, recognized Vichy as the legitimate government of France, sending Admiral Leahy to Vichy in December 1940 as United States ambassador. The British maintained contacts with Vichy. Lord Halifax, foreign minister until December 1940 and ambassador to Washington after that date, did not hide his hatred of de Gaulle and support of Vichy. Fortunately for de Gaulle, Anthony Eden took over from Halifax at the end of 1940. Eden would be the general's staunchest ally in the British government, vetoing several efforts by Churchill to cut ties with the irascible Frenchman. But the British mainly viewed de Gaulle and the French Resistance in practical terms: if they could advance the British cause, so much the better, but if they could not, Britain was willing to work with Pétain and Vichy to get things done. Of course, de Gaulle did not help matters any with his haughty concept of himself as the providential man. His obstreperous defense of French national honor, seemingly at all costs, became clear in 1941 when he and Churchill had a serious falling-out over the Middle East, an area of considerable interest to them both. Under the leadership of General Catroux, with significant British military support, Free French forces took Syria and Lebanon from Vichy in June 1941. To secure the support of the indigenous citizens of the region, de Gaulle had promised them immediate freedom and independence. But after Catroux's victory, de Gaulle violated his promise by appointing Catroux high commissioner, a position that he had agreed to abolish in a letter to Churchill. The British responded with the Acre agreement, which seemed to be an attempt to expel the French and incorporate the territory into the British Empire. At any rate, De Gaulle interpreted Acre as a hostile act and instructed Catroux to stop the British by taking control of Syria and Lebanon for France. This bold move led the British to back down. At the end of July 1941, Great Britain recognized France's historical rights in the Middle East and its "dominant and privileged position" in Syria and Lebanon. But the matter did not end there, as de Gaulle publicly accused Great Britain of desiring the dismemberment of France. Incensed by these remarks, Churchill ordered the Cabinet to cease dealing with the general and to cut off Free French access to the BBC. Eventually, in September 1941, the two men patched up their differences. The Free French were allowed to control Syria and Lebanon until the end of the war, at which time their fate would be decided through appropriate international agreements.[7]

To de Gaulle, such confrontations were necessary to maintain France's great power status and to bolster his credentials as leader of a Free France independent of British or American interests. If the French people saw him and Free France as puppets of the Anglo-Saxons, their denunciations of collaboration between Vichy and the Germans would lose credibility. Thus, de Gaulle maneuvered in the fall of 1941 to obtain the recognition of the Soviet Union for his movement, convinced that this would provide him independence from and a degree of leverage with his western allies. Despite his conservative, anticommunist background, de Gaulle expressed his support for the Soviets soon after the German invasion of 1941, going so far as to offer to send troops to fight alongside them on the Eastern Front. He eagerly embraced the Soviets' demand for a second front, pressuring the Allies to open it as soon as possible. And, on January 20, 1942, he celebrated the Soviet victory in the siege of Moscow by proclaiming on the BBC that the Germans had "suffered one of the great defeats of history," adding that all good Frenchmen rejoiced over this. De Gaulle's wartime diplomacy shaped the future of France in Europe and the world, as well as his relationship with the internal French Resistance, whose ranks included many communists by 1942.[8]

De Gaulle's diplomatic juggling act became more complex as the war progressed. In November 1941, he obtained two major advantages for his Free French movement. The United States opened up the Lend-Lease funds to it, allowing it to purchase war materiel from American firms, while the British recognized de Gaulle as the head of the French internal Resistance. But one month later, on Christmas Eve 1941, de Gaulle's troops invaded the tiny Vichy-controlled islands of St. Pierre and Miquelon, off the coast of Newfoundland, against the wishes of both Churchill and Roosevelt. Although the inhabitants of the islands rallied enthusiastically to Free France and American public opinion supported de Gaulle on the issue, Roosevelt's mistrust of the general increased. In 1942 de Gaulle would be kept out of the Atlantic Charter declaration agreed to by Roosevelt and Churchill and left in the dark about Allied plans to invade North Africa.[9]

Still, de Gaulle provided the Allies with enough reasons to give him grudging support. In November 1941, for example, he began using the republican slogan, Liberty, Equality and Fraternity, embracing democracy more firmly in the process. He increasingly called the war a struggle between democratic principles and their enemies. At Oxford, on November 25, 1941, he stated that "France and England are the foyers and champions of human freedom." Free France, he added, is "the party of liberty."[10] But none of these lofty sentiments convinced the Americans that de Gaulle was anything more than an "apprentice fascist" or, as one prominent figure in the American embassy at Vichy claimed, an "apprentice Hitler." The mistrust was mutual. Although de Gaulle reached an agreement with the United States on February 28, 1942, which gave the Americans landing rights in New Caledonia in return for U.S. recognition of Free French rights there and elsewhere in the Pacific, the general began referring to the Americans as imperialists in May 1942 on the basis of faulty information that they were trying to take over New Caledonia for themselves. Of course, the Anglo-Saxons did not help matters any when they took over Madagascar—a French colony—in May, without informing de Gaulle and with the accompanying U.S. State Department statement that the two allies would remain in control of the island until after the war. De Gaulle immediately sent a memo to his military commanders, warning them of an Allied effort to take over the French Empire in Africa. At the same time he opened discussions with the Soviet ambassador in London, asking for access to Soviet territory for Free French forces when the final break with the Anglo-Saxons occurred. The Soviets recognized the Free French as representing France and promised to aid them in their efforts to regain control of Madagascar and Martinique. In September 1942 the Soviets fully recognized de Gaulle and the Free French as the legitimate governing authority of the French people, the first recognition of total sovereignty from a major power. In the meantime, the British quarreled with de Gaulle over Madagascar, leading the general to mumble that he might break with the Allied powers. In September 1942, when Churchill and de Gaulle met to reconcile their differences, the two men reached the nadir of their stormy relationship: Churchill accused de Gaulle of making war on England rather than on Germany and made clear to the general that he did not recognize him as the legitimate head of the political Resistance in France. Unknown to de Gaulle, British intelligence had concluded by then that he had no support in the ranks of the Vichy military and no real political support in France beyond symbolic recognition as the leader of the Resistance. The British were so eager to replace de Gaulle that they had latched onto an Antibes agent named Carte who claimed to have 100,000 men ready to fight when the Allies invaded France. Churchill based his September conversation with de Gaulle on these faulty bits of intelligence, insisting that France combattante (as Free France was now called) was not France, but a purely military operation and that other groups existed that had as much claim to govern France as it did. De Gaulle replied, forcefully, that he was not fighting for England, as an auxiliary force, but rather for France, as its representative.[11]

In the wake of this stormy confrontation with Churchill, de Gaulle considered resigning as the head of the French Resistance, but he and others realized that no one else could fill the gap. By this point in the war—the fall of 1942—de Gaulle had become the linchpin of the French Resistance, without competition from internal or external rivals. He had organized a fighting force that had distinguished itself, especially in North Africa in the summer of 1942, when the Free French stood up to the Germans under Rommel at the bloody battle of Bir Hakeim. With the support of Jean Moulin, the French prefect-turned-Resistance organizer, de Gaulle had also begun to unite the internal Resistance under his leadership, despite petty squabbles within its ranks. Yet, as he stated on numerous occasions during and after the war, the legitimacy of the Free French movement was constantly questioned. The November 1942 invasion of the French Empire in North Africa was carried out by the British and the Americans without de Gaulle's knowledge. The Allies intended to appoint General Giraud as head of the external Resistance, bypassing de Gaulle completely in an attempt to marginalize him and his supporters. But this maneuver backfired, and during 1943 de Gaulle gradually marginalized Giraud despite the support Giraud obtained from the United States. But before we discuss the details of our hero's dramatic victory over Giraud we need to look at the internal Resistance, which had become a significant force by late 1942, both within France and in de Gaulle's bid for legitimacy.

To label the France of 1940 a nation of collaborators or resisters is misleading, if not inaccurate. For the most part the French people were like the characters in Samuel Beckett's *Waiting for Godot,* a play that is vaguely set in postwar France and in which the main characters are engaged in waiting for the title figure to appear. The French waited for the Germans to leave, for the British to win the war, for Vichy to fulfill its promises, for the Resistance to prevail, for something to happen that would end the interminable waiting that defeat had produced. At first, they hoped for the best from the terrible circumstances that defeat had brought. Many of them supported Vichy and, especially, Marshal Pétain who provided a sense of security. His values were the values of True France, of a rural utopia that no longer existed but which resonated in the hearts and minds of many. Why not let him carry out his National Revolution, many said in 1940, without realizing—or caring, in many instances—that this involved the exclusion, even the incarceration, of large groups of so-called undesirables. But, by the year's end, reaction against collaboration and Pierre Laval, as the public face of Vichy's detested policies, had turned a significant minority—even a majority in some areas—against the revolutionary regime in power. Out of this emerged a small Resistance movement by the end of 1940. It would gain increasing momentum as public opinion, measured by opening millions of letters and tapping telephones, turned increasingly against Vichy and the German occupiers, in favor of de Gaulle and the English. France went from being a nation of reluctant collaborators, in the wake of defeat, to a nation of reluctant resisters, in the agony of waiting for Liberation from Nazi occupation.

The Resistance that emerged within France, in contrast to its Gaullist counterpart in London, was extremely fragmented. In German-occupied France, Resistance was brutally repressed, which meant that it could not operate in the open. At the end of 1940, for example, the Germans acted without mercy against students involved in protest demonstrations commemorating Armistice Day on November 11 and against one of the first Parisian Resistance organizations, the Musée de l'homme group, which included a number of French intellectuals. In the south, by contrast, the Vichy regime had a more ambiguous attitude toward the Resistance—at least to begin with. Many anti-German resisters were not initially anti-Vichy, and therefore could be supported by Vichy as a potential ally in the effort to free France from German occupation. As a result, the purity of the Resistance on which de Gaulle insisted must be taken with a grain of salt. Later on, after Vichy was fully discredited, the complicated relationship between the Resistance and Vichy caused confusion about who really resisted and what the criteria were for determining whether one was a resister or a collaborator. A classic case of this confusion is that of François Mitterrand, who would be accused of collaboration and pro-Vichy sentiments, especially beginning in the 1990s. Another case, which still plagues historians, is that of the members of Uriage, a Vichy-financed school for future leaders of the new order. By looking at these two case studies in ambiguity we can begin to understand what Resistance meant in the Free Zone, where Gaullism was much weaker than in occupied France.

In 1940, François Mitterrand fought in the French army and was captured by the Germans. At the end of 1941, after numerous failed attempts, he escaped prisoner-of-war camp and returned to France, where he obtained a job in Vichy in March 1942 at the Légion française des combattants. As he later told Pierre Péan in a 1994 interview, his work involved creating files "on communists, Gaullists and those who were considered to be anti-French."[12] Although he claimed that he was a very minor figure at Vichy at the age of twenty-five, he moved quickly to the top, receiving one of the regime's highest awards, the Francisque, which the Marshal granted only to his most loyal followers. Mitterrand denied that he took an oath to support Vichy or that he submitted a written statement that he had no Jewish relatives, but he may have done both since these were often required of Vichy office holders. It is certain, however, that Mitterrand was loyal to Pétain and that he also engaged in acts of resistance during 1942 after he obtained a position at the Commissariat des prisonniers de guerre, a hotbed of opposition to the Germans, where he and his colleagues fabricated documents for themselves and prisoners of war. He also joined a Christian Resistance movement in June 1942 when he attended a meeting at Montmaur in the Hautes-Alpes. There he encountered a charismatic movement that resembled a phalanstery of Boy Scouts, Christian monks, and militant patriots. It appealed to his conservative, Vichyite, Catholic principles. But these did not conflict with his anti-German attitude: by the end of the year he had played a major role in creating a new, important Resistance group, the Mouvement de résistance des prisonniers de guerre.[13]

Clearly, Mitterrand was a member of a Resistance movement that had strong ties to the National Revolution and the Marshal. Those ties were only broken when Mitterrand and his fellow conservative Catholics realized that the regime was collaborating with Germany. For Mitterrand the turning point occurred in July 1943 when he publicly intervened at a meeting in the Salle Wagram in Paris to contradict the head of the official Vichy prisoners of war organization who claimed that for each French worker who went to Germany a POW was released. Mitterrand shouted out across the hall, for all to hear, "You are a liar!" Still, he remained skeptical of de Gaulle as head of the Resistance. Although Mitterrand denied vehemently that he supported General Giraud in his struggle against de Gaulle for control over the Resistance, his politics were closer to Giraud's than they were to de Gaulle's. Only after de Gaulle had definitely triumphed over Giraud did Mitterrand grudgingly recognize his leadership. Still, as late as 1996, Mitterrand refused to identify where he stood in the Resistance, except to say that the Resistance was not "a homogeneous bloc" and that the real Resistance, in his opinion, was the internal, not the Gaullist one.[14]

The same confusions and ambiguities existed among the members of the Uriage school, which was established to train a new elite for Vichy's National Revolution. Dunoyer de Segonzac, the head of Uriage in the early 1940s, was totally behind Pétain, believing, like many devout Catholics, in the values of the National Revolution. He demanded that all who taught there be absolutely loyal to the Marshal, whose ideas formed the basis for the school's pedagogy. He hoped to create a spiritual elite that would replace the old, bankrupt republican one mired in materialism and individualism. For this purpose he attracted such Catholic idealists as Hubert Beuve-Méry, the future principle founder of France's greatest post–World War II newspaper, *Le Monde,* Emmanuel Mounier, director of the influential leftist Catholic journal *Esprit,* and Jean-Marie Domenach, who was the driving force behind *Esprit* after Mounier's death in 1950. In short, some of the most important figures in the postwar French intellectual universe would be attracted, in the early 1940s, to this spiritualist, Pétainist venture to institutionalize the principles of the National Revolution. They wanted to create a "communitarian order" opposed to "anarchic individualism" and "the reign of money," as Beuve-Méry put it in June 1941.[15]

Without question, Uriage was solidly entrenched in the interwar critique of the Republic that attacked the reign of capital and political parties and called for a spiritual and personal revolution in order to transcend the status quo. Mounier's concept of personalism was closely connected with this, but so were the Resistance and Vichy's National

Revolution, both of which were revolutionary in ideology and contemptuous of capitalism and politics as usual. When Jean-Paul Sartre told Denis de Rougemont, in 1944, that "the personalists have won" since "everyone in France calls himself a personalist" he was only half right for personalism was part of a greater national longing for a solution to the seemingly insuperable problems of the interwar period. Still, there are significant differences between the concepts of the Catholic spiritualists at Uriage and the ideology of the National Revolution. Uriage, under de Segonzac, rejected National Socialism as an anti-Christian movement. Mounier privately protested Vichy's anti-Semitic laws. Over time, the close ties between Uriage and Vichy, based on seemingly common objectives, were called into question. Mounier, who initially thought of Vichy as an authoritarian state in which some freedom existed, became increasingly more critical of it, leading one Vichy official to label him a "Christian Bolshevik." In January 1942 he was arrested for attacking the regime in his journal *Esprit,* although he was soon released for lack of evidence. Virtually everyone at Uriage turned against Vichy in the spring of 1942, when Pierre Laval returned to power, confirming that collaboration with the Germans rather than spiritual rebirth would dominate national politics. At that point, de Segonzac, for one, began to reach out to such Resistance groups as the Témoignage chrétien movement in Lyon. By the end of 1942, de Segonzac and his Uriage school had joined Henri Frenay's Resistance movement. In October 1942, the leaders of Uriage met and accepted a manifesto that rejected racism, embraced the equality of all men, emphasized liberty as the basis of spirituality, and called for a communitarian solution to the age's spiritual crisis. On November 3, 1942, on the eve of the German invasion of southern France, Hubert Beuve-Méry condemned the National Revolution and Hitler's national socialist revolution in a speech at Uriage. In February 1943 the Milice took over Uriage, kicking out the intellectuals who had deserted Pétain and the National Revolution by this time. Finally, in 1944 de Segonzac met de Gaulle in North Africa and accepted him as the head of the Resistance. Uriage had come full circle.[16]

François Mitterrand and Uriage were not isolated examples of the ambiguities of Resistance. The internal Resistance, in contrast with De Gaulle's Free French movement, contained countless examples like these. The French police, for instance, harbored a significant number of resisters whose duties required them to arrest and interrogate their comrades. If they did not show sufficient ruthlessness toward them they endangered their ability to convey information about police activities to the Resistance. After the war it was often difficult to determine the Resistance credentials of these policemen, as those who had suffered directly from their interrogations accused them of being collaborators. Alfred Angelot was one of these. Angelot was a Resistance mole in the antiterrorist police. He used his position to warn the Resistance about police activities, but this required him to engage in occasional torture sessions against members of the Resistance in order to maintain his cover. When the war ended, Angelot spent a year trying to clear his name against accusations that he was a collaborator. Those who had been tortured by him could not believe that he was a leading figure in the police Resistance.[17]

Similar suspicions of duplicity or outright collaboration emerged about important Resistance figures that had close ties with Vichy. Henri Frenay is a prominent example of this. Frenay was close to the far right prior to and during the war. As a military man he had great respect for Marshal Pétain. To him, the National Revolution seemed to be the perfect response to the corrupt Third Republic. Although he objected to the armistice and collaboration, which he believed to be due to the influence of Pierre Laval, Frenay felt at home with Vichy's anti-Bolshevik, anti-Freemason, and anti-Semitic positions. Therefore, when Frenay organized a number of fellow military officers into a Resistance group in Marseille and established a network in southern France, he believed that the Marshal's government would support him against the German menace, which was the primary, if not the only, objective of his organization. He openly discussed his Resistance objectives with members of the Vichy government and was even invited by Vichy's head of intelligence, Colonel Rivet, to merge his movement with the intelligence organization in early 1941. But Frenay refused the offer. Over time he gravitated toward the Catholic left, away from the influence of Vichy, although in early 1942 he engaged in discussions with Pierre Pucheu, the minister of the interior, about the role of Resistance movements such as his in Vichy's National Revolution. Those talks tainted Frenay as a collaborator in some Resistance circles, even though he rejected totally Pucheu's overtures and turned against Pétain and the National Revolution, convinced that Vichy was locked into collaboration with the Nazis.[18]

Out of this morally dubious beginning, Henri Frenay created one of the leading organizations in the internal French Resistance, the National Liberation Movement. In Lyon he encountered Mounier, Father Chaillet, and numerous other figures in the Catholic leftist Resistance. Like them, Frenay had a deep-seated hatred of Nazism as a barbaric threat to the Christian faith and the values of Western civilization. Although he despised bolshevism as much as Nazism, he maintained that the real enemy was Nazi Germany and was willing to ally with groups with which he disagreed as long as they focused on ridding France of the German occupiers. In 1941 and 1942 this meant creating a united Resistance movement with Lyon and eventually Paris as its headquarters. To achieve this, Frenay cooperated with Jean Moulin, whom he met in June 1941. He told Moulin at the time that only de Gaulle could possibly bring the numerous Resistance groups together, even though most people in the Resistance had only a vague idea of the general's position. Then, in the fall of 1941, Frenay's National Liberation Movement engaged in discussions to merge with two other Resistance organizations in southern France. One of them, called Liberté after the journal that it published, began as a network of Catholic law professors from Lyon, Montpellier, Clermont-Ferrand, and other university towns. They were acutely aware of the dangers of Nazism, which some of them had written about before the war. Like Frenay, they tended at first to believe in the virtues of Vichy, but this soon ended in disillusionment. Yet, Vichy did not pursue them. On the contrary, when one of their members, the Montpellier law professor Pierre-Henri Teitgen, openly called for an American victory over the

Germans in December 1941, Vichy did nothing to silence him. Teitgen and his fellow law professors united with Frenay's movement in December 1941 to form the Movement for French Liberation, which published what became the greatest of the French Resistance newspapers, *Combat*.[19]

The merger of these two groups was relatively easy to accomplish, since Catholic religious values dominated both of them. Far more problematic, however, was the complete unification of the Resistance in southern France, although this was the primary objective of de Gaulle and his brilliant political agent Jean Moulin. Two or three major Resistance organizations existed outside of the *Combat* nexus. They tended to lean more to the Left, including in their ranks members of trade unions and leftist political parties. A number of fellow travelers, sympathetic with the outlawed Communist Party, gravitated toward one of these, the Front National. It, like most of these movements, had very few members during the first years of the war. The southern Resistance organizations were noted more for their newspapers, which provided them with a sense of identity, than they were for their ability to recruit large numbers of resisters. Franc-Tireur and Libération were among these newspaper/Resistance movements. Of the two, Libération was the most important organization. Under the leadership of Emmanuel d'Astier it recruited widely among trade unionists and socialists, gaining the support of the SFIO leader André Philip as well as the backing of Léon Morandat, the head of the Savoy branch of the Catholic union, the CFTC. D'Astier also recruited Raymond and Lucie Aubrac, who organized a Resistance paramilitary group in Lyon, where Libération established its headquarters. In contrast, Franc-Tireur was known almost entirely in these early days for its newspaper, which circulated throughout the south from its Lyon base. Protestant and Jewish militants made up a considerable part of its leadership, which was in constant contact with members of both Combat and Libération.[20]

These more or less organized groups do not exhaust the ranks of the Resistance, which was spread widely and thinly during the early years. A culture of Resistance existed in numerous parts of the south, fueled by memories of opposition to authoritarian governments that had preceded the Third Republic. In Marseille, where such memories were strong, the Resistance emerged rapidly among such diverse groups as Catholics, socialists, communists, and the police. The socialist leaders of the Marseille Resistance, Gaston Defferre and Félix Gouin, essentially rebuilt the French Socialist Party during the war. On July 14, 1942, thousands took to the streets in Marseille to protest the rule of Vichy as the police stood by, refusing to break up these illegal demonstrations. In Grenoble, a similar urban Resistance emerged, fueled by a combination of refugees, intellectuals, and metallurgical workers. During the course of the war it spilled over into the surrounding mountains, creating some of the most tenacious Maquis Resistance units. Other groups of resistors emerged in southern cities such as Toulouse and Montpellier. They were not always connected to the larger movements that have dominated the official story of the Resistance. The communists created a host of newspapers (*L'Humanité de la femme* and *L'Humanité des paysans,* for example, as well as scores of local papers) that attacked Vichy policies and, in some local cases, even the Nazis before the invasion of the Soviet Union in June 1941. In contrast to pro-Vichy Resistance movements, many of these communist journals were early opponents of the National Revolution, including its anti-Semitic policies. Communists and socialists combined to publish another prominent journal, *L'Insurgé,* in Lyon. With the Lyonnais *canut*'s motto "Live working or die fighting" in its masthead, this independent paper reached an impressive circulation of about 25,000 copies in southern France alone. Another leftist group, Libérer et fédérer, emerged in Toulouse, where it had close connections with Archbishop Saliège. At the local level leftist unions also succeeded in winning victories against Vichy. The miners' strike at Montceau-les-Mines in January 1942 ended in success as Vichy agreed to provide the workers with extra rations. Later that year another small victory was won by the metalworkers of La Ciotat. Even Jews began to organize into small Resistance groups in the south: by 1942 they had created a group called the Jewish Army, as well as one or two communist newspapers in Yiddish. And finally, by 1942, women had taken matters into their own hands in large parts of the south, by rioting against food shortages and demanding, sometimes successfully, their fair share of the food supplies.[21]

For the most part, the early Resistance in the south—and in the north as well—was urban in nature. Rural areas were immune to it until they came into contact with Vichy's requisitioning of food at fixed prices and Nazi forms of governance later in the war. Peasant France experienced no significant modifications in the usual rhythm of life immediately after defeat in 1940. Village life did not change much either. Existing political divisions and quarrels continued in most small towns as though nothing had happened. In addition, Pétain's reassertion of rural values appealed to these groups at first. As a result, very few peasants or rural workers joined the Resistance until the end of the war. Even after the Maquis was created in 1943, the peasants played a more or less passive role, aiding members of that organization but not joining it. Thus, throughout France the sociology of the Resistance was primarily urban (possibly two-thirds). With very few exceptions, overwhelmingly rural departments did not possess a strong Resistance movement at any time during the war.[22]

The local incidents of Resistance that historians value as evidence of opposition to Vichy and the Germans did not, however, impress de Gaulle and his agent Jean Moulin. They wanted a united movement that could be used to bolster the claims of the Free French to represent France as a sovereign state. To achieve this, they were willing to negotiate with the political extremes, as long as their interlocutors accepted a few fundamental points: the imperative need to defeat Nazi Germany and the Vichy regime with the support of the Allies; the dominance of de Gaulle and the Free French movement over the internal Resistance; and the commitment to democratic values and institutions as the essential framework for creating a new French Republic. Communists, members of the extreme right Action française, former Vichyites, union members, Freemasons, Jews, Protestants, and even Third Republic politicians were all more or less welcomed into this large tent if they supported these points. On this basis, Jean Moulin proceeded in early 1943 to unite the southern Resistance, notably Combat, Libéra-

tion, Franc-Tireur, and the Front National into one umbrella organization, the Mouvements unis de la Résistance (MUR). No group
completely lost its separate identity in the process, although everyone
feared that this would happen. The net winners were the Free French
and de Gaulle, which now gained some control over the southern internal Resistance and the support of a small, secret army within France
that would eventually play a role in its Liberation.[23]

In the north, the Resistance emerged under the yoke of German
occupation and became disillusioned early with Vichy, which seemed
remote due to the demarcation line and German restrictions on Vichy
propaganda. Henri Frenay's cautious support of the National Revolution was viewed poorly by the northern Resistance. As in the south,
however, the Resistance was fragmented into numerous groups, which
were mostly extremely small and limited in influence. Paris, like Lyon
in the south, became their capital. Certain parts of the north, especially
the Nord/Pas-de Calais region, which stretched across the Belgian border to the Channel, emerged early as centers of Resistance, based on
local memories of German occupation during World War I and deep-
seated Anglophile sympathies. By the end of 1940, acts of sabotage
against the Germans, which numbered fifty-one in December, were
commonplace in these northern departments. Nazi retaliation against
the region's Resistance was brutal: when the coal miners of Nord/Pas-
de-Calais went on strike in 1941, the Germans executed nine and deported 224 of them. Despite this devastating blow, the outlawed trade
unions from the communist-dominated CGT to the Catholic CFTC
united to resist the Nazis through strikes, production slowdowns, sabotage operations, and the hiding of resisters in the mines.[24]

The Resistance in Paris dwarfed that of other parts of northern
France. Yet during 1940 Resistance developed very slowly there. The
first major act occurred on November 11 when a group of students
protested the German occupation and heralded the Gaullist Resistance
while commemorating the World War I armistice at the Arc de Triom-
phe. Clandestinely, groups began to organize late in the year. One,
centered around intellectuals and scholars at the Musée de l'Homme,
was discovered and broken up by the occupiers in early 1941. Mean-

while, the Nazis executed several individuals for acts of sabotage and Resistance, driving home the point that these would not be tolerated. Although the communists continued to emphasize immediate, direct action, the northern, Parisian Resistance remained otherwise underground throughout most of the war, waiting for the moment to rise up in support of the Allied forces. *Attentisme* prevailed in its ranks, not armed acts of resistance.[25]

Most of the early acts of resistance in the north were carried out by individuals, not organized groups. They hid soldiers in order to keep them from being taken as prisoners of war. They buried weapons, with the hope that they could be used later to liberate France. They wrote anti-German graffiti on walls and attacked German soldiers. Although these isolated acts of resistance made little if any contribution to winning the war, they advertised the existence of continued opposition, bolstering the morale of thousands who wanted to defy the Germans. Out of them eventually emerged organized groups that opposed the occupation more effectively.[26]

The major northern Resistance groups tended to have links to those in the south. Thus, a Libération-Nord developed, closely tied to its southern counterpart, with the prominent CGT trade union leader Christian Pineau in charge of it. It remained, primarily, a political and propaganda organization which played only a minor role in the armed Resistance.[27] Frenay's Resistance organization also had a northern relative, but it was almost completely destroyed by Nazi infiltrators. Eventually, in early 1943, it was replaced by a new organization called Ceux de la Résistance, which refused to take a political stand and committed itself to a military solution to the occupation. Similarly, the communists organized the Front national in the north. Its influence was much greater there than in the south, although both fronts were open to all who resisted the Nazis, regardless of political affiliation.

Two significant, independent Resistance movements emerged in the north that had no southern counterpart: Défense de la France and the Organisation civile et militaire (OCM). Défense de la France was the smaller of the two. It was founded in late 1940 by a number of conservative university students and professors who opposed German occupation, English influence over France, and Gaullism. At first, they believed that Pétain and the National Revolution were their best hope, but by late 1942 they began to rally to de Gaulle. Like the Catholics who resisted in the south, the members of Défense de la France maintained a spiritual, *attentiste* position, rejecting armed Resistance, but emphasizing the barbarity of Nazism. Over time they gravitated toward a more confrontational attitude. In 1943, in the conflict between de Gaulle and Giraud for leadership of the Resistance, Défense de la France initially chose Giraud. This doomed the movement's prospects for gaining recognition as a part of the internal Resistance, even though scores of its members were executed or deported to German camps. De Gaulle and his close advisors did not trust it and kept it out of the inner circle of the National Council of the Resistance created in 1943. Despite the fact that Défense de la France had become a devoted follower of de Gaulle by the end of the war and did not deviate from the mainstream Resistance on major issues, its last minute rallying to de Gaulle prevented it from gaining favor in Resistance circles, in contrast to Henri Frenay's equally conservative movement.[28]

The OCM was the largest and most important of the northern Resistance movements. It was a catchall organization that included Pétainists, Gaullists, pro-communist railroad workers, prominent military figures, and businessmen in its ranks. It began in the fall of 1940 as a small group of right-wing Parisian resisters who espoused anti-Semitic and pro-Vichy sentiments. In the course of 1941, however, the OCM shed most of its Pétainist sympathies for Gaullist ones and recruited broadly to create cells in virtually every part of the Occupied Zone. Although its members yearned to undertake direct action against the Nazis, the organization maintained an *attentiste* position, engaging in espionage operations to determine German war plans and the railroad routes that transported German military supplies. Valuable information was relayed from the OCM to London through networks set up by Rémy and other agents of the Free French movement. By 1943 the OCM claimed to have at least 50,000 members, but this was clearly an exaggeration, since the Resistance in all of France probably had no more than 80,000 bona fide members by then. Still, it was probably the largest Resistance organization, the equal in the north of Frenay's Combat movement in the south. Like Combat, the OCM was politically ecumenical, although it believed that the Resistance had to create a strong state and executive to revive the nation after the war. The OCM, whether it knew so or not, was similar to other Resistance movements in advocating a new French revolution at Liberation.[29]

As separate, independent organizations, these northern Resistance movements had very little influence or power. In fact, as individual units they were either worthless or dangerous rivals as far as the Free French were concerned. And in the eyes of the British and the Americans they were unimportant to the war effort. To de Gaulle, however, the unification of these organizations would help the Free French gain legitimacy and achieve the rapid revival of France as a great power after the defeat of Germany. To accomplish those goals, de Gaulle met with leaders of the northern Resistance and dispatched emissaries to them for the purpose of uniting these disparate movements under his leadership. Pierre Brossolette, a dedicated socialist who became one of the general's most loyal and passionate supporters, organized the north behind de Gaulle in early 1943, just in time for Jean Moulin to complete the process of national union in May of that year by creating the National Council of the Resistance, a governing body which brought together all of the leading Resistance organizations—both north and south—plus the major French trade unions and republican political parties under de Gaulle's leadership. Despite serious misgivings from Henri Frenay—and others—about the inclusion of discredited political parties from the Third Republic, the council received enthusiastic, unanimous approval from the groups included. More importantly, the council helped de Gaulle convince the skeptical British and Americans of his national legitimacy by creating a hegemonic Liberation force that could instantly replace Vichy once the Nazis had been seriously challenged on French soil.[30]

Resistance was not confined exclusively to these relatively organized movements. Throughout France numerous networks (*réseaux*) also emerged during the war. They were involved in countless activities that ranged from sabotaging war production to transporting downed British pilots back to England. The first networks were created in Brittany and Normandy, where fishermen took Free French fighters across the Channel as early as the summer of 1940. Others soon emerged in places like the Vosges Mountains, whose inhabitants helped thousands of French prisoners of war escaping German camps make it to unoccupied France. In the Pyrenees, hundreds of mountain guides formed networks to help refugees—most of them Jews—flee the Nazis. Under British direction the Special Operations Executive set up units throughout France to organize and carry out sabotage and intelligence activities. The radio operators among them undertook an especially risky task; their average life expectancy on the job was about six months. In all, as many as 266 networks were established in France between 1940 and 1945, mobilizing about 150,000 French men and women over the course of the war. Whether they made a major differ- ence or not is debatable. The great historian of the Resistance, Henri Michel, has argued that with proper Allied support they could have accomplished far more than the ineffective and inaccurate bombing missions that the Allies carried out in France. As it was, the Allies were highly skeptical of the military effectiveness and political reliability of the Resistance and refused to provide it with sufficient material to carry out sustained attacks.[31]

Allied skepticism followed from a lack of confidence in the military effectiveness of irregular fighters and the slow development of mass Resistance to German occupation beyond minor acts of defiance such as the singing of the Marseillaise or shunning German soldiers in cafes and other public places. Furthermore, when a more or less mass Resis- tance developed in 1943, it seemed to be tainted with an anarchical, sometimes pro-communist political orientation that the Allies feared. The British and Americans did not want to defeat the Germans in order to see them replaced by an unruly leftist government. But Allied assessments of communist influence in the Resistance were inaccurate. We now know that the Communist Party's role in the Resistance was never as great as it seemed during the war. The party of the so-called 75,000 *fusillés* probably lost only a few thousand men to German firing squads. The front organization, the Front National, was never very powerful and mainly comprised of non-communists, while the most important communist-led Resistance organization, the Franc-Tireurs Partisans, probably included no more than 20,000 fighters at its peak, many of whom were not party members. Furthermore, from the beginning of the war the French Communist Party leadership, both in Moscow and in France, proclaimed that the party was interested exclusively in national Liberation and not revolution. Maurice Thorez, the party's leader in exile in the Soviet Union, repeatedly called for "unity of action," appealing to French communists to unite with other forces from the Left to the extreme Right, including La Rocque and his followers, for the purpose of defeating the Nazis. At no point did Thorez and the party challenge de Gaulle's leadership of the Resistance. They were clearly nationalists first and revolutionaries a distant second.[32]

Still, some observers have pointed to the Maquis as a communist-led part of the Resistance that could have carried out a socialist revolution after the war. But there is no evidence for this: communists helped individuals join the Maquis, providing them with false papers and connections, but very few members of the Maquis were communists. What is certain is that the most important development in the creation of a mass Resistance movement was the Nazis' attempt to requisition French laborers, many of whom were on the Left politically, to work in Germany. When that happened, beginning in late 1942, French workers fled to the countryside to escape, forming the legendary, seemingly anarchical "Maquis," named after the shrubs that dominated the southern French rural landscape. In 1943, following the implementation of the STO (the compulsory labor service), the Maquis mushroomed. The Allies and the Free French now called on French workers to join it, in an effort to channel them into this new form of Resistance. Robert Schumann, speaking on the BBC in the fall of 1943, encouraged workers to desert the STO and hide out in small groups in the French countryside. He implied that the Allies would come to their aid, but this never materialized in any major way. At the same time some leaders in the Church broke with long-standing theological positions on matters of conscience and faith, in light of this massive opposition to legal authority. They proclaimed that Catholics could decide according to their individual conscience whether or not to obey the call-up for the STO. Overnight, Catholic clerics grudgingly adopted a Protestant conception of conscience that had been anathema to them since the Reformation, if not before.[33]

The STO brought about a qualitative and quantitative change for the internal French Resistance: from a small, marginal movement that was basically urban and middle class, the Resistance suddenly became a mass movement that included workers and peasants in its ranks. By late 1943 or early 1944 it was a formidable force that could potentially challenge the Germans in large parts of France, especially in the south where the Maquis was most solidly entrenched. But, as we shall see in the next chapter, the Maquis had serious problems of organization and armament that limited its strength in the last year or two of the war. And it faced serious opposition from many in France who viewed its members as nothing more than bandits. In contrast to the myth of the Maquis, public opinion as measured by Vichy and the Germans was not always on its side in 1944. In order to survive, the Maquis often had to resort to robbery in the small towns of southern France that bordered its mountain redoubts. Banks, bakeries, grocery stores, and other providers of fundamentals were targeted by these "primitive rebels," who believed that their cause transcended the normal rules of conduct and should be supported by all good French men and women. The public condemned most of these acts, but generally refused to take action against the Maquis. Only when the Maquis attacked the Germans directly did the French support its activities, and even then German reprisals against people unassociated with the Maquis turned some against it. Still, the Maquis was an enormous success overall. Largely because of it only 1.6 percent of the French went to Germany as laborers during the war, compared to 6.6 percent of Belgians. And, the Maquis also succeeded in pinning down German troops that could have been used to fight the invading Allied forces.[34]

By about the middle of 1943 the French Resistance had been brought together into one organization, led by General de Gaulle, despite the efforts of the Americans and, to a lesser extent, the British, to prevent de Gaulle from gaining the upper hand. De Gaulle had been deliberately kept in the dark in late 1942 when the Allies launched the North African campaign, despite the fact that French territory in Morocco, Algeria, and Tunisia was involved. The Americans hoped to place their men in power, but the American choice, General Giraud, lacked legitimacy and soon lost out to de Gaulle in the struggle for control over the Resistance. Giraud was too close to Vichy and too oblivious to politics, unlike de Gaulle whose solid anti-Vichy and pro-democratic credentials gained him solid support from French political leaders ranging from communists and socialists on the Left to members of the Action française on the Right. In the first half of 1943 de Gaulle outmaneuvered Giraud to gain the grudging acquiescence of even staunchly anti-Gaullist American diplomats.

De Gaulle prevailed because of his own strengths and Giraud's glaring weaknesses. In early 1943, de Gaulle gained the support of the great socialist leader, Léon Blum, as well as the backing of the French Communist Party. With the creation of the National Council of the Resistance in May 1943 every major party, trade union, and Resistance organization in France recognized de Gaulle as the leader of the national Resistance. Even before this, de Gaulle had gained the support of the National Committee, which had been set up early on for the purpose of broadening the legitimacy of the Free French movement. De Gaulle also had on his side a rising military star, General Leclerc, who had joined de Gaulle in London in 1940 and whose army played a significant role in the defeat of the Germans in North Africa. With Leclerc, the bulk of the French Empire, and the internal and external Resistance behind him, de Gaulle dominated the scene. Only Roosevelt's obstinate support of General Giraud stood in his way.

Giraud had none of the advantages that de Gaulle possessed. In fact, General Leclerc, following significant victories in Libya and Tunisia, wrote Giraud in April 1943 instructing him to rally behind de Gaulle: "You have no other choice, and make sure you do it immediately." Giraud lacked political credentials to lead the Resistance. He was a typical authoritarian officer, totally contemptuous of the democratic process and happy with the politics of Vichy and the National Revolution. He saw no reason to change the Vichy-imposed legal order, which had instituted anti-Semitic laws and incarcerated thousands of Jews in concentration camps. To rescue Giraud from his worst political instincts, Jean Monnet rushed from Washington to North Africa in February 1943 to inform him that the Americans would not accept a reactionary, racist administration in the region. Monnet even wrote a speech that Giraud delivered on the virtues of democracy. But no one, not even Giraud, believed in his conversion.[35]

Totally outclassed by de Gaulle, Giraud eventually gave in to the general, and his most ardent backers, such as Monnet and Maurice Couve de Murville, accepted de Gaulle's leadership. By late May 1943, Giraud realized that de Gaulle had the upper hand, following the creation of the National Council of the Resistance, and he agreed to share power with de Gaulle in the French Committee of National Liberation (CFLN), which was to be the sovereign authority for France as long as the war lasted. Once more, Giraud's base of support was eroded by the exclusion of supporters of the National Revolution from the CFLN and by the requirement that everyone pledge allegiance to the Republic and condemn the Pétainist "arbitrary regime of personal power." Roosevelt and the Americans tried to counter this setback by insisting that they would provide arms to the Fighting French only if Giraud was commander-in-chief of the military forces. Despite Giraud's resulting formal military leadership, de Gaulle remained in charge, since he was appointed to head the "military committee" that had jurisdiction over all fighting forces. Consequently, by the end of July, de Gaulle had total command of the civil and military powers of the French government-in-exile. He reinforced his authority by rallying important Vichy military leaders such as General Juin to the Fighting French. And in the fall of 1943 he consolidated his political power when the CFLN created a Consultative Assembly to meet in Algiers until a provisional government could be established on French soil. It included a broad spectrum of representatives from both the internal and external Resistance, bringing together in one body all political parties and groups that opposed Vichy and Pétain. In a November 3, 1943, speech that inaugurated the assembly, de Gaulle proclaimed that it was "a first step in the resurrection of the French representative institutions upon which the future of our democracy depends." Significantly, the Allied powers thought the same thing. De Gaulle had won their reluctant, grudging support by establishing that Fighting France was based on democratic political values and had the backing of the leading democratic forces within France.[36]

General de Gaulle, in his war memoirs, best captured the essence of this struggle with Giraud. To de Gaulle, Giraud was a superb military leader, but one who lacked political understanding. When the two met in Casablanca in January 1943, Giraud told de Gaulle that he had no interest in politics, "that, de Gaulle wrote, he never listened to anyone who tried to interest him in a theory or a program, that he never read a newspaper or turned on the radio." He criticized Vichy only for its refusal to fight the Germans. He had no use for the internal Resistance, which he found "incomprehensible if not reprehensible" because of its "revolutionary character." De Gaulle was certain that such a man could never lead the Liberation of France, for the French, he correctly understood, needed a government that would "condemn Vichy, proclaim that the armistice was always null and void, and identify itself with the Republic and, in the eyes of the world, with the independence of France."[37]

Were all French resisters? Or collaborators? Or neither? Or both? France was probably no better or worse than most European countries in resisting the Nazis. Nevertheless it is more accurate to call France a nation of resisters than one of collaborators, although neither appellation is totally appropriate or accurate. Resistance was greatest among those groups that had a history of rebellion against authority, such as the Protestants of the Cévennes or various marginal ethnic groups such as the Bretons and the Basques. It was also high among persecuted groups such as Jews, Spanish refugees, and communists. In addition, workers and peasants whose labor and products were demanded by the Germans and Vichy joined the Resistance to escape forced mobilization. Workers' adherence to the Maquis in 1943 made the Resistance a mass movement that vastly outstripped the forces of collaboration by the end of that year.

Of course there were many groups that did not eagerly or openly embrace Resistance. Among them were members of the extreme right political parties of the Third Republic, many of whom collaborated during the war. Less obvious were members of the Radical Party, which had been the backbone of the Third Republic, but deserted it in 1940 and mostly eschewed the Resistance movement. Catholics, too, were reluctant to resist. Catholic culture, in general, favored the status quo, which in this case was Pétain and Vichy. The one major exception to this rule was the Catholic Left, which embraced the Republic and accepted the Enlightenment as a secular interpretation of the Christian dispensation. The military, too, found itself tied to a culture of obedience. Although there was a small military Resistance movement, the Organisation de Résistance de l'Armée, it was dwarfed by the large numbers of officers who adhered to Vichy and accepted without question the German dissolution of the French military in late 1942. Finally, big business tended to cooperate with the Germans, the most notorious case being the Renault automobile company. Still, a number of businesses tried to protect their workers from the STO forced labor requirement, including the Michelin tire company.[38]

Intellectuals comprise a special category in the Resistance. In a sense, the Resistance was an intellectual movement. The main activity of most Resistance organizations was to publish clandestine newspapers, which were intended to inform people of events unreported in the censored press and to bolster morale among the faithful. Perhaps the best known of these journals was *Combat,* which Albert Camus edited in the last years of the war. Beyond that, intellectuals formed numerous small Resistance groups, such as the communist-inspired Comité national des écrivains, which oversaw the politics of intellectuals. They also wrote and published novels, plays, and essays, some of which were subversive of the Nazi status quo. Without doubt, Jean-Paul Sartre's play, *The Flies,* which attacked the German occupation before hundreds if not thousands of theatergoers, was a cultural high point in the Parisian intellectual Resistance. But not all intellectuals sided with Sartre and the Resistance. Some, such as Drieu la Rochelle, backed the Nazis and collaborated openly. Under his editorship, the prestigious French intellectual journal, the *Nouvelle Revue française,* was transformed into a collaborationist mouthpiece in which Resistance intellectuals mostly refused to publish, choosing instead to use such journals as the Marseille-based *Cahiers du sud* and various clandestine Parisian publications. Probably the most successful of these Resistance presses was Éditions de minuit, the publisher of the great Resistance novel by Vercors, *The Silence of the Sea,* which propagated the Manichean myth that the good French man or woman refused to carry on any sort of relationship with the occupier, no matter what the circumstances might be. Such purity never existed, not even among intellectuals, but the book served the purpose of projecting the concept of a nation united against the enemy. For the most part, the intellectual Resistance was a limited, Parisian phenomenon that very few people experienced firsthand.[39]

Yet, however limited, the impact of intellectuals' words in French life both during and immediately after the war should not be underestimated. Although not without wartime moral shortcomings himself, Jean-Paul Sartre, in particular, emerged out of the ranks of French intellectuals as the dominant voice of Resistance. He expressed the mentality, the spirit, of the war in his 1944 essay, "La République du silence," when he proclaimed famously, "We have never been so free as under German occupation." He added: "We were on the brink of the deepest knowledge that man can have of himself. Because man's secret is not his Oedipus complex or his inferiority complex, it is the limit of his freedom, it is his power to resist torture and death."[40] More than anyone else, Sartre captured the existential moment that the vast majority of French people had experienced, either firsthand or indirectly, during these dismal years of occupation, collaboration, and Resistance.

Women provide us with another aspect of the complexities of determining who resisted. As we shall see in the next chapter, a significant number of women collaborated with the enemy and were severely punished for it. The story of these collaborationist women has been told over and over, while the more important involvement of women in the Resistance has been muted, if not suppressed. On a day-to-day level, women both resisted and collaborated, just as men did. Life was too complex under Vichy and the Germans to follow a Manichean agenda. At least this was true for most people, including the Sartres, Camus, and Beauvoirs of the world.[41] The haute couture industry, which was dominated by women entrepreneurs and clients, provides a striking example of the fine line between Resistance and collaboration. To survive, the heads of the Parisian establishments had to collaborate with the Germans, but they resisted the Nazis in various subtle ways, among them producing whimsical hats that mocked the occupation. The jeweler, Cartier, created a piece called "The Bird in a Cage" that depicted the captivity of the French and their future Liberation, which occurred when the cage opened to free the imprisoned bird.[42]

Women also joined the Resistance to do the same things that men did. In most cases they were excluded from military matters and were relegated to clerical tasks and liaison operations. Yet, they often risked their lives in dangerous assignments such as transporting Resistance materials. Some women were involved in running the networks stretching from Belgium to the Pyrenees that smuggled downed British pilots and other important individuals out of the continent. Others rescued Jews. Jewish children, in particular, were protected by extensive networks of women, many of whom were nuns, as we saw in the previous chapter. In general, women who joined the Resistance came from families that had a history of activism. A disproportionate number of them were Jewish, socialist, communist, Catholic leftist, or Protestant. In that sense, the composition of the female Resistance mirrored that of the male. But unlike the members of the male Resistance, the women who resisted never gained significant public recognition of their actions. Many women who returned from the German camps, where they had been interred for their Resistance activities, received no sympathy from their compatriots. In one case, a female teacher who asked for leave in order to restore her health was told that she had already had a vacation in Germany. For the most part, French men, whether they were Pétainists or Gaullists, believed that women belonged in the home. Basking in the glory of the Resistance was a man's job.[43]

Still, the moment of the Resistance remained for all to remember, no matter how much it would be tarnished in the years after the war.

By 1944, on the eve of the Allied invasion, the Resistance had become a formidable movement in France. By then there were 100 national Resistance newspapers and as many as 500 regional ones. Their total circulation was about 2 million; their readership was probably several times that number. Before the Allied landings in June, the Resistance had about 1 million more-or-less active members within France. Outside of France, de Gaulle and the Fighting French had amassed 550,000 troops, of whom 250,000 were from the French colonies. In comparison, the forces of collaboration in France never surpassed 250,000 during the course of the war. Yet, the overwhelming concern of the French in 1944 was not the Resistance but survival. Food was the number one topic discussed in the letters opened by Vichy and the Germans. If anything, the Resistance, at least in the form of the Maquis, was viewed with suspicion, if not hostility, by the majority. And yet the Resistance would soon sweep all before it as the French joined the cause in massive numbers after D-Day. France may not have been the nation of resisters that de Gaulle believed it was, but it clearly was not a nation of collaborators. As one historian of the period has claimed, more French men and women participated in public affairs during the Liberation of France than at any other time in the history of the country.[44]

6

By the end of 1943, the Resistance had become a powerful, united force, with Charles de Gaulle in charge of both the Fighting French headquartered in London and Algiers and the internal Resistance. No other Western European country under Nazi occupation had developed such an efficient, united movement to oppose it. The constituent members of this Resistance agreed that the new France must be a parliamentary democracy, with a strong state that provided for the general welfare of the people by reigning in the worst excesses of capitalism, nationalizing vital sectors of the economy, and extending health, unemployment, and old age insurance to all people. Socialists, communists, and Christian democrats all adhered to these principles, despite differences regarding their practical implementation. Both advocates of a market economy and of socialism generally believed that the French economic system needed some form of planning, although not the heavy-handed kind that Vichy advocated. Out of their different positions would emerge the postwar planning mechanism inaugurated by Jean Monnet: democratic planning centered around a set of national priorities that allowed the state and the market, along with employers and workers, to play major roles in determining what should be done to achieve productive, equitable economic growth. Although many members of the Resistance were disillusioned by the failure to fully implement the Resistance Charter of social, political, and economic objectives as the revival of Third Republic–style politics undermined the revolutionary élan of wartime politics, still the legacy of the Resistance became an integral part of the Fourth and Fifth Republics, shaping the role of the state, the welfare of French citizens, and the parameters of debate on crucial issues.[1]

In late 1943 and early 1944, however, the Resistance was not yet a hegemonic, mythical movement. On the contrary, its powers were greatly circumscribed by the reluctance of the United States to recognize it as the legitimate representative of the French people and the related weakness of its military forces. At times, the United States attempted to divide the Resistance and, it seems, conquer it. For example, when Henri Frenay and Combat desperately needed financial resources in early 1943, the United States channeled it to them through Geneva, without consulting de Gaulle or providing aid to the Free French in general. But most of the time the Americans refused any dealings with the Resistance. The State Department even refused to negotiate with de Gaulle and the CFLN on what the status of France would be after the D-Day invasion. The U.S. government.intended to set up a military government called AMGOT (Allied Military Government for Occupied Territories) in liberated France as it had in Italy. Not until July 1944, after the massive popular support of the CFLN became evident, did Washington recognize it as "competent to ensure the administration of France."[2]

American reluctance to recognize de Gaulle and the CFLN contributed to the problem of military weakness. Neither the Americans nor the British were willing to give the French Resistance a significant role in the war. De Gaulle was kept deliberately out of the planning for the invasion of France, although he was told that his troops would participate in it. Allied weapons that could have aided the internal Resistance in its struggle against Vichy and the Germans were not provided, or were insufficient for the task. As a result, the size of the Resistance was limited by lack of military supplies, if nothing else. The promise made by the British to aid all Frenchmen who evaded German labor conscription was not fully kept. Consequently, the Maquis lacked even basic necessities. Not until the very end of the German occupation, when the balance was tipping in favor of the Allies and the French were joining the Resistance in massive numbers, did the Allies begin to provide for this burgeoning, important anti-German movement, re-inforcing its numbers in the process. But it would be wrong to assume that the weakness of the Resistance was due exclusively to the failure of the Allies to supply it. We should also keep in mind that General de Gaulle's Fighting French movement failed to obtain many recruits, despite years of pleading. Less than one-half of De Gaulle's Liberation army of about 575,000 came from metropolitan France. The rest came from the Empire mainly from the North African army formerly con-trolled by Vichy.[3]

Despite serious limitations and the fact that the Allied forces played the dominant role in liberating France, de Gaulle and the Resistance rehabilitated French honor and glory through their actions in 1944 and 1945. France emerged out of the ashes of the war as one of the four powers occupying Germany, with one of the five permanent seats in the United Nations Security Council, and with its citizens believing that the nation had risen up en masse to overthrow the Nazi occupiers. By December 1944, almost two-thirds of the French believed that the nation was once again a great power.[4]

This miraculous turnaround from pariah status among nations to the self-image as a great power occurred within the course of a year or less and was a consequence of the success of the Liberation of France from Nazi occupation. This success led the French to believe that, as a nation, they had stood up against the German occupation.[5] Only a small portion of them had collaborated, the French believed at the war's conclusion. And those who did collaborate were punished, in some cases severely, during the postwar purges. In every part of France, every region, every province, every major or even minor city, Resistance forces had risen up to oppose the enemy and take control of matters in what most perceived to be a smooth transition from rule by Vichy to governance by the Fourth Republic. Paris, the greatest city in the French-speaking world, was liberated by French forces, not by the Allied powers. All the French knew this, they were all aware of what had happened in their community, and almost all of them be-lieved that they had participated in the Resistance, however small a role they might have played. All of France, the French thought, had resisted the enemy, or at least opposed collaboration. It would take a long time—over twenty years—for this powerful myth of total Resistance to be punctured.

The history of what happened in 1944 and 1945 is probably not as Manichean in nature as Resistance triumphing over collaboration. Although the overwhelming majority opposed collaboration, most were *attentiste* regarding the Resistance and the overthrow of German rule. In fact, as late as the summer of 1944, as Allied troops were flooding into France, the French were focused on food shortages and bombing raids. In the 2 million letters that the authorities opened and analyzed in July 1944, the Resistance ranked only sixth in importance, far behind the omnipresent subject of staying alive.[6] By that point, however, the Resistance had become a major player in the Liberation of France, gaining more recruits every day and taking open military action against the Germans. The *attentiste* phase of the Resistance had come to an end with D-Day if not before. Increasingly during the course of 1944 the French became involved in freeing themselves, with mixed results. The story of their Liberation from Nazi rule, seen almost totally from their perspective, without the retelling of the Allied victories in 1944 and 1945, is what follows.

The struggle for Liberation began in 1943 with two major French offensives. General Giraud, in a maneuver that surprised everyone including de Gaulle, invaded Corsica in September 1943, taking the island from the Italians in a quick campaign with the support of the local communist Resistance. Despite the Corsican success, however, Giraud did not avoid eventual disgrace. De Gaulle successfully used Giraud's supposedly duplicitous secrecy and pro-communist tactics against him to obtain from the CFLN his dismissal as commander-in-chief in April 1944. Also in 1943, General Juin commanded the 120,000 French troops who fought with the Allies in Italy, in which they performed remarkably well until they were redeployed in August 1944 for the invasion of southern France. Although the number of troops Juin commanded was small, the French military in Italy accomplished its main objective, which was to be a significant part of the Allied coalition on the continent in the effort to restore France to great power status and gain complete sovereignty for the nation after the Liberation.[7]

Just as significant for regaining status and sovereignty were the actions of the internal Resistance. Here the difficulties were far greater. For one, after the German invasion and occupation of southern France in late 1942, the internal Resistance could no longer rely on the Vichy government to tolerate its activities. The Nazis now called the shots in the south, and they soon began infiltrating and breaking up the Resistance. In the summer of 1943, the Lyon Resistance, which was the center of the movement in the south, was devastated by the arrest of leading figures, including de Gaulle's emissary to the internal Resistance, Jean Moulin. Most of the Lyon leaders who escaped the Nazi roundup left for Paris, where they remained for the rest of the war. The Vichy administration, which had been infiltrated by numerous Resistance moles—as many as 2,000 by the end of 1943—still provided valuable information, but could offer little protection, especially after the fascist Milice began ruthlessly uprooting anyone who opposed collaboration with the Germans.[8]

With the Germans in control of the entire country, the Resistance faced serious obstacles to carrying out military actions without major Allied support. Yet, prior to D-Day, Resistance forces undertook a number of actions, which made the Germans feel increasingly isolated and highly suspicious of even friendly French. Acts of sabotage increased greatly in late 1943 and early 1944, as part of the campaign to destabilize the Germans. In December 1943 and January 1944 the Resistance destroyed 111 railroad locomotives in an effort to undermine Nazi use of the French transportation system. From that point on, the railroads were seriously disrupted by the Resistance, culminating after D-Day in the massive destruction of rail lines and trains in a successful effort to delay if not prevent the deployment of German troops and equipment to the western front. But acts of sabotage were not limited to the railroads, as can be seen in the examples of Marseille and Clermont-Ferrand. In Marseille, beginning in January 1943 with the Nazi destruction of the quarters around the Old Port, acts of sabotage became a daily occurrence, even though the police arrested thousands of citizens. The Germans eventually discovered that their efforts to stop these acts were thwarted by the police intendant for Marseille and the regional prefect, both of whom belonged to the Resistance. Similarly, in Clermont-Ferrand and the surrounding Auvergne, confrontations between Germans and the Resistance increased dramatically during the last years of the war: between November 1943 and August 1944 over 2,400 incidents were recorded ranging from raids on city halls to sabotage of factories. After D-Day, the police in the area deserted their posts in large numbers to join the Resistance, while those who remained in their jobs were reluctant to support the Germans against their compatriots.[9]

Beyond the cities a good part of the southern countryside had gone over to the Maquis by early 1944. As H. R. Kedward has pointed out, Vichy had lost the support of the rural areas in the south by 1944 through misguided policies of excessive taxation and requisitioning of food at prices below market value, while the Maquis had gained peasant backing through attention to local concerns and support of regional cultures. The Protestant culture of the Cévennes was openly antiauthoritarian, as we have seen, but the same was true of the Haute-Savoie where the memory of Resistance to the Revolution and even, in some places, to Richelieu, fueled Resistance to Vichy and the Germans. Other areas, such as Quercy, had similar antistatist traditions, while the Aude modeled its Resistance after the Cathars. These local, cultural factors may not entirely explain why the Maquis took hold in the south, but they were often more important than allegiances to political movements such as the Popular Front. Most members of the Maquis did not join it to back political causes, such as the Communist Party's concept of revolutionary upheaval. There is no evidence to support the commonly accepted interpretation of the Maquis as a tool of the French communist cause. The number of communists in the Maquis was never large and they were, above all, French patriots, fully supportive of de Gaulle and the Liberation of the nation. Whatever the reasons, by 1944 the rural areas of the south were solidly behind the Resistance. The subprefect of Le Vigan, in the Cévennes, informed his superiors in the spring of 1944 that many of the cantons in his part of the department of the Gard "live in absolutely independent fashion, immune to all control." The Germans, who were aware of this, began to act in early 1944, moving into the mountains to break up the opposition, massacring the local population and burning their homes in an effort to prevent sabotage. In the south the battle for the Liberation of France began well before D-Day.[10]

By this point, in early 1944, the Maquis was ready to confront the Germans openly, in pitched battle if necessary, but serious obstacles emerged to caution restraint. For one, de Gaulle did not trust the Maquis to be loyal to his agenda; he feared that the communists would dominate it and use it for their own political purposes. He advocated restraint rather than confrontation, hoping to unleash the Maquis only after D-Day and then for narrow military objectives that he would determine. For that purpose, de Gaulle worked hard to centralize power in the hands of the CFLN, over which he presided. He parachuted his military delegates into France in September 1943 with orders to bring all paramilitary Resistance organizations under their control. By D-Day these groups were theoretically under the command of General Koenig, the head of the French Forces of the Interior (FFI), and directly accountable to de Gaulle. At the same time, de Gaulle worked with reliable elements of the internal Resistance to create a new administrative apparatus in liberated France, again under his control. By D-Day he had already selected half of the departmental prefects who would take over from Vichy. In short, de Gaulle restricted as much as possible the internal Resistance's influence over postwar government. And, on this point he was in total agreement with Churchill and the British. As a result, neither de Gaulle nor the British offered much support to the southern French freedom fighters when they battled Vichy and the Germans in early 1944.[11]

In the Hautes-Alpes, on the plateau of Glières, the Maquis chose to fight openly against Vichy in February and March 1944, after being harassed by the Milice for an extended period of time. The Allies had promised to parachute weapons and supplies into the area to support it, but little help materialized. Even so, the Resistance prevented Vichy's forces from taking the plateau, making it necessary for the Germans to finish the job. After heavy bombardment of the Maquis's positions, 20,000 Wehrmacht troops stormed the plateau and subdued the Maquis in late March. The Germans lost 300 men in combat, while the Maquis suffered 250 deaths. Vichy courts martial added to the casualty total by sentencing numerous members of the Resistance to death, and the Germans shot survivors on the spot or hauled them off to concentration camps. Although this represented a major defeat for the guerillas, it also discredited Vichy totally in the eyes of the local population and contributed slightly to Allied victory by diverting thousands of German troops that could have been used elsewhere. But Glières would also become one of the sacred places of the Resistance, where the French stood up alone, without Allied support, and fought heroically in a losing battle against all odds. In the French story of the war, Glières was the first battle in the Liberation of southern France and facilitated the rapid success of the Allied invasion of Mediterranean France in August 1944.[12]

After the Glières fiasco the Resistance chose to wait for the Allied invasion before confronting the Germans again. By this point, in the spring of 1944, everyone knew that D-Day was imminent. Allied bombardments had been stepped up greatly. Major northern French cities such as Le Havre, Nantes, and Rouen were flattened by heavy bombing. Even Paris suffered from almost daily Allied bombing by the end of May 1944. As many as 5,000 Parisians died in such raids during the course of the war. Altogether, the Allies carried out 7,444 bombing raids that killed 36,000 French during 1944. Vichy reacted to these with a propaganda campaign that condemned the Allies for "aiding" France by killing her people and destroying her cities, but the French overwhelmingly blamed the Germans for their situation.[13]

The average French citizen who lived through these bombing raids in the spring of 1944 probably knew as much about D-Day as de Gaulle, who was kept out of the inner circle of military planning for the invasion of France. The Allies had no intention of using the French army in Operation Overlord, as the invasion was called. Nor did they want to give de Gaulle's provisional government any sort of recognition or authority on French soil. They merely wanted to use the Resistance for their own military purposes. This led to serious conflict between de Gaulle and Churchill over the issue of the recognition of the French government-in-exile just before the Normandy invasion. In a meeting between the two in early June, Churchill burst out in anger against de Gaulle's obstinate refusal to accept the Allied plan: "Every time I have to decide between you and Roosevelt, I shall always choose Roosevelt." This led de Gaulle to refuse to speak on the BBC in support of the invasion. He claimed that he could not tell his countrymen to accept the "occupation" of their country. Churchill responded that he wanted de Gaulle locked up, adding, "He must not be allowed to set foot in France!" But de Gaulle gave in at the last moment and spoke on the radio on June 6, appealing to the French to coordinate their actions "as closely as possible with those carried out at the same time by the Allied and French armies." Still, Churchill fumed over their confrontation and did not allow de Gaulle to set foot on French soil until June 14. Shortly after this, the British government recognized the French provisional government as the government of France. De Gaulle won Roosevelt over to his position in July 1944 during a hastily arranged trip to Washington.[14]

What had happened after D-Day to change the attitudes of these reluctant allies? Simply put, as the U.S. intelligence service, the OSS, reported, the Fighting French and the internal Resistance quickly revealed in battle that they were united behind the general and his provisional government and that they were a formidable force in the Liberation of France. The careful, methodical preparation that de Gaulle and his supporters had undertaken for the invasion and defeat of the Germans and Vichy began to pay off within weeks, if not days, after June 6, 1944. After the war General Eisenhower would state that the French contributed greatly to the Allied victory. Although that claim has been used by the Resistance to inflate its importance, it is nevertheless true. Recently, it has been corroborated by evidence from the German archives, which indicates that the Wehrmacht viewed the French Resistance as a formidable force that had to be neutralized if the Germans were going to prevail after D-Day. As a result, considerable German troops were dispatched to western and southern France in an unsuccessful effort to eliminate the Maquis. Clearly, the evidence indicates that without the serious involvement of the French in their Liberation, World War II in Europe would have lasted much longer. The Resistance was not an insignificant movement, but rather one that helped defeat the Nazis, forced Vichy to capitulate without a major struggle or civil war—such as occurred in Yugoslavia—and aided the nation in making the transition from the disruptive, dangerous period of warfare in 1944 to the government of the Fourth Republic.[15]

By D-Day, therefore, the Resistance was ready to fight. It had developed carefully thought-out plans to be implemented throughout France once the invasion began. Plan Vert, to which we have already alluded, aimed at incapacitating the railroads. Plan Tortue, later renamed Plan Bibendum, sought to disrupt German highway traffic in northern France. Plan Violet strove to stop German telephone and telegraph communications. And Plan Bleu aspired to sabotage the nation's electrical system. All of them worked well. During the first days of the Allied invasion, the Resistance carried out 950 acts of sabotage. In June and July 1944, it derailed 600 trains and put 1,800 locomotives out of commission. It blocked roads and disrupted traffic, seriously delaying tanks and troops moving from the German border to Normandy. It routinely cut telephone and electrical lines, disturbing communications. It also provided the Allies with significant intelligence data about German troop movements, weapons, and the like. By D-Day, an extensive network of as many as 1,400 "pianists" (radio operators) located primarily in the north were transmitting essential intelligence information to Britain.[16]

Only a handful of French soldiers were part of the original Overlord invasion, but others soon joined the fight. In Brittany, for example, the local Maquis rose up to overthrow the German occupier. As many as 30,000 Resistance troops participated in that successful operation in the summer of 1944. Elsewhere, in the south, the "Plan Montagnard" that Jean Moulin and General Delestraint, the head of the Secret Army of the Resistance, had drawn up in the spring of 1943 was put into action. Under the leadership of Colonel Gaspard, the Auvergne rose up in conjunction with the Allied invasion. At Vercors, in June 1944, about

4,000 men gathered to fight the Germans in pitched battle, believing that the Allies would provide them with significant aid. Unfortunately Vercors, while tying down the Nazis, turned out to be like Glières as not enough supplies materialized and the Germans massed enough troops to prevail. Around Toulouse, in the department of Tarn, the Maquis, joined by Vichy deserters in places such as Albi and Redon, was especially successful in using guerrilla tactics to keep the Germans occupied for almost two months. Beyond the Tarn, guerrilla uprisings occurred in virtually every southern department. The Germans responded to them by destroying towns and massacring villagers. When they finished their operations in the south, the Nazis had massacred civilians in over 100 locations. In Tulle, for example, they executed 120 citizens for aiding the Resistance. The most notorious case took place in Oradour-sur-Glane, where SS troops en route to Normandy killed 642 of the town's 725 residents in cold blood on June 10, 1944. This brutal incident was the culmination of a series of attacks that the Germans had carried out in the Limousin region against the civilian population since March 1944 in an effort to eliminate the Maquis. Instead of success, however, the Germans discovered that every massacre bred more Resistance that tied down more German troops. The hunt for the Maquis became a minor German obsession; the Nazis depicted these rebels as illegal combatants inspired by the Jews, leading Hitler, in July 1944, to call for the elimination of the Maquis "by all means possible." Nothing of the sort occurred as the Germans retreated from the inhospitable south shortly thereafter. In what can only be called a compliment to the tenacity of the Resistance, the Nazis called the Massif Central "the little Ukraine" in recognition of the stiff opposition they faced there.[17]

None of these vicious encounters between the Resistance and the Germans was typical, but that in Saint-Amand-Montrond in the Cher, a town of 10,000 that was located just north of the city of Vichy, can provide us with one powerful, complex example of what this nasty war entailed. On D-Day, the Resistance, with the support of the local gendarmerie, took over the city hall and the subprefecture, as well as the headquarters of the local Milice. They took thirty-six miliciens, including women, as hostages against a possible counterattack by Vichy and German forces. They soon realized that they could not defend Saint-Amand and left to join their comrades in Guéret, the capital of Creuse, where a much larger uprising had put the Resistance in power and taken a number of German soldiers and Vichy miliciens prisoner. The Guéret Resistance even succeeded in fending off a German attack on June 8, solidifying support for its cause. Meanwhile, however, the Germans took Saint-Amand without much effort, set fire to a number of houses, and rounded up 200 hostages, 8 of whom were executed immediately. By the end of the day, June 8, the Germans had killed 19 citizens and burned six houses. They handed over power to the Milice, which governed the city until the end of August 1944 with a reign of terror that included pillaging, arrests, and executions.

The Saint-Amand case was complicated by the fact that one of the hostages held by the Resistance was Simone Bout de l'An, the wife of the head of the Vichy Milice. He threatened to execute sixty hostages from the town and to bomb and set fire to what remained of Saint-Amand unless the Resistance released his wife. This set off a complicated round of negotiations with the Archbishop of Bourges playing a key role in pleading with both the Germans and Vichy to spare the lives of these innocent citizens. Bout de l'An, who was convinced that the "terrorists" holding his wife hostage were atheistic communists, took the wives of the Resistance leaders hostage and proposed a swap as the solution to the problem. The swap was made, but the Maquis continued to hold twenty miliciens and the Nazis sent more troops to free them and eliminate what remained of the opposition. They arrived around mid-July and immediately wiped out most of the Maquis, taking sixty-two Maquisards prisoner, sending them to camps in Germany. Others, however, escaped capture and continued to fight until the Germans retreated from the department later in the summer.

In the midst of these skirmishes, the Nazis rounded up the Jews of Saint-Amand arresting about seventy of the 200 Jews who lived there. Thirty-six of them were executed on an isolated farm, their bodies thrown into three deep wells from which they were recovered after the war. By the time that Saint-Amand was liberated, over 100 citizens of the city had lost their lives, mostly at the hands of the Germans, although the Milice played a role in this bloody affair as well.

Did the citizens of Saint-Amand lose their lives in vain? Should the Resistance have remained passive after D-Day, waiting for the Allies to liberate their small city? Did they really accomplish anything in resisting the Nazis? These are questions that have no easy answers, in part because we do not know the degree to which a relatively insignificant uprising in an isolated city such as this one contributed to the defeat of the Nazis and their Vichy allies. We only know that such incidents contributed greatly to the myth of universal Resistance that helped the French rehabilitate themselves after the ignominious defeat of 1940.[18]

Similar doubts could be raised concerning the sacrifices that many French made, either willingly or not after D-Day. For example, was the taking of the important Norman city of Caen worth the loss of lives and property? The city of William the Conqueror was totally destroyed during the siege that lasted seventy-eight days from D-Day until mid-August, left only 400 out of 18,000 homes undamaged, and killed between 3,000 and 5,000 civilians. One French observer—from a distance—noted in her diary entry for June 22, 1944, "What a costly and terrible 'liberation!'" After the war, the people of Caen came to a similar conclusion: the Liberation had cost too much. They had been willing to endure a short struggle but not an endless destructive battle.[19]

On June 14, General de Gaulle landed in France. At Bayeux, not far from Caen, an enthusiastic crowd of supporters greeted him. He discovered that the liberated parts of Normandy had been brought under the control of the Free French, in what seemed to be an effortless transition from Vichy's administration. On August 1, French troops under General Leclerc landed in time to participate in the Allied breakthrough out of Normandy begun in late July. They joined General Patton's march eastward, south of Caen through the Avranches toward Paris and the north. Although Leclerc's army was quite small, only a little over 15,000 men, it was one of the best trained units in the war. Leclerc had spent nine months putting together a first-rate tank division for the invasion and had the support of the French Forces of the

Interior and most of the French Resistance. Leclerc was intent on taking Paris, which the British and Americans had chosen to bypass to pursue the Germans into northern France and beyond. With General Eisenhower's reluctant support the battle for Paris began in early August. Paris would be liberated exclusively by the French, which was precisely what de Gaulle wanted.[20]

The battle for Paris offers a microcosm of how the united French Resistance worked in 1944. The battle began on August 10 when the railroad workers went on strike. They were soon followed by others, and by August 15 the city was paralyzed by a general strike. On that day the police joined the effort. By August 22, barricades had been erected throughout Paris, shutting the Germans out of the center. When General Leclerc's troops entered the city two days later the Germans were in retreat. One day later, on August 25, General von Choltitz, the commander of the German troops in Paris, surrendered. Among the French about 3,000 regular soldiers, French Forces of the Interior, Resistance members, and civilians were killed. The Germans suffered about the same, 2,800 deaths. General von Choltiz had totally misunderstood the extent of the Parisian Resistance and had missed his opportunity to nip it in the bud before the barricades went up. After that, Resistance mushroomed and his forces proved incapable of stopping it.[21]

In the midst of the fighting, which continued in the suburbs until late August, de Gaulle entered Paris, triumphant at having accomplished the impossible task of restoring the republican government of France in its capital city against the opposition of the Germans, the Vichy regime, and even his Allied supporters. De Gaulle knew exactly what needed to be done, as he tells us in his memoirs: "I would mold all minds into a single national impulse, but also cause the figure and the authority of the state to appear at once." He wanted to make sure that the more unruly elements of the Resistance did not gain power and undermine the State. Thus, he required that General von Choltitz capitulate to Leclerc and the army, not to the Resistance. Upon entering Paris de Gaulle demonstrated the continuity of the State by going to his old office in the Ministry of War where he had been under secretary for national defense. Only then did he visit city hall, from which provisional revolutionary governments had traditionally been proclaimed, where he gave his famous speech, congratulating the people of Paris for liberating the city "with the help of the army and the support of all of France." When he was goaded by Georges Bidault, the head of the internal Resistance, to proclaim the Republic, he replied in typical Gaullist fashion: "The Republic has never ceased. Free France, Fighting France, the French Committee of National Liberation have successively incorporated it. Vichy always was and still remains null and void."[22]

On Saturday, August 26, de Gaulle marched down the Champs d'E-lysée, swarmed by hundreds of thousands of liberated Parisians. The mass that he attended at Notre Dame Cathedral was a first, rather tentative step toward the reconciliation of Church and State, as de Gaulle shunned Archbishop Suhard and the Church showed its lukewarm support by having the choir sing "Magnificat" rather than "Te Deum." On August 28, he integrated the French Forces of the Interior into the regular army and dissolved the National Council of the Resistance, which had been superseded by the restoration of the Republic in Paris. With these acts, de Gaulle had fulfilled his mission of 1940: "[a] call to honor from the depths of history, as well as the instinct of the nation itself." This had provided him legitimacy to "call the nation to war and to unity, impose order, law and justice, demand from the world respect for the rights of France." He concluded his memoirs for this period of the war with one of his most moving and messianic statements: "Gradually, the call was heard. Slowly, severely, unity was forged. Now the people and the leader, helping each other, were to begin the journey to salvation."[23]

Meanwhile, many mundane things remained to be done. On August 15 the bulk of the French army—200,000 men, many of whom had fought in the Italian campaign—invaded the south along with several hundred thousand Allied troops. Under the leadership of General de Lattre de Tassigny they took both Toulon and Marseille with unanticipated speed. Marseille fell after only five days of fighting, compared with a preinvasion estimate of thirty-one. This rapid advance took the Germans completely by surprise, since they expected to stop the Allied forces long enough for an orderly retreat up the Rhône River. It also allowed the Allies to unload massive amounts of supplies through the port of Marseille, more than went through any other European port during the last months of 1944. By September 3, 1944, French troops had reached Lyon, disrupting the German plan to establish a line from Sens to Dijon and the Swiss border. Three weeks later the French had established a front from the northern Vosges Mountains to the Swiss border. The German strategic retreat up the Rhône valley thus failed to achieve its objective of preventing the southern Allied army from linking up with the Normandy forces. This was due not only to the rapid pursuit of the Germans by the French and Allied armies but also to the actions of the internal Resistance, which harassed the Germans, pecking away at them as they went through Gap and Grenoble, taking 3,500 of them prisoner in the Haute-Savoie area, and inflicting heavy losses on them at Montélimar, where 11,000 German casualties occurred. The Resistance and the FFI prevented about 40 percent of German troops in the south from joining forces with their compatriots in the north. By September 12, 1944, the French had 120,000 German prisoners in custody, about one-third of the total number that the Allies had taken by then. In the course of these triumphant events, the Resistance mushroomed in size, the FFI increasing from 100,000 in June to 500,000 in September. Nothing succeeds like success.[24]

By the end of 1944, the French had liberated almost the entire country, with a bit of help from the British and the Americans. After the Liberation of Paris and the quick triumph of the Mediterranean invasion, French troops under General de Lattre de Tassigny took Strasbourg and Alsace with Allied support in November 1944. In late December, however, Allied troops pulled out of Alsace to defend the Ardennes against the final, desperate German offensive, known as the Battle of the Bulge. De Gaulle refused to follow the Allied withdrawal and allow Strasbourg to be retaken for fear that French morale would plummet. He ordered General de Lattre to defend the city, against the wishes of the Allies, and informed General Eisenhower on January 3,

1944, that retreat from Alsace "would be a national disaster. For Alsace is sacred ground." Eisenhower finally accepted de Gaulle's position, and Strasbourg was defended successfully. From this point, de Gaulle's primary objective was to obtain a de facto right to participate in the occupation of postwar Germany. To achieve this, he instructed General de Lattre to carve out a French sphere of influence in southwestern Germany. De Lattre's troops crossed the Rhine on March 4, 1945, established themselves in the Black Forest-Baden-Württemberg sector, and took Stuttgart before the Americans arrived. By the end of April they had accomplished their mission. On May 9, 1945, France joined the three Allied powers in signing the act that proclaimed the capitulation of Germany. Due largely to the contribution of the nation's military forces and Resistance to the liberation of Europe, de Gaulle had adroitly restored France to the ranks of the great powers.[25]

While France was being liberated from Nazi control, the collaborationist Vichy government disintegrated completely and acquiesced in a cockamamie scheme to go into exile in Germany. Pétain, who had refused to leave France in 1940 to continue the war against the Nazis from North Africa, now left his native soil under very questionable circumstances. Beginning with D-Day, Pétain counseled the French to reject Liberation, although he also warned his supporters to avoid fratricidal warfare. Nevertheless, the paramilitary Milice followed the bloody path of summary executions and torture that had become commonplace since early 1944 when its head, Joseph Darnand, had been elevated to Pétain's cabinet. Darnand believed that Pétain supported the Milice's actions, since he had proclaimed on April 28, 1944, "Whoever participates in the Resistance compromises the future of the nation." On that basis, Darnand instructed the Milice to carry out total war against the anti-France of the Resistance, which it did with a vengeance after D-Day. One incident, in particular, stands out among many. On June 28, the Resistance assassinated the Vichy radio commentator, Philippe Henriot, whose virulent anticommunist, anti-Semitic and anti-Resistance broadcasts appealed to a large audience. Paul Touvier, the head of the Lyon Milice, ordered the execution of seven Jewish hostages in reprisal. After the war Touvier would be protected from prosecution by Catholic clerics who hid him until he was finally apprehended and tried for crimes against humanity in the 1990s. More immediately, however, such summary actions were rewarded by Vichy, which on July 6, 1944, decorated the miliciens who had fought against the Maquis on the Glières plateau in March. They were also remembered by the Resistance, which in August 1944 executed seventy-seven miliciens in the Haute-Savoie for treasonous collaboration with the Germans. With the Nazis retreating and Vichy collapsing in August 1944, the Milice—6,000 in number—revealed its true colors by marching east to Germany.[26]

The beginning of the ignominious end of Vichy can be dated August 19, 1944, when the Nazis gave Pétain an ultimatum to either go to Germany willingly or be forced to do so against his will. The Marshal protested to Hitler, but once again this amounted to nothing. By September, Pétain and about 1,500 die-hard collaborationist followers, including Laval and the French fascist leaders, had settled in Sigmaringen. There, on September 6, Pétain's advisors created the Délégation gouvernementale française pour la défense des intérêts français en Allemagne, which replaced Vichy as the government of these collaborationist fanatics. Pétain himself played no public role in this new entity. He left everything to his subordinates, who created the illusion that the Marshal was still in charge. Fernand de Brinon, the Vichy ambassador to the German occupying forces in Paris, took over as head of the delegation, appointed theoretically by Pétain but in reality by Hitler's representative, Ribbentrop. In that capacity, de Brinon issued an "Appeal to all French" that challenged the authority of the Free French and the Resistance: "The head of the French State, Marshal Pétain, has traveled from Belfort to Germany in order to defend the true interests of the French against the Gaullist usurpers and the English and American exploiters of the people." He concluded by proclaiming that Pétain remained "the only source of French legal authority." About a month later, in early October, the German Foreign Office issued a communiqué that stated that Pétain stood solidly behind a policy of "collaboration with Germany in the attempt to reestablish peace on French soil." Although he had serious doubts about collaboration, the Marshal allowed his name to be used in support of this unproductive and treasonous policy until the end of the war.[27]

At Sigmaringen, the diehard collaborationists joined forces to continue the Vichy regime in exile, working to return eventually to a "liberated" France in which communists, Gaullists, and other undesirable groups were eliminated. The Parisian fascist leaders, Déat, Doriot, and company, led the way, with a handful of followers—not more than 15,000—accompanying them. They hoped to rally French prisoners of war and French workers in Germany to their crusade against Jews, Bolsheviks, and Gaullists, but the hundreds of thousands of French men and women in German camps wanted nothing to do with Vichy. Although at one point, early in the war, many of them had been pro-Pétain, by late 1944 the POW and labor camps were overwhelmingly pro-American and Gaullist. Even some of the fascist leaders, such as Déat, knew that the Sigmaringen crowd had little chance to win over the French. He told Ribbentrop that three-fourths of the French believed that the Allies would win the war. Still, they struggled on against all odds and with considerable opposition within their own ranks.[28]

When the Rundstedt offensive—better known as the Battle of the Bulge—occurred in December 1944 the fascists began packing their bags for the return to Paris. Over the radio, de Brinon called on French soldiers under de Gaulle to resist and disobey: "Only if we are victorious will you see the end of your troubles," he claimed. Pétain, however, wanted to return to France to face the high court that had been set up on November 18 to try him, while Laval was intent on fleeing to Silesia. Others who were followers of Pétain and Laval wanted to return to France to unite with the right-wing resistance against the communists. They had no hope in the German cause despite the Rundstedt offensive.

Meanwhile, the fascists came increasingly under the control of their Nazi protectors. Possibly 2,500 members of the Milice joined the SS in November 1944. Another 2,000 went to work for the Reich, while others joined the Charlemagne division, which brought together miliciens, legionnaires, and other collaborationist soldiers to fight for Germany against the Soviets on the Eastern front. In all of these cases, the

Sigmaringen government-in-exile lost command over its few remaining military resources. Jacques Doriot wanted to reverse this by employing the 8,000 members of the Charlemagne division to fight for the Liberation of France. On January 8, 1945 he founded the Committee for the Liberation of France that called for a new "resistance" against bolshevism and the Anglo-American occupation of the nation, which he characterized as worse than the German one. Doriot, who conceived of himself as the de Gaulle of the new resistance, was killed on February 22, 1945. By then the French fascist cause had lost all hope.

Within France, in the waning months of the war, many feared that the Resistance would take power and carry out a revolution, purging all collaborationists and placing in control men who favored massive social, economic, and political change. Nothing of the sort happened. The Communist Party, which had emerged as a major element of the Resistance, cooperated completely with de Gaulle and the mainstream, opting for law and order rather than civil war. In fact, de Gaulle used the communists for his own political purposes, knowing that no communist threat existed in 1944–45. The leaders of the Communist Party had assured him on several occasions that they supported the Free French without reservation. In Moscow, for example, the head of the French Communist Party in exile, Maurice Thorez, told de Gaulle's ambassador that the party had no intention of seizing power. Beyond that, de Gaulle had ample evidence from events and individuals in France indicating that the communists would not stir up trouble. Yet, he scapegoated the communists as troublemakers in 1944 and 1945, claiming that they planned to take over Paris, had established a dictatorship in Marseille, and had created a soviet form of government in Toulouse. If we can believe the letters written by the noted American historian of France, Crane Brinton, who traveled 1,600 miles across southern France between October 8 and 15, 1944, visiting major cities and rural hamlets, no evidence of revolution existed anywhere in the south, and de Gaulle was recognized by everyone as the leader of the liberated nation: "a symbol of continuity of France rather than as a potential or actual *Fuhrer*."[29]

Although revolution did not occur and no group of importance plotted to undermine the restoration of democracy and take over power, elements of civil war erupted in this period from D-Day to the final Liberation of France. Much of what occurred can be classified as spontaneous revenge by the Resistance and its fellow travelers against collaborators. The Milice, in particular, was hated for its execution of thousands of Resistance fighters in 1944. In retaliation, the Resistance targeted miliciens and other collaborators for execution, either with or without trial, killing 6,000 of them by the end of the year.[30]

Other examples of revenge, such as the shaving of the heads of collaborationists, seemed to be more complicated and less rational. Approximately 20,000 women had their heads shaved for collaboration between 1943 and 1946, with the majority of these—about two-thirds—punished during the Liberation period after D-Day. By contrast, only about thirty-five to fifty men suffered from this form of retribution. Almost half of the women shaved were found guilty of having sexual relations with the enemy, but none of the men were. Nor were prostitutes included among the guilty. Most of them were considered to be earning a living and not collaborating in any sexual sense. The courts that tried these more or less ordinary French women had a very traditional view of gender and sexual relations, viewing all females as naturally immoral and conceiving of sleeping with the enemy as a form of crossbreeding (*métissage*) that undermined the nation. In short, the courts believed that cohabitation with German males was a form of treason that had to be punished by a public act of purification witnessed by the entire community. Thus, most shavings were performed by Resistance members in central places such as the town square, in patriotic acts of communion that united everyone, including the mayor, the police, and other local authorities, behind the Liberation of France and against the stain of collaboration with the Germans. Shavings were expiations of guilt at the expense of a female scapegoat, similar to the witch hunts of the late medieval period, but they were also festive occasions, carnivals, in which communities carried out what might be their only act of violence—if it can be called that—against the defeated enemy in an attempt to make things right after years of living in an alien world. Often shavings were accompanied by boisterous renditions of the Marseillaise, in celebration of this renewed national unity against the Germans.[31]

Of course this form of punishment and reconciliation excluded women from the ritual activities involved, unless they were willing to accept the terms established by "virile" France. Shavings represented an attempt to overcome the defeat of 1940 and to reconstruct French identity as one of male superiority and female inferiority. The female body was the source of evil, of immorality, that had to be chastised and marked. France had been liberated, in this version of history, through male combat, not through the acts of women. The picture of woman in the Resistance was the picture of the good mother, someone who accepted traditional female roles and did not challenge male authority, very similar to what Vichy had established in its propaganda. Female collaborators violated that image and had to be punished accordingly so that the gender order could be reestablished. Reverting to archaic medieval rituals for designating and punishing adulteresses, French males in every corner of the nation acted in almost identical, collective fashion, as though planned by a central committee! In as many as fifty cities women were not only shaved but also undressed and forced to walk around nude and in a few cases endure spankings.

Purging those who had collaborated was a major part of the Resistance mentality and the Liberation of France, as this massive outpouring of vengeance against horizontal collaborators demonstrates. Planning for the purges was methodical and among the first acts undertaken by the French government-in-exile. As early as mid-1943 the French government in Algeria established norms for trying high officials of the Vichy regime, including Marshal Pétain. The CFLN set up a Purge Commission for that purpose. Its first victim was the former Vichy Minister of the Interior Pierre Pucheu, who was tried and executed in March 1944, months before the Normandy invasion. De Gaulle refused to commute Pucheu's sentence, mainly because he wanted to set an example. But de Gaulle also wanted to place the authority to purge collaborators in the hands of the State. He refused to sanction vigilante justice, carried out indiscriminately by members of the Resistance, just as he refused to grant local Resistance units sovereign governing authority. Still, despite de Gaulle's strict guidelines on the matter and numerous attempts by his government to crack down on vigilante justice, at least 8,000 suspected collaborators were executed without a trial in the Liberation period.[32]

Like all purges in history, that of French collaborators was very uneven. Some groups were punished fairly severely, while others were let off with minor penalties. Those who left a published paper trail often suffered more than economic collaborators or civil servants working in anonymous bureaucracies. In general, those who were tried immediately after D-Day received harsher penalties than those who were tried later on. In turn, it seems that virulent anticommunist collaborators were given more severe sentences than others, probably because juries comprised of members of the Resistance thought of the communists as the mainstay of the internal Resistance. At first the purges targeted Vichy officials, especially the police and the judiciary. No French government, including Vichy, had ever carried out a major purge of the police. But French police collaboration with the Germans during World War II made a purge necessary, even though 150 policemen had died fighting to liberate Paris and almost all of the city's police force had gone out on strike against the Germans in August 1944. Surprisingly, however, the purge tribunals did not pursue the French police for the role they played in the arrest of approximately 90 percent of all Jews rounded up for deportation. For the reasons discussed in the chapter on exclusion, the fate of the Jews was not considered to be either unique or important in 1944–45. In addition, many policemen argued successfully that they arrested Jews as cover for their Resistance activities or that they were just following German orders. Only two members of the notorious Police aux questions juives were sentenced to prison for arresting and deporting Jews. In contrast, the anticommunist police were purged with a vengeance, largely because the communists had emerged from the war as a powerful political force and used their position to act forcefully against collaborators. Of 230 police in the anticommunist Brigades Spéciales, 195 were put on trial and 163 were found guilty. The French Jewish community, which had been seriously weakened by the Final Solution, was not capable of launching a similar legal offensive at the time. Still, despite these uneven results, the French police force underwent the greatest purge in its history: possibly one-fifth of the police was affected in some way by the purges, although only about 5 percent were imprisoned or dismissed from the force.[33]

When the purge trials ended, about 5,000 civil servants had been dismissed and 6,000 had been sanctioned for collaboration out of approximately 1 million state officials. The purge of the military may have affected another 5,000 individuals, although only a few hundred were dismissed without a pension or tried for collaboration. Among civil servants, the Vichy prefects suffered the most from the purges: well over half of them—sixty—were dismissed permanently and a handful was shot for collaborating with the Germans. In contrast, the tribunals generally ignored minor acts of collaboration committed by local officials, such as mayors and city councilors. Judges, too, were treated leniently. A special commission suspended 266 from the bench in 1944, but most were eventually restored to office. However, those at the top of the judicial hierarchy were punished more severely: of fifty presidents and procureurs généraux in France, only fifteen kept their posts after the war.[34]

The purge of economic collaborators was not as extensive or severe as that of state officials and the military. Businessmen were often able to make credible arguments that exonerated them. For example, Michelin, which was forced to collaborate with the Germans or close its doors, pointed to the role it played in protecting its workers from being conscripted by the Nazis. Countless other vital war businesses, with less convincing records than Michelin's, made similar claims and were cleared of guilt. A few, such as Renault, pleaded extenuating circumstances but failed to convince anyone. In Renault's case, the company was nationalized by the French State for the role that Louis Renault played in support of the German cause during the war. But Renault was the exception, along with Berliet and Acéries du Nord (a Marseille firm). The CGT, the pro-communist trade union, wanted to purge all industrialists who had collaborated with the Germans, but only a handful of individuals was found guilty.[35]

Other elite groups mostly escaped punishment. The Catholic Church hierarchy, for example, included a number of blatant collaborators. After the war the head of the National Council of the Resistance, the Christian Democratic politician Georges Bidault, wanted the resignation of all three French cardinals, as well as four archbishops and sixteen bishops, but he ran into serious opposition from Rome. After considerable negotiation, the Church reluctantly agreed to dismiss three bishops and to promote a number of pro-Resistance clerics, the most prominent of whom was Archbishop Saliège of Toulouse, who became a cardinal in October 1945. Similar leniency existed in the ranks of the professions. Very few doctors and lawyers were purged, despite considerable evidence of collaboration. Union leaders, however, were not as lucky. Several hundred of them were excluded from membership in a union, in some cases for life, because of their acts during the war.[36]

The most publicized and best-known purges occurred in those areas that were most subject to public scrutiny, such as politics and intellectual life. These were also areas in which a lengthy paper trail existed, documenting acts or statements of collaboration. In politics the trials of Pétain and Laval took center stage, while in the intellectual arena the case of Robert Brasillach became a mini-Dreyfus affair, dividing the nation's thinkers into two camps. Other politicians and intellectuals were purged during the Liberation, but did not attract the same attention. Of the two groups, however, politicians suffered more for their actions during the war. Although several writers such as Céline, Drieu la Rochelle, and Charles Maurras had their books banned and four members of the Académie française were expelled from that organization after the war—Marshal Pétain being one of them—no major purge of university professors occurred. In contrast, political parties removed large numbers of collaborators from political life. The Socialist Party, at its November 1944 congress, expelled the eighty-four socialist members of parliament who had voted full powers to Pétain in

1940. Although no other party went as far as this, a total of 321 members of the 1940 parliament, 56 percent of those who voted for full powers, were eliminated from political life after the war. In addition, after the war the Liberation courts tried 8.5 percent of all living members of the 1940 parliament, compared with only 1 percent of all French. As the result of these measures taken against the political elite of the defunct Third Republic, 80 percent of those elected to the Constituent Assembly in 1945 had never sat in the national legislature before.[37]

The most discussed purges were the ones that raised moral and ethical questions about the entire process. Among intellectuals, the trial of Robert Brasillach did this, while among politicians the trial of Pétain divided the nation for decades. Of the two, Brasillach's trial had the most immediate divisive impact. At the time, the nation was united against Pétain; only later did the French raise serious questions about his guilt, although most of these were brought up by the defense in his trial.

Brasillach was one of the most hated of French intellectuals by war's end, despite having been heralded as a literary genius in the 1930s, receiving a nomination for the Goncourt literary prize for his openly pro-fascist work, *Les Sept Couleurs.* During the war his repeated calls for the execution of Léon Blum, Georges Mandel, and Paul Reynaud, along with his vicious anti-Semitic articles in *Je suis partout,* earned him the reputation as one of the most collaborationist of Parisian intellectuals. In February 1944 he added considerable fuel to the fire when he stated publicly, "Frenchmen given to reflection, during these years, will have more or less slept with Germany—not without quarrels—and the memory of it will remain sweet for them." Since Brasillach had openly expressed his homosexual orientation, this statement took on a meaning that placed him in the company of collaborationist women under the occupation. Like them, he was a traitor to male France. Of course his case was not helped by the fact that he had advocated the arrest of leading literary figures and the execution of all of his supposed Resistance enemies. The prosecution had no difficulty making Brasillach into a sort of "horizontal collaborator." The subtext

of homosexual submission to the dominant German occupier perme-
ated the case made by the chief prosecutor, who used forceful sexual
metaphors of invasion, penetration, submission, and the like to make
his points. Brasillach accepted German dominance, the prosecution
maintained, and attacked anyone who opposed the Nazi yoke, denouncing politicians, intellectuals, and others for refusing to collaborate.
Since these denunciations were part of the public record, published in
newspapers, journals, and books, the defense resorted to the argument
that Brasillach was a literary genius. But this had no appeal to the jury,
which was made up of ordinary Frenchmen who had resisted the
Nazis. They were unmoved when François Mauriac, one of the nation's
greatest intellectuals with impeccable Resistance credentials, came to
Brasillach's defense by writing: "It will be a loss for French letters if
this brilliant mind is forever extinguished." More to the point was
Brasillach's claim that he had merely done what everyone else did during the war, which was to cope with the German occupation, to get by
the best he could in his chosen profession. He added to this the stan-
dard anticommunist argument that the Germans were better than the
Soviets and the idea that German atrocities were no worse than others.
He went on to claim that he was 100 percent French in his ideas:
his anti-Semitism was not inspired by the Germans, his fascism was
homegrown, and his hatred of Gaullists, communists, Jews, and so-
called Resistance leaders was inspired by patriotism. He concluded by
arguing for the ambiguity of moral responsibility, claiming that one
could be a resister or a collaborator in good faith.

But the crowning argument in Brasillach's defense was made by
his lawyer, Jacques Isorni, who attacked the French judiciary—even
the prosecution lawyers—for collaborating in the deaths of communists, Jews, and members of the Resistance by practicing law throughout World War II, despite the "illegality" of Vichy. He asked pointedly
whether Brasillach was guiltier than the lawyers and judges who had
sent innocent victims of the Nazis to their deaths. Then Isorni turned
to the chief prosecution lawyer and said: "You did your duty as a mag-
istrate. You thought that if it wasn't you who was in the business of
judging the communists, it would be the Germans who did it and that

there would be more deaths. You were a collaborator in order to save what could be saved in the judiciary realm" just as others collaborated elsewhere to save French lives and protect the nation.[38]

Isorni's plea for a form of moral relativism, based on a questionable historical understanding of events, did not convince many Frenchmen in the aftermath of the war. The court convicted Brasillach and sentenced him to death. Even though a number of intellectuals, such as Mauriac, Albert Camus, Jean Cocteau, and Paul Valéry petitioned de Gaulle to pardon him, the death penalty was carried out. Perhaps more significantly, Brasillach's trial and execution raised questions about the legitimacy of the purge trials. A large number of French intellectuals attacked the purges for being morally equivalent to the actions of the Vichy regime. Even though the courts sentenced only a handful of intellectuals to death, the impression emerged that the Resistance had turned on the intellectual class with a vengeance. The moral purity of the Resistance was tarnished by such impressions. When Jean Paulhan proclaimed in 1952 that the purge trials were like the terror, only carried out by communists, the myth of what these trials entailed had already been established. On both counts, Paulhan was completely wrong, but his words were not seriously questioned.[39]

The trial of Marshal Pétain provided another opportunity to muddy the moral waters, much more so than that of Pierre Laval, who was universally detested. Over three-fourths of the French wanted Laval executed in 1945, even though his trial had been seriously flawed. Charles de Gaulle considered a retrial but decided against it. Laval was executed on October 15, with almost no one regretting his demise. To the end he defended his policy of collaboration with the Nazis as a great success for the French nation. He saw no merit in the charge of treason that the prosecution made against him, nor in the particulars of that charge, which included his implementation of the forced labor program and the exclusionary laws against the Jews.[40]

Pétain, however, was seen in a different light. In contrast to Laval, Pétain was the hero of Verdun, revered by millions for his role in World War I. By 1945, however, that glorious reputation had been seriously tarnished; polls indicated that a solid majority wanted him punished for his collaboration. Pétain defended himself by claiming that the armistice had led eventually to Allied victory and that he had played the role of the leader of the French at home while de Gaulle had done the same for the French abroad. This idea of a double game of collaborating and resisting at the same time gained him some support, for many French had done something similar. But the evidence against Pétain proved too great for this tendentious argument to hold. The prosecution convincingly and successfully depicted the Marshal as a defeatist who willing accepted collaboration and condemned his enemies to death, including de Gaulle. Against these charges, the defense offered a picture of Vichy as total resistance to the Nazis. Pierre Laval took the stand in defense of Pétain, claiming that the two leaders had protected the nation from far worse scenarios. When he was asked directly about the Jews he responded that he had protected French Jews from the Nazis. The prosecution accepted none of these arguments. In its summation of the charges, it accused Pétain of depriving France of its sovereignty by signing the armistice agreement and undermining the Republic through the July 1940 "coup d'état." At no point, it argued, did Pétain or the Vichy government support the Resistance; absolutely no evidence existed for this. Furthermore, it maintained, after destroying the Republic, Pétain continued to act in a treasonable manner, giving up Alsace-Lorraine to the Germans, agreeing to collaborate with Hitler at the Montoire meeting of October 1940, ceding the fleet to the Germans, implementing anti-Semitic policies that mimicked those pursued by the Nazis, and generally submitting and subordinating France to the enemy until the end of the war. The narrow fourteen-to-thirteen margin by which the jury sentenced Pétain to death revealed that the internal divisions still prevailed, at least in regard to the old Marshal. Even General de Gaulle was reluctant to punish a fellow soldier and World War I hero too severely. When Pétain appealed for a pardon, de Gaulle exempted him from the death penalty, but not from a sentence of life imprisonment. Still, the trial had laid the foundations for the famous "shield" argument propagated by Colonel Rémy, one of de Gaulle's closest wartime companions, a few years later when he claimed that Pétain acted as the shield that protected de Gaulle and the Resistance from the Germans. It was an argument that flew in the face of the historical record, but one that many wanted to believe, especially those who collaborated openly or had flirted with collaboration before joining the Resistance at the last minute.[41]

One last point of importance regarding these trials needs to be mentioned. Henry Rousso has argued convincingly that the issue of anti-Semitism, which many believed was overlooked or swept under the carpet in the purges of 1944–45, played a role in a number of trials, including those of Pétain and Laval. As we have seen, the charges against both Pétain and Laval included the racial laws that they had implemented. Both men defended themselves with self-serving comments about how many Jewish friends they had or how much they worked to protect French Jews. In addition, both Brasillach and Charles Maurras were tried and convicted, in part, on the basis of their virulent anti-Semitic positions. In the notorious case of René Bousquet the courts accepted his argument that not he, but Darquier de Pellepoix had been responsible for the 1942 roundups of Jews, but in the 1980s the evidence against him became so great that he was arrested on the charge of crimes against humanity, only to be assassinated before the trial could be held. And finally, in the trial of the guards at the notorious Drancy camp, which served as the transit camp for Jews who were to be exterminated at Auschwitz, a total of fifty-six witnesses described in detail the inhuman conditions that existed there, leading to the imprisonment of several gendarmes and their superiors. The charge of anti-Semitism was clearly part of the purge trials, although at the time it was not considered to be as serious a crime as treason and collaboration.[42]

In gross numbers, in the purges 132,828 people were tried in civil courts, of whom 37,413 were acquitted. Of those found guilty, 7,037 were condemned to death (but only 791 were actually executed), 39,200 were sentenced to either prison or hard labor, and 49,178 were subjected to "national degradation," which entailed loss of political and civil rights for a period of time. In addition, French military tribunals also carried out purges, trying 20,127, of whom 769 were executed, a far higher percentage of executions per case than in the civil courts. The grand total for all purges, whether carried out through the courts or through vigilante justice, was 8,000 to 9,000 executed in cold blood, 1,500 to 1,600 executed through the judicial process, 44,000 condemned to prison, 50,000 condemned to national degradation, as many as 28,000 bureaucrats reprimanded in some fashion—half of whom lost their jobs—and 126,000 people imprisoned for some period of time, whether they were convicted of a crime or not. The French executed more, per capita, than any other nation in Europe, with the exception of Yugoslavia and Greece, but they jailed a fairly low number. Overall, the purges were not as severe as the supporters of Vichy or Jean Paulhan would have us believe, nor as lenient as die-hard members of the Resistance maintained. They neither disrupted economic and governmental activities nor created insuperable obstacles to national reconciliation. They were not perfect, by any means, but they did help settle, in a very minor but important way, the outstanding issues left over from the dark years of the 1930s and 1940s. After the purges, France was ready to move forward under a new republic, one that would be responsible for the *trente glorieuses*—the thirty years of unprecedented economic prosperity that followed the debacle of World War II.[43]

Epilogue

We can no longer view France as a nation of collaborators, any more than we can say it was a nation of resisters. On the contrary, the historical narrative on the "dark years" has revealed a nation that opposed collaboration virtually from the beginning and gradually accepted Resistance as the only solution to Nazi domination, much like other Western European nations under the Nazi yoke. Although opposition to anti-Semitic measures came somewhat late in the day, the French people's response to the Holocaust was largely exemplary: despite the existence of widespread anti-Semitic attitudes in France, a culture of universal humanitarianism, inspired by either the ideals of the Enlightenment and the French Revolution or Christian compassion for the persecuted, helped save thousands of Jews from the Nazi camps and contributed to Vichy's less cooperative response to German roundups of Jews after 1942. French gentiles did not necessarily like the Jews in the abstract, but they came to their aid as much as if not more than any other European nation.

The France that failed in World War II was the official, institutional France. The debacle of 1940 was not due to low morale or a lack of patriotism among the rank and file French soldiers. France could have defeated the Nazis in 1940 or earlier, but the military and political elite refused to take the initiative by attacking Germany when it was vulnerable in the fall of 1939 and then failed to interpret their own intelligence information properly in the spring of 1940. The French military elite was sclerotic, tied to antiquated policies of defense in an age of German blitzkrieg. Rather than accept their responsibility, most of these same military and political elites, led by Pétain and Laval, accepted an armistice that subjected France to Nazi Germany and then imposed upon the nation, with Catholic Church support, the so-called National Revolution, justified by a series of lies about French decadence and the need to atone for the sins of the nation that had led to the defeat of 1940. The National Revolution was quickly rejected by the bulk of the population; neither it nor Vichy's collaborationist policies had much legitimacy with the French people by the time Germany occupied the "Free Zone" in November 1942.

Out of this came, in time, the Resistance. Not the heroic movement depicted in postwar hagiography, it had many flaws. The Resistance was comprised of French men and women, some of whom, made compromises with Vichy, believed in some of the ideals of the National Revolution, expressed anti-Semitic attitudes, adhered to a narrow nationalist agenda, or joined the cause for unworthy reasons to engage in despicable, criminal activities and so on and so forth, ad infinitum. But not everyone in the Resistance was a Lucien Lacombe, the anti-hero of Louis Malle's film about Resistance and collaboration. The Maquis was not the mirror image of the fascist Milice. For all of its faults, the Resistance adhered to a set of ideals that made it different from Vichy or the National Revolution. Those ideals, embodied in the Resistance Charter, aimed to create in France a democratic, egalitarian political, economic, and social order in place of the authoritarian police state that the Nazis and Vichy had created. In the spirit of that charter, the Resistance fought the dual enemy of Vichy and Germany, succeeding remarkably in liberating Paris, Brittany, the South of France, and a good part of Alsace. The republican and revolutionary values that formed the core of the Resistance, both internal and external, corresponded with the goals and aspirations of the vast majority of the French people. Out of it and de Gaulle's extraordinary leadership abilities came one of Europe's smoothest transitions to postwar government. Vichy faded away and the French Resistance filled the gap, without serious disruption of governmental activities, civil war, or the need for an Allied government on French soil. Whatever its faults, the French Resistance enabled the French to play a major role in recovering their freedom.

France suffered severely from World War II. The total loss of lives directly related to the war was roughly 600,000, most of whom were civilians. Only 210,000, including 40,000 conscripted from Alsace and Lorraine into the German military, lost their lives in combat operations. As many as 5 million or 12.5 percent of the nation was displaced by the war, most to Germany and eastern Europe where they were prisoners of war for five long years or reluctant workers or political prisoners or racial undesirables slated for elimination in the Nazi extermination camps. The physical devastation was greater than in the First World War. One-quarter of all buildings were destroyed, compared with only 9 percent during World War I. Less than half of all railroad lines remained intact by 1945. The merchant fleet had shrunk to one-third of its prewar size. Coal production was 60 percent of its 1938 level. Industrial production totaled only 29 percent of its 1938 output. The cost of living had tripled, while salaries had lagged far behind. Public debt had almost quadrupled over six years and grew rapidly after the war, due to the high demand for state services. Food supplies had been devastated by the war and German requisitioning. In 1945 grain production was one-half of prewar output. Food rationing remained in place well into the postwar period, although caloric intake per capita increased dramatically from 900 calories per day in 1944 to 1515 by May 1945.[1]

Yet, World War II did not kill France; it killed a certain idea of France. Vichy succeeded, through its massive failure as a government and an ideology, in discrediting the reactionary and fascist visions of France. The dark years ended with some light shining, pointing toward a way out from the stalemate society that France had been during the interwar period. Clearing away the debris from the past was an important aspect of this process, Not that 1945 brought a republican utopia in the wake of such incompetence. Hardly. But the new Republic at least was given the opportunity to break through the cake of custom, in a moment that can be called a revolutionary epiphany. It would succeed where the veil of illusion had been torn by the actions of Vichy and the Nazis. It would fail where the Resistance itself had created illusions. European union, the welfare state, economic planning, and the like would be the positive creations of this new republic. Continued efforts to restore French *grandeur* combined with a blinkered attitude toward the rights of the colonized peoples who had helped liberate France had, on the other hand, the negative effect of making French decolonization reluctant, painful, and costly. Overall, though, a better France emerged, one in which Catholicism and communism were reconciled with the republican tradition, anti-Semitism was relegated to the extreme of the political spectrum, and women were granted the beginnings of full citizenship.

France recovered rapidly from the war and enjoyed its greatest period of economic expansion and social change in the thirty years that followed the war, the so-called *trente glorieuses*. While there was little reckoning with Vichy in the first postwar decades, it would come with a vengeance beginning in the early 1970s. Now, three decades later, the specter of Vichy no longer haunts the nation. The French have come to grips with their history, realizing that their sins and heroic acts were about par for the course during World War II, not much better or worse than those of their neighbors. As François Furet told the French in the late 1970s, the French Revolution is over; the same is true of Vichy. It is a history that has now passed to the point that the Resistance has regained some of the luster lost to the grand narrative of collaboration during the course of the 1970s and 1980s.

But is not the threat of a return to the dark years palpable in today's France? Does not France have fuel for fascism in high unemployment and a stagnant economy? Do not anti-immigrant sentiment, the outlawing of Muslim headscarves in French schools, French opposition to globalism led by the sheep farmer José Bové, and the French vote against the European Constitution in 2005 indicate that France is turning in on itself, seeking a return to "True France"? And does not the second-place finish of the fascistic Jean-Marie Le Pen in the 2002 presidential election show that France is on the verge of fascism? Nothing could be further from the truth, the anti-French screeds in the American media since the second Gulf War notwithstanding.

Although the French economy, like that of other advanced economies, has grown at a slower rate since the oil shock of the mid 1970s than during the *trente glorieuses,* it has shown considerable dynamism. Consumer purchasing power growth after the oil shock rivals that of the earlier period. Average family wealth grew more in the period 1970–2001 than in any other period in French history. The poverty rate has declined by over 50 percent since the early 1970s, and life expectancy has increased by an average of more than eleven years since 1961. Although France has low rates of participation in the workforce, its workers are highly productive. French productivity per hour worked rivals all other nations and now exceeds that of the United States. If France has high unemployment this is not a consequence of a poor economy, but rather of public policy which has increased the cost of low-skilled labor through a high minimum wage and payroll taxes to the extent that it is priced out of the market. Unemployment is a serious problem, but unlike the 1930s, it is a problem that occurs in a generally prosperous economy. Although the French may express pessimism in public opinion polls, their behavior is generally optimistic. The French birthrate, which was among the lowest in Europe before World War II, is now among the highest and is growing while that of other European countries is not.[2]

To see French opposition to globalism as a sign of French decadence or proto-fascist xenophobia is likewise misleading. Despite the leading role that the French have taken in criticizing globalization, France is among the most successfully globalized advanced economies. There are eight French companies among the world's hundred largest industrial and service companies and seven French banks among the world's fifty largest banks. Many major French companies, such as Michelin, Alcatel, and Dassault, depend on international sales for their profits. France has had a positive trade balance every year but one since 1993 and is now the world's fourth largest exporter. In 1997 total trade accounted for 49 percent of France's GDP, compared to 25 percent for the United States. In 2000 France was the second largest overseas investor. And foreign investment has come to France. Roughly 40 percent of the shares on the French stock market are owned by foreigners, far more than the United States where foreigners own only 7 percent. Perhaps most striking is that the French, historically unwilling to emigrate, have begun to live abroad in record numbers; the net outflow is now 50,000 per year. France today is by many measures much more globalized than the United States. In no area is this more evident than in culture. Films made in languages other than English account for only 1 to 2 percent of films shown on U.S. movie screens. Despite government subsidies and quotas which have made the French film industry a comparative success within Europe, French movies account for only 38 percent of movie tickets sold in France. French opposition to globalization is generally not a refusal of it, not a sign of a return to an insular True France. Rather, the mainstream French critique of globalization emphasizes the need for it to be managed so as to protect culture, the environment, the food supply, and the like. Even the critique of globalization of the rabble rousing Bové, who spent part of his youth in California, stems less from a defense of True France than from the post-1968 ecological movement[3]

Perhaps what makes us most confident that a return to the dark years is unlikely is the enormous transformation of French society since the 1960s. Pétain's National Revolution hoped to build on the traditional family, the peasantry, and the institutions of the army and the Church, yet all of these have been completely transformed since World War II. The agricultural workforce declined from 6 million in 1946 to 1 million in 1986 by which time the uneducated, technologically conservative peasant had been replaced by the educated, technically savvy farmer who in modernizing his operations doubled French agricultural production and made France the world's second largest exporter of food. As the former homes of peasants became secondary residences for city dwellers and farmers adopted lifestyles increasingly similar to others, the differences between urban and rural France diminished and the sociological foundation of True France vanished. In the same time period the army became reconciled with the Republic and lost much of its prestige, and the Catholic Church declined in importance. Today, monthly Mass attendance is below 10 percent of the population, and the Catholic Church has limited its ambition to serving the remaining believers. More importantly, the rise of individualism and the move toward gender equality in French society have

profoundly transformed authority relations and the most basic of social institutions, the family. Authority is now more negotiated and
flexible than in the past. Families have become more diverse as they
have adapted to the needs of individuals, particularly of women. Thus,
between 1975 and 1990 the number of marriages declined by nearly
45 percent while the number of divorces nearly doubled. Today, France
exceeds all European countries outside of Scandinavia in the percentage of births outside of marriage. Opinion polls indicate that French
tolerance of difference has grown. For example, only 32 percent of the
population considered homosexuality "unjustifiable" in 1999, whereas
62 percent considered it so in 1981. One 1999 study ranked the French
alongside the Dutch as the most permissive people in Europe. With
the Church and the army diminished and transformed, the traditional
patriarchal family in tatters, and a permissive and individualistic population, today's France offers barren ground for a revival of the National
Revolution.[4]

To be sure, contemporary France has its share of problems. The
political elite has become increasingly disconnected from and dis-
trusted by the population. High unemployment is creating an excluded
underclass. It, plus racism, has prevented non-European immigrants
and their descendants from being fully integrated into French society
as the unrest of the fall of 2005 revealed in spectacular fashion. Yet,
these are limited, manageable, and potentially solvable problems. Discontent with the political elite and concern about security may have
gotten Le Pen to the second round of the 2002 presidential election,
but he was still defeated in it by Jacques Chirac who received 82.2
percent of the vote. And the descendants of non-European immigrants
are, despite the serious obstacles created by unemployment and racism, clearly being assimilated to the norms of French culture. The
youth who took to the streets in the fall of 2005 did not do so flying the
banners of Arab nationalism or Islamic jihad. Rather, they protested to
demand full inclusion in French society with which they identified. If
French politicians could muster the political courage to adopt both
serious measures against discrimination and policies that reduce unemployment, the integration of this population would undoubtedly im-

prove. Whatever boost the extreme Right might receive from a backlash against anti-discrimination measures would likely be offset by an improvement of the employment picture. In short, given France's prosperity and long democratic traditions, there is no reason to believe that either the exclusion of France's minority youth population or the extreme Right's electoral success are insolvable problems leading France to a political meltdown.[5]

No one can say with total confidence that the dark years will never return, but the evidence is overwhelming that the conditions that helped create them have disappeared. As Pierre Birnbaum has argued, the old France of the imagined, unitary community has passed away, with the exception of such relatively marginal extremist groups as the National Front. Birnbaum, a prominent scholar of French Judaism who has been critical of the treatment of French Jews in the past, cites the German Jewish exile Heinrich Heine to make the point that France may be, for all of its horrendous faults, the best hope in Europe for Jews, immigrants, and refugees. "Long live France! Despite everything," Heine exclaimed, for France is like Penelope, engaged in the eternal process of spinning her fabric, "making it and tearing it apart." To Heine, and to Birnbaum, France has the potential to be the haven for peoples of all cultures and memories, a place that provides all citizens equal rights and respect, in a civic space where no one individual or group is favored. Today, that potential is greater than ever, but it still must be tempered with the skepticism of those who have been blinded with sight by history.[6]

Further Reading in English

General histories of the period include Julian Jackson's encyclopedic *France: The Dark Years, 1940–1944*, trans. Janet Lloyd (New York: Oxford University Press, 2001) and Philippe Burrin's excellent *France under the Germans: Collaboration and Compromise* (New York: New Press, 1996). Older, but still useful is Jean-Pierre Azéma, *From Munich to Liberation, 1938–1944*, trans. Janet Lloyd (Cambridge: Cambridge University Press; Paris: Editions de la Maison des sciences de l'homme, 1984). Robert O. Paxton, *Vichy France: Old Guard and New Order 1940–1944* (New York: Columbia University Press, 1972) remains fundamental, especially for state collaboration. Collecting recent scholarship are Sarah Fishman, Laura Lee Downs, and Ioannis Sinanoglou, eds., *France at War: Vichy and the Historians* (New York: Berg, 2000), a *Festschrift* for Robert O. Paxton, and Hanna Diamond and Simon Kitson, eds., *Vichy, Resistance, and Liberation: New Perspectives on Wartime France* (New York: Berg, 2005), a *Festschrift* for H. R. Kedward. *Collaboration and Resistance: Images of Life in Vichy France, 1940–1944* (New York: Harry N. Abrams, 2000) offers a visual perspective. On the French defeat of 1940 recent general histories include Julian Jackson, *The Fall of France: The Nazi Invasion of 1940* (New York: Oxford University Press, 2003) and Andrew Shennan's brief *The Fall of France* (New York: Longman, 2000). Ernest R. May, *Strange Victory: Hitler's Conquest of France* (New York: Hill and Wang, 2000) focuses on France's intelligence failure and looks at both the German and French sides. Recent scholarship is collected in Joel Blatt, ed., *The French Defeat of 1940: Reassessments* (Providence, R.I.: Berghahn Books, 1998). Still important is Marc Bloch, *Strange Defeat: A State-*

ment of Evidence Written in 1940, trans. Gerard Hopkins (New York: Norton, 1968).

The period may be approached from the top through biographies of key actors such as Jean Lacouture, *De Gaulle, the Rebel, 1890–1944,* trans. Patrick O'Brian (New York: Norton, 1990); Alan Clinton, *Jean Moulin, 1899–1943: The French Resistance and the Republic* (New York: Palgrave, 2002); Geoffrey Warner, *Pierre Laval and the Eclipse of France 1931–1945* (London: Eyre and Spottiswoode, 1968); and Nicholas Atkin, *Pétain* (New York: Longman, 1998), or from below through local studies: Robert Gildea, *Marianne in Chains: Daily Life in the Heart of France during the German Occupation* (New York: Metropolitan Books, 2003); Robert Zaretsky, *Nîmes at War: Religion, Politics and Public Opinion in the Gard, 1938–1944* (University Park, Pa.: Pennsylvania State University Press, 1995); Paul Jankowski, *Communism and Collaboration: Simon Sabinani and Politics in Marseille, 1919–1944* (New Haven: Yale University Press, 1989); and John F. Sweets, *Choices in Vichy France: The French under Nazi Occupation* (New York: Oxford University Press, 1994), the most important of the lot.

No specific aspect of the French wartime experience is served better by the English language literature than the Holocaust. Among the better works are Susan Zuccotti's general history, *The Holocaust, the French and the Jews* (New York: Basic Books, 1993); Vicki Caron, *Uneasy Asylum: France and the Jewish Refugee Crisis, 1933–1942* (Stanford: Stanford University Press, 1999); Michael Robert Marrus and Robert O. Paxton, *Vichy France and the Jews* (New York: Basic Books, 1981), which focuses on Vichy policy and its implementation; and Donna F. Ryan, *The Holocaust and the Jews of Marseille: The Enforcement of Anti-Semitic Policies in Vichy France* (Urbana: University of Illinois Press, 1996). Denis Peschanski, *La France des camps: l'internement, 1938–1946* (Paris: Gallimard, 2002) is fundamental on the question of exclusion and should be translated into English. Women, family, and gender issues have recently been examined notably by Miranda Pollard, *Reign of Virtue: Mobilizing Gender in Vichy France* (Chicago: University of Chicago Press, 1998); Francine Muel-Dreyfus, *Vichy and the Eternal Feminine: A Contribution to a Political Sociology of Gender*, trans. Kathleen A. Johnson (Durham, N.C.: Duke University Press, 2001); and Sarah Fishman, *We Will Wait: Wives of French Prisoners of War, 1940–1945* (New Haven: Yale University Press, 1991). Specific studies of other aspects of wartime France include Bertram Gordon, *Collaborationism in France during the Second World War* (Ithaca: Cornell University Press, 1980) on the Paris collaborationists; Robert O. Paxton, *Parades and Politics at Vichy: The French Officer Corps under Marshal Pétain* (Princeton: Princeton University Press, 1966) on the army; W. D. Halls, *Politics, Society and Christianity in Vichy France* (Providence, R.I.: Berg, 1995) on religion; W. D. Halls, *The Youth of Vichy France* (New York: Oxford University Press, 1981) on youth; Eric Thomas Jennings, *Vichy in the Tropics: Pétain's National Revolution in Madagascar, Guadeloupe, and Indochina, 1940–1944* (Stanford: Stanford University Press, 2001) on the colonies; Alan S. Milward, *The New Order and the French Economy* (Oxford: Clarendon Press, 1970) on German exploitation of the French economy; Richard Kuisel, *Capitalism and the State in Modern France: Renovation and Economic Management in the Twentieth Century* (New York: Cambridge University Press, 1981) on French economic planning; Gilles Perrault and Jean-Pierre Azéma, *Paris under the Occupation* (New York: Vendome Press, 1989) on the City of Light; Dominique Veillon, *Fashion under the Occupation*, trans. Miriam Kochan (New York: Berg, 2002) on the world of haute couture; and Herbert Lottman, *The Left Bank: Writers, Artists, and Politics from the Popular Front to the Cold War* (Boston: Houghton Mifflin, 1982) on intellectuals.

On the Resistance, the work of H. R. Kedward is fundamental: *Resistance in Vichy France: A Study of Ideas and Motivation in the Southern Zone 1940–1942* (New York: Oxford University Press, 1978) and *In Search of the Maquis: Rural Resistance in Southern France 1942–1944* (Oxford: Clarendon Press, 1994). See also the essays collected in Roderick Kedward and Roger Austin, eds., *Vichy France and the Resistance: Culture and Ideology* (Totowa, N.J.: Barnes and Noble, 1985); Henri Michel, *The Shadow War: European Resistance, 1939–1945*, trans. Richard Barry (New York: Harper and Row, 1972); and James D. Wilkinson, *The Intellectual Resistance in Europe* (Cambridge, Mass.: Harvard University Press, 1981). Andrew Shennan, *Rethinking France: Plans for Renewal* (New York: Oxford University Press, 1989) covers the Resistance's ideas for postwar change. On the Liberation and purges there are H. R. Kedward and Nancy Wood, eds., *The Liberation of France: Image and Event* (Washington, D.C.: Berg, 1995), Fabrice Vigili, *Shorn Women: Gender and Punishment in Liberation France,* trans. John Flower (New York: Berg, 2002); Peter Novick, *The Resistance versus Vichy: The Purge of Collaborators in Liberated France* (New York: Columbia University Press, 1968); Alice Kaplan, *The Collaborator: The Trial and Execution of Robert Brasillach* (Chicago: University of Chicago Press, 2000); and Megan Koreman, *An Expectation of Justice: France, 1944–1946* (Durham, N.C.: Duke University Press, 1999), which studies three towns. On postwar memory, see Henry Rousso's fundamental *The Vichy Syndrome: History and Memory in France since 1944,* trans. Arthur Goldhammer (Cambridge, Mass.: Harvard University Press, 1991); Rousso's follow-up publications; Sarah Farmer, *Martyred Village: Commemorating the 1944 Massacre at Oradour-sur-Glane* (Berkeley: University of California Press, 1999); and *Memory, the Holocaust and French Justice: The Bousquet and Touvier Affairs* (Hanover: University Press of New England, 1996) and *The Papon Affair: Memory and Justice on Trial* (New York: Routledge, 2000), both edited by Richard J. Golsan.

Finally, one should not forget the memoirs of the participants, only a few of which are listed here. Charles de Gaulle, *The Complete War Memoirs of Charles de Gaulle,* trans. Jonathan Griffin and Richard Howard (New York: Carroll and Graf Publishers, 1998) is fundamental. Henri Frenay, *The Night Will End,* trans. Dan Hofstadter (New York: McGraw-Hill, 1976) and Claire Chevrillon, *Code Name Christiane Clouet: A Woman in the French Resistance* (College Station: Texas A & M University Press, 1995) offer perspectives from the internal resistance, while Marie-Louise Osmont, *The Normandy Diary of Marie-Louise Osmont, 1940–1944,* trans. George L. Newman (New York: Random House/The Discovery Channel Press, 1994) gives the account of a civilian caught in the middle of the D-Day invasion. Father Benoît's rescue of Jews is related by one of his accomplices in Fernande

Leboucher, *Incredible Mission,* trans. J. F. Bernard (Garden City, N.Y.: Doubleday, 1969). Gilbert Michlin, *Of No Interest to the Nation: A Jewish Family in France, 1925–1945* (Detroit: Wayne State University Press, 2004), offers the perspective of a victim of the Holocaust and emphasizes France's complicity in it.

Notes

Chapter 1   Defeat of France

1. See Philippe Pétain, *Discours aux Français, 17 juin 1940–20 août 1944* (Paris: Albin Michel, 1989), 66; Herbert Lottman, *The Left Bank: Writers, Artists, and Politics from the Popular Front to the Cold War* (Boston: Houghton Mifflin, 1982), 130; Philippe Burrin, *France under the Germans: Collaboration and Compromise,* trans. Janet Lloyd (New York: New Press, 1996), 19; Andrew Shennan, *The Fall of France* (New York: Longman, 2000), 13.

2. Eugen Weber, *The Hollow Years: France in the 1930s* (New York: Norton, 1994), 11–15, 88–90; Leonard V. Smith, Stéphane Audoin-Rouzeau, and Annette Becker, *France and the Great War 1914–1918*, trans. of French sections by Helen McPhail (New York: Cambridge University Press, 2003), 69–71, 96.

3. Benjamin F. Martin, *France and the Après Guerre, 1918–1924: Illusions and Disillusionment* (Baton Rouge: Louisiana State University Press, 1999), 18–24; Philippe Bernard and Henri Dubief, *The Decline of the Third Republic, 1914–1938*, trans. Anthony Forster (Cambridge: Cambridge University Press, 1985), 93.

4. A point emphasized by Smith, Audoin-Rouzeau, and Becker, *France and the Great War*, 146–47.

5. Lloyd George quoted in John C. Cairns, "A Nation of Shopkeepers in Search of a Suitable France, 1919–40," *The American Historical Review* 79, 3 (June 1974): 713.

6. Weber, *The Hollow Years*, chap. 2; Julian Jackson, "1940 and the Crisis of Interwar Democracy in France," in *French History since Napoleon*, ed. Martin S. Alexander (London: Arnold, 1999), 224–33.

7. Robert Soucy, *French Fascism: The Second Wave, 1933–1939* (New Haven: Yale University Press, 1995), passim and 32 for the number of deaths.

8. Ibid., 108.

9. Julian Jackson, *The Popular Front in France: Defending Democracy, 1934–38* (New York: Cambridge University Press, 1988), chap. 1.

10. Ibid.; Jackson, "1940 and the Crisis of Interwar Democracy in France," 229–32.

11. William D. Irvine, "Fascism in France and the Strange Case of the Croix de Feu," *The Journal of Modern History* 63, 2 (June 1991): 280.

12. Daniel R. Brower, *The New Jacobins: The French Communist Party and the Popular Front* (Ithaca: Cornell University Press, 1968), 227–30.

13. On "True France," see Herman Lebovics, *True France: The Wars over Cultural Identity, 1900–1945* (Ithaca: Cornell University Press, 1992).

14. Georges Duby and Armand Wallon, eds., *Histoire de la France rurale* (Paris: Editions du Seuil, 1977), vol. 4, *La Fin de la France paysanne depuis 1914,* 54–59, 94–95, 360, 375.

15. Maurice Barrès, *The Faith of France,* trans. Elisabeth Marbury (Boston: Houghton Mifflin, 1918); Robert Paxton, *French Peasant Fascism: Henri Dorgères's Greenshirts and the Crisis of French Agriculture, 1929–1939* (New York: Oxford University Press, 1997).

16. On education, see Jean-Michel Barreau, *Vichy contre l'école de la République* (Paris: Flammarion, 2000).

17. The best work on this trend in the 1930s is Jean-Louis Loubet del Bayle, *Les Non-conformistes des années 30: Une tentative de renouvellement de la pensée politique française* (Paris: Seuil, 2001). See also Richard Kuisel, *Seducing the French: The Dilemma of Americanization* (Berkeley: University of California Press, 1993), chap. 1.

18. Gérard Noiriel, *Les Origines républicaines de Vichy* (Paris: Hachette, 1999), 201–4, 257–59.

19. Ibid., 142–48.

20. Vicki Caron, "The Politics of Frustration: French Jewry and the Refugee Crisis in the 1930s," *Journal of Modern History* 65, 2 (June 1993): 311–56; Denis Peschanski, *La France des camps: L'internement 1938–1946* (Paris: Gallimard, 2002), 40.

21. Vicki Caron, *Uneasy Asylum: France and the Jewish Refugee Crisis, 1933–1942* (Stanford: Stanford University Press, 1999), 189, 197–99; 99 and 289 for the quotes.

22. Alice Kaplan, *The Collaborator: The Trial and Execution of Robert Brasillach* (Chicago: University of Chicago Press, 2000), 24–26. See also Simon Epstein, *Les Dreyfusards sous l'Occupation* (Paris: Albin Michel, 2001), 16, 338.

23. Weber, *The Hollow Years*, 19.

24. Ibid., 24.

25. R. J. B. Bosworth, *Italy, the Least of the Great Powers: Italian Foreign Policy before the First World War* (New York: Cambridge University Press, 1979).

26. Pierre Guillen, "Franco-Italian Relations in Flux, 1918–1940," in *French Foreign and Defence Policy, 1918–1940*, ed. Robert Boyce (New York: LSE/Routledge, 1998), 149–63; Robert J. Young, *In Command of France: French Foreign Policy and Military Planning, 1933–1940* (Cambridge, Mass.: Harvard University Press, 1978), 83–92, 99–114, and 133–36; Charles Antoine Micaud, *The French Right and Nazi Germany 1933–1939: A Study of Public Opinion* (New York: Duke University Press, 1943), chap. 4.

27. Michael Jabara Carley, "Prelude to Defeat: Franco-Soviet Relations, 1919–1939," in *The French Defeat of 1940: Reassessments*, ed. Joel Blatt (Providence, R.I.: Berghahn Books, 1998), 171–203 and 188 for the Laval quote; Young, *In Command of France*, 147–49; Micaud, *The French Right and Nazi Germany*, 103–5; Nathan Greene, *Crisis and Decline: The French Socialist Party in the Popular Front Era* (Ithaca: Cornell University Press, 1969), 43 and 96; Jackson, *The Popular Front in France*, 195–98.

28. Stephen A. Schuker, "France and the Remilitarization of the Rhineland, 1936," *French Historical Studies* 14, 3 (Spring 1986): 299–338; Ernest R. May, *Strange Victory: Hitler's Conquest of France* (New York: Hill and Wang, 2000), 142–43; Young, *In Command of France*, 118–29; Robert A. Doughty, "The French Armed Forces, 1918–40," in *The Interwar Years*, eds. Allan R. Millet and Williamson Murray, vol. 2 of *Military Effectiveness* (Boston: Allen and Unwin, 1988), 43–44, 52.

29. Peter Calvocoressi, Guy Wint, and John Pritchard, *The Penguin History of the Second World War* (London: Penguin Books, 1999), 104–6; Ernest R. May, *Strange Victory: Hitler's Conquest of France* (New York: Hill and Wang, 2000), 92; Young, *In Command of France*, 203 and 297, n. 33.

30. William D. Irvine, "Domestic Politics and the Fall of France in 1940," in *The French Defeat of 1940*, 95; Young, *In Command of France*, 208–9; Richard Overy with Andrew Wheatcroft, *The Road to War*, 2nd ed. (New York: Penguin Books, 1999), 152; May, *Strange Victory*, 168.

31. May, *Strange Victory*, 167–68; Young, *In Command of France*, 209–12.

32. Micaud, *The French Right and Nazi Germany*, chap. 11; Irvine, "Domestic Politics and the Fall of France in 1940," 94–97; May, *Strange Victory*, 191;

Julian Jackson, *France: The Dark Years 1940–1945* (New York: Oxford University Press, 2001), 101; Robert J. Young, *France and the Origins of the Second World War* (New York: St. Martin's Press, 1996), 120 and 127; Jean-Pierre Azéma, "La France de Daladier," in *La France des années noires,* eds. Jean-Pierre Azéma and François Béderida, vol. 1, *De la défaite à Vichy* (Paris: Seuil, 2000), 29, 38; Young, *In Command of France,* chap. 9.

33. Marc Bloch, *Strange Defeat,* trans. Gerard Hopkins (New York: Norton, 1968), 134–70.

34. This point is most convincingly made by Doughty, "The French Armed Forces, 1918–40," 66.

35. Doughty, "The French Armed Forces, 1918–40," 43, 55; Julian Jackson, *The Fall of France: The Nazi Invasion of 1940* (New York: Oxford University Press, 2003), 13–15; Ernest May, *Strange Victory,* 208–9, 403–4.

36. Jackson, *The Fall of France,* 17–21; Young, *France and the Origins,* 106–8.

37. Young, *In Command of France,* 181 for the quote; Martin S. Alexander, "In Defence of the Maginot Line: Security Policy, Domestic Policy and the Economic Depression in France," in *French Foreign and Defence Policy,* 164–94; Doughty, "The French Armed Forces, 1918–1940," 55–57; Jackson, *The Fall of France,* 21–24.

38. Doughty, "The French Armed Forces, 1918–1940," 54–61.

39. Guy Rossi-Landi, *La Drôle de guerre: la vie politique en France 2 septembre 1939–10 mai 1940,* Travaux et recherches de science politique, no. 14 (Paris: Armand Colin, 1971), part 2, chap. 3; Georges Vidal, "Le Haut Commandement et la crainte de 'l'ennemi intérieur' en juin 1940: origines caractéristiques de la peur du complot communiste dans la hiérarchie," in *La Campagne de 1940,* ed. Christine Levisse-Touzé (Paris: Tallandier, 2001), 357–81.

40. Vicki Caron, "The Missed Opportunity: French Refugee Policy in Wartime, 1939–1940," in *The French Defeat of 1940,* 126–59. See also Peschanski, *La France des camps,* 72–77, which makes the point that France was no worse than other nations in handling refugees.

41. Both quotes can be found in Elisabeth du Réau, "Edouard Daladier: The Conduct of the War and the Beginning of Defeat," in *The French Defeat of 1940,* 107, 110.

42. Quoted in François Bédarida, "Huit mois d'attente et d'illusion: la 'drôle de guerre,'" in Azéma and Bédarida, eds., *La France des années noires,* 1:52.

43. The quote comes from Jean Lacouture, *De Gaulle the Rebel, 1890–1944,* trans. Patrick O'Brian (New York: Norton, 1993), 172; see also Charles de Gaulle, *The War Memoirs of Charles de Gaulle: The Call to Honour (1940–1942),* trans. Jonathan Griffin (New York: Viking Press, 1955), 28–29; Calvocoressi, Wint, and Pritchard, *The Penguin History of the Second World War,* 118; and especially Stefan Martens, "La défaite française: Une heureuse surprise Allemande?" in *La Campagne de 1940,* 403–11; and Ernest R. May, *Strange Victory,* 275–78.

44. See Georges-Henri Soutou, "Introduction," in *La Campagne de 1940,* 24; and Patrick Facon, "L'Armée de l'air dans la bataille de 1940: mythes, légendes et réalités," in *La Campagne de 1940,* 210–20.

45. See du Réau, "Edouard Daladier," 113; and May, *Strange Victory,* 333–36.

46. May, *Strange Victory,* 286–87, 331, 341–45.

47. Warner, *Pierre Laval,* 149–51, 154–57, and 160 for the quote of Pétain; Rossi-Landi, *La Drôle de guerre,* part 1, chap. 3.

48. Azéma, *De Munich à la Libération,* 51–53; Rossi-Landi, *La Drôle de guerre,* part 1, chap. 4; Andrew Shennan, *The Fall of France,* 143–44.

49. Soutou, "Introduction," in *La Campagne de 1940,* 29 and Nicole Jordan, "Strategy and Scapegoatism: Reflections on the French National Catastrophe of 1940," in *The French Defeat of 1940,* 22–23 and 26, n. 32.

50. De Gaulle, *The Call to Honour (1940–1942),* 35.

51. According to General Jean Delmas in *La Campagne de 1940,* 184.

52. May, *Strange Victory,* 261–62, 368, 371. May is the source of much of what follows.

53. Ibid., 268.

54. Ibid., 357–58, 371; Olivier Forcade, "Le Renseignement face à l'Allemagne au printemps 1940 et au début de la campagne de France," in *La Campagne de 1940,* 131 for the quote.

55. Jordan, "Strategy and Scapegoatism," 28–29.

56. May, *Strange Defeat,* 392–95, 399, 407–12, 419–20, 429–31; Jackson, *The Fall of France,* 42–54.

57. Most of this paragraph is based on *New York Times* dispatches from Paris during the second half of May 1940, but see also Jean-Paul Cointet, *Paris 40–44* (Paris: Perrin, 2001), 16.

58. Lacouture, *De Gaulle the Rebel,* 188; de Gaulle, *The Call to Honour (1940–1942),* 48–49; Calvocoressi, Wint, and Pritchard, *The Penguin History of the Second World War,* 136–37; Jackson, *The Fall of France,* 60–62 and 85–92.

59. See especially Colonel Jacques Vernet, "La Bataille de la Somme," in *La Campagne de 1940*, 198–208.

60. Cointet, *Paris 40–44*, 21–26; *New York Times*, June 13 and 16, 1940.

61. Jean-Pierre Azéma, "Le Choc armé et les débandades," in Azéma and Bédarida, eds., *La France des années noires*, 1: 123; de Gaulle, *The Call to Honour (1940–1942)*, 55.

62. Jacques Marseille, "L'Empire," in Azéma and Bédarida, eds., *La France des années noires*, 1: 285–86 provides a strong case against the feasibility of the North African option. For the June 16 debate see Lacouture, *De Gaulle the Rebel*, 202–5, 209.

63. Pétain, *Discours*, 57–58. For the demoralizing impact of Pétain's speech on the troops see the memoir of Jean Dutourd, *The Taxis of the Marne*, trans. Harold King (New York: Simon and Schuster, 1957). See also Philippe Lasterle, "Autopsie d'un exode maritime: L'évacuation des ports par la marine," in *La Campagne de 1940*, 265–85.

64. Sarah Fishman, *We Will Wait: Wives of French Prisoners of War, 1940–1945* (New Haven: Yale University Press, 1991), 26–27.

65. Quoted in Robert Frank, "Les Incidences nationales et internationales de la défaite française: le choc et le trauma et le syndrome de quarante," in *La Campagne de 1940*, 527.

Chapter 2   The National Revolution

1. See Andrew Shennan, *The Fall of France* (New York: Longman, 2000), 49; Jean-Pierre Azéma, *De Munich à la Libération 1938–1944* (Paris: Editions du Seuil, 1979), 73–74.

2. Robert O. Paxton, *Parades and Politics at Vichy* (Princeton: Princeton University Press, 1966), 48; Philippe Burrin, *France under the Germans: Collaboration and Compromise*, trans. Janet Lloyd (New York: New Press, 1996), 140–42.

3. *New York Times*, June 24, 1940; Philippe Pétain, *Discours aux français, 17 juin 1940–20 août 1944* (Paris: Albin Michel, 1989), 66.

4. W. D. Halls, *Politics, Society and Christianity in Vichy France* (Oxford: Berg, 1995), 38–39, 48–49.

5. Olivier Wieviorka, *Les Orphelins de la république: Destinées des députés et sénateurs français (1940–1945)* (Paris: Editions du Seuil, 2001), 63.

6. For the quote see Joel Colton, *Léon Blum: Humanist in Politics* (Cambridge: MIT Press, 1974), 350. See also Michèle Cointet, *Pétain et les français: 1940–1951* (Paris: Perrin, 2003), 38–40.

7. Colton, *Léon Blum*, 383. See also Wieviorka, *Les Orphelins*, 407–9.

8. Dominique Rémy, *Les Lois de Vichy* (Paris: Romillat, 1992), 31–46.

9. An excellent analysis is Michèle Cointet-Labrousse, *Vichy et le fascisme* (Paris: Complexe, 1987), 9–25. For Pétain's stand on Dreyfus see Simon Epstein, *Les Dreyfusards sous l'Occupation* (Paris: Albin Michel, 2001), 187. The Pétain quote is from Henry Rousso, *Vichy: l'événement, la mémoire, l'histoire* (Paris: Gallimard, 2001), 60. See also Jean-Pierre Azéma, "Le Régime de Vichy," in Jean-Pierre Azéma and François Bédarida, eds., *La France des années noires* (Paris: Editions du Seuil, 2000), vol. 1, *De la défaite à Vichy*, 170–71.

10. Michael Marrus and Robert O. Paxton, *Vichy France and the Jews* (Stanford: Stanford University Press, 1995), 3–5; Rémy, *Les Lois*, 51–52, 55–56, 68–70, 74.

11. See Rémy, *Les Lois*, 53, 57, 60–62, 82.

12. Ibid., 83–91; Marrus and Paxton, *Vichy France and the Jews*, 3–5, 9–10.

13. Eugen Weber, *Action Française: Royalism and Reaction in Twentieth-Century France* (Stanford: Stanford University Press, 1962), 442.

14. Michel Winock, *Le Siècle des intellectuels* (Paris: Seuil, 1999), 438–40. See also Eugen Weber, *My France: Politics, Culture, Myth* (Cambridge, Mass.: Harvard University Press, 1991), especially the chapter entitled "Nationalism, Socialism, and National Socialism."

15. Michèle Bordeaux, *La Victoire de la famille dans la France défaite, Vichy 1940–1944* (Paris: Flammarion, 2002), 126.

16. Pétain, *Discours*, 60.

17. Francine Muel-Dreyfus, *Vichy et l'éternel féminin, contribution à une sociologie politique de l'ordre des corps* (Paris: Seuil, 1996), 106.

18. Bordeaux, *La Victoire*, 46.

19. Muel-Dreyfus, *Vichy et l'éternel féminin*, 101.

20. Ibid., 98–101, 111–15, 132–33; Bordeaux, *La Victoire*, 84–88, 96–97, 139–42, 179–80, 189, 197, 221–33.

21. Bordeaux, *La Victoire*, 58–60, 66, 74–75.

22. Sarah Fishman, *We Will Wait: Wives of French Prisoners of War, 1940–1945* (New Haven: Yale University Press, 1991), 46–54, 58–59, 99–100.

23. Bordeaux, *La Victoire*, 157–58, 161–64; Miranda Pollard, "La Politique du travail féminin," 243–47, in Jean-Pierre Azéma and François Bédarrida, eds., *Le Régime de Vichy et les français* (Paris: Fayard, 1992).

24. Pétain, *Discours*, 133.

25. Muel-Dreyfus, *Vichy et l'éternel féminin*, 136–42, 148, 356.

26. Rémy Handourtzel, *Vichy et l'école, 1940–1945* (Paris: Noêsis, 1997), 60.

27. Jean-Michel Barreau, *Vichy contre l'école de la République* (Paris: Flammarion, 2000), 232–35, 265.

28. Muel-Dreyfus, *Vichy et l'éternel féminin*, 163, 173–74, 185.

29. Renée Bédarida, *Les Catholiques dans la guerre, 1939–1945* (Paris: Hachette, 1998), 41, 49, 52, 64–67.

30. Pétain, *Discours*, 80–81.

31. Christian Faure, *Le Projet culturel de Vichy* (Lyon: Presses Universitaires de Lyon, 1989), 40–43, 67–68, 73–75, 164 ff., 230–31.

32. Ibid., 139, 144–49, 180–83.

33. Jean-Pierre Rioux, ed., *La Vie culturelle sous Vichy* (Brussels: Éditions Complexe, 1990), 167–81.

34. Faure, *Projet culturel*, 103.

35. Studies of the Dordogne, Franche-Comté, Brittany, and Alpes-Maritimes can be found in Azéma and Bédarida, eds., *Le Régime de Vichy*. See also Bernard and Gérard Le Maroc, *L'Alsace dans la guerre 1939–1945* (Le Coteau: Horvath, 1988) and Philippe Joutard, Jacques Poujol, and Patrick Cabanel, eds., *Cévennes terre de refuge, 1940–1944* (Montpellier: Presses de Languedoc, 1994).

36. *New York Times,* Aug. 21, 1940.

37. Robert O. Paxton, *Vichy France: Old Guard and New Order 1940–1944* (New York: Columbia University Press, 1982), 205–9, 215. See also Azéma, *De Munich,* 98, n. 3.

38. Isabel Boussard, *Vichy et la corporation paysanne* (Paris: Presse de la fondation nationale des sciences politiques, 1980), 135 for the quote. This paragraph relies almost exclusively on this monograph.

39. Ibid., 204.

40. Pétain, *Discours,* Mar. 7, 1942.

41. Georges Duby and Armand Wallon, eds., *Histoire de la France rurale* (Paris: Editions du Seuil, 1977), vol. 4, *La Fin de la France paysanne depuis 1914,* 94–95, 98–99, 101, 103.

42. Burrin, *France under the Germans,* 140–41, 284.

43. Pétain, *Discours,* 111–13, 127–30, 249–51. See also Henry Rousso, "L'Impact du régime sur la société: ses dimensions et ses limites," in Azéma and Bédarida, eds., *Le Régime de Vichy,* 577–80, who points out that artisans received nothing from Vichy.

44. Pétain, *Discours,* 188–89.

45. Jean-Pierre le Crom, *Syndicats Nous Voilà! Vichy et le corporatisme* (Paris: Les Éditions de l'Atelier/Éditions ouvrières, 1995). Henry Ehrmann is

quoted by Rousso, *Vichy: l'événement,* 97. On questions of economic planning and modernization see Rousso, "L'impact du régime ," 581–82 and Richard Kuisel, *Capitalism and the State in Modern France: Renovation and Economic Management in the Twentieth Century* (Cambridge: Cambridge University Press, 1981); Burrin, *France under the Germans,* 215–17.

46. Pétain, *Discours,* 66, 68–71.

47. Ibid., 73–78, 81–82.

48. Ibid., 86–94.

49. Ibid., 150–55.

50. Ibid., 197–200.

51. Ibid., 212–15.

52. Richard H. Weisberg, *Vichy Law and the Holocaust in France* (New York: New York University Press, 1996), 8–9, 19, 132.

53. Cointet-Labrousse, *Vichy et le fascisme,* 177–96; Bordeaux, *La Victoire,* 58–60, 74–75.

54. Cointet-Labrousse, *Vichy et le fascisme,* 185–96.

55. Cointet, *Pétain et les français,* 248.

56. This paragraph is based on the excellent article by Sonia Mazey and Vincent Wright, "Les Préfets," 267–86 in Azéma and Bédarida, eds., *Le Régime de Vichy.*

57. Gérard Noiriel, *Les Origines républicaines de Vichy* (Paris: Hachette, 1999), 163–204. Noiriel emphasizes the continuity between the Republic and Vichy probably more than is warranted by the evidence.

58. Robert O. Paxton, *Parades and Politics at Vichy,* 146–47, 152–53; Pierre Giolitto, *Histoire de la Milice* (Paris: Perrin 2002), 32; Pétain, *Discours,* 218–21.

59. Jean-Paul Cointet, *La Légion française des combattants, 1940–1944: La tentation du fascisme* (Paris: Albin Michel, 1995), 40, 54–55, 60, 64, 101, 110.

60. Giolitto, *Histoire de la Milice,* 46–55. On the spiritual festivals see Cointet, *La Légion française,* 340–48.

61. Ibid., 127, 129; Pétain, *Discours,* 304–5.

62. Henry Rousso, *Pétain et la fin de la collaboration: Sigmaringen 1944–1945* (Bruxelles: Éditions Complexes, 1984).

Chapter 3 Collaboration

1. *New York Times,* July 11 and 25, 1940.

2. For the quote see Robert O. Paxton, *Vichy France: Old Guard and New Order 1940–1945* (New York: Columbia University Press, 1982), 71. See also

Jean-Pierre Azéma, *De Munich à la Libération 1938–1944* (Paris: Éditions du Seuil, 1979), 110–11, 114; Geoffrey Warner, *Pierre Laval and the Eclipse of France 1931–1945* (New York: Macmillan, 1968), 218, 222–24; Philippe Burrin, *France under the Germans: Collaboration and Compromise,* trans. Janet Lloyd (New York: New Press, 1996), 96–97.

3. Burrin, *France under the Germans,* 79–93. The quote, from Abetz, is on page 93.

4. Philippe Pétain, *Discours aux français, 17 juin 1940–20 août 1944* (Paris: Albin Michel, 1989), 73–78, 86–89. See also the report in *New York Times,* Oct. 11, 1940 and Warner, *Pierre Laval,* 231–32.

5. *New York Times,* Oct. 31, 1940 and Nov. 1, 1940; Paxton, *Vichy France,* 72, 80; Pétain, *Discours,* 95.

6. *New York Times,* Oct. 22, 1940 and Nov. 22, 23, and 25, 1940; Pierre Laborie, *L'Opinion française sous Vichy* (Paris: Seuil, 1990), 239–40.

7. Michèle Cointet, *Pétain et les Français, 1940–1945* (Paris: Perrin, 2002), 219–21, 224–26; Laborie, *L'Opinion française,* 244; *New York Times,* Nov. 19, 1940.

8. Pétain, *Discours,* 101; Paxton, *Vichy France,* 100–5; *New York Times,* Dec. 16, 1940.

9. Dominique Rémy, *Les Lois de Vichy* (Paris: Romillat, 1992), 105–11; Robert Frank, "Pétain, Laval, Darlan," in Jean-Pierre Azéma and François Bédarida, eds., *La France des années noires* (Paris: Editions du Seuil, 2000), vol. 1, *De la défaite à Vichy,* 324–36; Paxton, *Vichy France,* 110–12.

10. Denis Peschanski, *Vichy 1940–1944: Contrôle et exclusion* (Brussels: Éditions complexes, 1997), 42–50; Laurent Gervereau and Denis Peschanski, eds., *La Propagande sous Vichy* (Nanterre: BDIC, 1990), 16–27.

11. *New York Times,* Feb. 10 and 18, 1941; Paxton, *Vichy France,* 114–18; Burrin, *France under the Germans,* 116–17, 120–21.

12. Historians disagree about the precise reasons for the failure of the Protocols. Some believe that French officials had sought to scuttle them by making unacceptable demands. Others hold that the Germans simply lost interest in them. For a summary of the debate see Julian Jackson, *France: The Dark Years, 1940–1944* (New York: Oxford University Press, 2001), 180–81.

13. Paxton, *Vichy France,* 122–26, 387–90 and 123 for the Ribbentrop quote; Burrin, *France under the Germans,* 121–27; Azéma, *De Munich,* 118 for the Pétain quote; Jackson, *France: The Dark Years,* 183–84.

14. Paxton, *Vichy France,* 114 and 144 for the quote; Burrin, *France under the Germans,* 249–58.

15. Richard Kuisel, *Capitalism and the State in Modern France: Renovation and Economic Management in the Twentieth Century* (Cambridge: Cambridge University Press, 1981), 131–32, 141–42.

16. Burrin, *France under the Germans*, 252, 263–67; Henry Rousso, *Vichy: l'événement, la mémoire, l'histoire* (Paris: Gallimard, 2001), 80–93, 201 (for the quote), 219–24, 228; Azéma, *De Munich*, 218–19.

17. The quotes are from Warner, *Pierre Laval*, 285, 292, 300–1; Frank, "Pétain, Laval, Darlan," 337–39.

18. Warner, *Pierre Laval*, 299; Burrin, *France under the Germans*, 142. See also Robert Gildea, *Marianne in Chains: Daily Life in the Heart of France during the German Occupation* (New York: Henry Holt, 2003), 273, 277. Gildea is one of the only historians who does not believe that the STO helped create the Resistance: "This is a myth that dies hard," (285).

19. Quoted in Burrin, *France under the Germans*, 155.

20. Michael Marrus and Robert O. Paxton, *Vichy France and the Jews* (Stanford: Stanford University Press, 1995), 244.

21. Warner, *Pierre Laval*, 310–11 for the quote. See also, Burrin, *France under the Germans*, 150.

22. Warner, *Pierre Laval*, 322–24, 329–34, 337–38, 343, 347, 351.

23. Robert O. Paxton, *Parades and Politics at Vichy: The French Officer Corps under Marshal Pétain* (Princeton: Princeton University Press, 1966), 396–99; Pétain, *Discours*, 302.

24. Jean-Pierre Azéma, *Les Archives de guerre 1940–1944* (Paris: La Documentation Française, 1996). See the newsreels for the summer of 1943, especially those for June 25, July 2 and 9, and Sept. 3. See also the newsreel for Dec. 24.

25. Warner, *Pierre Laval*, 380–86; Henry Rousso, *Pétain et la fin de la collaboration: Sigmaringen 1944–1945* (Bruxelles: Éditions Complexes, 1984), 72–74.

26. Cointet, *Pétain et les français*, 71.

27. Michèle Cointet, *Vichy et le fascisme* (Paris: Complexe, 1987), 224–26, 235–39; Pierre Giolitto, *Histoire de la Milice* (Paris: Perrin, 2002), 203–5, 210–13, 235–41, 245, 249.

28. Giolitto, *Histoire de la Milice*, 382–83, 448–49; Pétain, *Discours*, 325–26.

29. The long, and futile, history of collaboration after August 1944 is detailed in Rousso, *Pétain et la fin de la collaboration*.

30. Burrin, *France under the Germans,* 427–36.

31. This definition of collaboration is, more or less, the one used by Gildea in *Marianne in Chains.*

32. Burrin, *France under the Germans,* 207; André Halimi, *La Délation sous l'occupation* (Paris: Alain Moreau, 1983), 24, 33–34, 87–88, 119.

33. On the west of France see Gildea, *Marianne in Chains.* For Brittany see Jacqueline Sainclivier, "La France de l'Ouest," 381–98 in Jean-Pierre Azéma and François Bédarida, eds., *La France des années noires* (Paris: Editions du Seuil, 2000), vol. 2, *De l'Occupation à la Libération* and Hervé le Boterf, *La Bretagne sous le gouvernement de Vichy: une tentative de régionalisation?* (Paris: Éditions France-Empire, 1982).

34. Burrin, *France under the Germans,* 362–65; Sarah Farmer, *Martyred Village: Commemorating the 1944 Massacre at Oradour-sur-Glane* (Berkeley: University of California Press, 1999), 136–57; Pascal Ory, *Les Collaborateurs, 1940–1945* (Paris: Seuil, 1980), 184–90.

35. Robert Zaretsky, *Nîmes at War: Religion, Politics and Public Opinion in the Gard, 1938–1944* (University Park: Pennsylvania State University Press, 1995), 145–50; Jean-Pierre Azéma and Réné Bédarida, eds., *Le Régime de Vichy et les français* (Paris: Fayard, 1992), 545–51; John F. Sweets, *Choices in Vichy France: The French under Nazi Occupation* (New York: Oxford University Press, 1994), 84.

36. Paul Jankowski, *Communism and Collaboration: Simon Sabiani and Politics in Marseille, 1919–1944* (New Haven: Yale University Press, 1989), chaps. 7 and 8; Azéma and Bédarida, eds., *Le Régime de Vichy,* 556–59.

37. Germaine Brée and George Bernauer, eds., *Defeat and Beyond: An Anthology of French Wartime Writing, 1940–1945* (New York: Random House, 1970), 147–58; Jean-Paul Cointet, *Paris 40–44* (Paris: Perrin, 2001), 33, 49–53, 67, 70, 95.

38. Cointet, *Paris 40–44,* 97, 157–61, 174–75.

39. Dominique Veillon, *La Mode sous l'Occupation* (Paris: Payot, 2001), 119–20, 142–44, 153, 162, 166–70.

40. Gisèle Sapiro, *La Guerre des écrivains 1940–1953* (Paris: Fayard, 1999), 82–83, 100, 159–60; Alice Kaplan, *The Collaborator: The Trial and Execution of Robert Brasillach* (Chicago: University of Chicago Press, 2000), 82–91.

41. Herbert Lottman, *The Left Bank: Writers, Artists, and Politics from the Popular Front to the Cold War* (Boston: Houghton Mifflin, 1982), 142–47; Michel Winock, *Le Siècle des intellectuels* (Paris: Seuil, 1999), 450–52; Julian

Jackson, *France: The Dark Years, 1940–1944* (New York: Oxford University Press, 2001), 205, 313, 316.

42. Lottman, *The Left Bank,* 160–62.

43. On the roles of Sartre and Beauvoir see Ingrid Galster, *Sartre, Vichy et les intellectuals* (Paris: L'Harmattan, 2001) especially 85–87.

44. Lottman, *The Left Bank,* 168; Brée and Bernauer, eds., *Defeat and Beyond,* 97–99, 101, 342–45; Eugen Weber, *Action Française: Royalism and Reaction in Twentieth-Century France* (Stanford: Stanford University Press, 1962), 468, 479 for the quotes from Maurras.

45. Simon Epstein, *Les Dreyfusards sous l'Occupation* (Paris: Albin Michel, 2001), 300–1, 332–38.

46. The discussion of Doriot and other political leaders is based on the following secondary sources: Burrin, *France under the Germans;* Ory, *Les Collaborateurs;* and Bertram Gordon, *Collaborationism in France during the Second World War* (Ithaca: Cornell University Press, 1980).

47. See especially Gordon, *Collaborationism in France,* 145–50.

48. In addition to the sources above, see Zeev Sternhell, *Neither Left nor Right: Fascist Ideology in France* (Princeton: Princeton University Press, 1996), 174–83.

49. See especially Burrin, *France under the Germans,* 384, 400–10.

50. Ibid., 466.

51. This section is based on Renée Bédarida, *Les Catholiques dans la guerre 1939–1945* (Paris: Hachette, 1998) and W. D. Halls, *Politics, Society and Christianity in Vichy France* (Berg: Oxford, 1995).

52. The quotes are from Halls, *Politics, Society and Christianity,* 20, and Bédarida, *Les Catholiques,* 52. See also the *Petit Robert* entry for *vénérer.*

53. The quotes are from Bédarida, *Les Catholiques,* 188, 191 and Halls, *Politics, Society and Christianity,* 325.

54. See Halls, *Politics, Society and Christianity,* 350 ff.

55. But, see Gildea, *Marianne in Chains,* who seems to believe that the many close ties between the French and the Germans were based on genuine friendship, at least in the west of France. The evidence is not totally convincing.

56. Philippe Burrin, "Le Collaborationisme," in Azéma and Bédarida, eds., *La France des années noires,* 1:402–3; Olivier Wieviorka, *Les Orphelins de la République: Destinées des députés et sénateurs français (1940–1945),* 177, 194–95, 293.

57. In addition to Paxton's *Vichy France,* see his succinct contribution , "La collaboration d'État," to Azéma and Bédarida, eds., *La France des années noires,* 1: 349–83.

58. See the important articles by Dick van Galen Last, "The Netherlands," and Hans Kirchhoff. "Denmark" in Bob Moore, ed., *Resistance in Western Europe* (Oxford: Berg, 2000).

Chapter 4 Exclusion

1. Pierre Péan, *Une Jeunesse française: François Mitterrand, 1934–1947* (Paris: Fayard, 1994), 210. In a later conversation with Elie Wiesel, Mitterrand claimed that he was far more affected by the defeat of France than by the fate of the Jews because that defeat was a very personal one for him: "It has left an indelible mark on my life, and every time I have had occasion to protect France's sense of itself as a nation I think about this time. Never again will the country find itself in that situation." See François Mitterrand and Elie Wiesel, *Memoir in Two Voices,* trans. Richard Seaver and Timothy Bent (New York: Arcade, 1996), 111.

2. Studs Terkel, *"The Good War": An Oral History of World War Two* (New York: Pantheon Books, 1984).

3. Vicky Caron, *Uneasy Asylum: France and the Jewish Refugee Crisis, 1933–1942* (Stanford: Stanford University Press, 1999).

4. Michèle Cointet, *Pétain et les français, 1940–1951* (Paris: Perrin, 2002), 138.

5. Philippe Pétain, *Discours aux Français, 17 juin 1940–29 août 1944* (Paris: Albin Michel, 1989), 81–82. The section in which he referred openly to the anti-Semitic laws was removed at the last minute.

6. Dominique Rémy, *Les Lois de Vichy* (Paris: Éditions Romillat, 1992), 48–56.

7. Ibid., 68–70, 74.

8. Ibid., 87–90; André Kaspi, *Les Juifs pendant l'Occupation* (Paris: Seuil, 1997), 66.

9. Rémy, *Les Lois,* 116–23; Michael Marrus and Robert O. Paxton, *Vichy France and the Jews* (Stanford: Stanford University Press, 1995), 98–99; Susan Zuccotti, *The Holocaust, the French, and the Jews* (New York: Basic Books, 1993), 61.

10. Richard H. Weisburg, *Vichy Law and the Holocaust in France* (New York: New York University Press, 1996), 69, 76–78, 164–69, 186–89. Weisburg

has little patience for the law under Vichy, but his account indicates clearly that the law did provide some recourse for Jews, despite the anti-Semitism of many who were involved with the legal process.

11. Rémy, *Les Lois,* 126–29, 148–60, 178–82.

12. According to Pierre Laborie in Richard J. Golsan, ed., *Memory, the Holocaust, and French Justice: The Bousquet and Touvier Affairs* (Hanover: University Press of New England, 1996), 94–96.

13. Weisberg, *Vichy Law,* 281. Donna F. Ryan, *The Holocaust and the Jews of Marseille: The Enforcement of anti-Semitic Policies in Vichy France* (Urbana: University of Illinois Press, 1996), 72–73, points out that only half of all Jewish businesses in Marseille were Aryanized. She believes that this was due to the low value of many of them.

14. Marrus and Paxton, *Vichy France and the Jews,* 191–93; Weisberg, *Vichy Law,* 300, 307, 317–19.

15. Marrus and Paxton, *Vichy France and the Jews,* 82–83, 108–10; Weisberg, *Vichy Law,* 8–10, 13 for the quote.

16. Marrus and Paxton, *Vichy France and the Jews,* 84–85, 116 for the quote, 135–36.

17. Claudia Koonz, *The Nazi Conscience* (Cambridge, Mass.: Belknap Press, 2003) on this phenomenon in Germany.

18. Kaspi, *Les Juifs pendant l'Occupation,* 108–9.

19. Jean-Paul Cointet, *Paris 40–44* (Paris: Perrin, 2001), 227–28; Zuccotti, *The Holocaust, the French, and the Jews,* 81–89.

20. Zuccotti, *The Holocaust, the French, and the Jews,* 90–94.

21. Denis Peschanski, *La France des camps: l'internement, 1938–1946* (Paris: Gallimard, 2002), 322, 346–47.

22. On Annie Kriegel, see Margaret Collins Weitz, *Sisters in the Resistance: How Women Fought to Free France, 1940–1945* (New York: Wiley, 1995), 33. On the Toulouse case, see Stacy Cretzmeyer, *Your Name is Renée: Ruth Kapp Hartz's Story as a Hidden Child in Nazi-Occupied France* (New York: Oxford University Press, 1999), 37–40. The doctor quote comes from Cointet, *Paris, 40–44,* 235–36. The figures, quoted in this and the previous paragraph, are now common knowledge, used by everyone involved with the issue.

23. Peschanski, *La France des camps,* 108–16, 250–55; Marrus and Paxton, *Vichy France and the Jews,* 256.

24. Both quotes are from Zuccotti, *The Holocaust, the French, and the Jews,* 155–56.

25. Kaspi, *Les Juifs*, 232–33. The French Red Cross made a similar comment about public opinion.

26. Marrus and Paxton, *Vichy France and the Jews*, 276. The quote is from Denis Peschanski, *Vichy 1940–1944: Contrôle et exclusion* (Brussels: Éditions complexes, 1997), 188.

27. Pierre Laborie, "1942 et le sort des juifs: Quel tournant dans l'opinion?" *Annales ESC* 48, 3 (May–June 1993): 661.

28. Quoted in *New York Times*, Nov.14, 1940.

29. W. D. Halls, *Politics, Society and Christianity in Vichy France* (Oxford: Berg, 1995), 27, 98, 104 for the quotes.

30. Ibid., 106–9; Bernard Comte, "Conscience Catholique et persécution antisémite: L'engagement de théologiens lyonnais en 1941–1942," *Annales ESC* 48, 3 (May–June 1993): 642–43, 652–53. For a more robust defense of the Church see Henri de Lubac, *Christian Resistance to Anti-Semitism: Memories from 1940–1944* (San Francisco: Ignatius Press, 1990).

31. Halls, *Politics, Society and Christianity*, 118–20.

32. Philippe Joutard, Jacques Poujol, and Patrick Cabanel, eds., *Cévennes terre de refuge, 1940–1944* (Montpellier: Presses de Languedoc, 1994), 138–39, 236–37.

33. There is some disagreement about the effect of Laval's protest to Oberg. Serge Klarsfeld seems to believe that it had an immediate impact on French policies toward the Jews, while Robert Paxton believes that not until mid-1943 did Laval try to stop the roundups. See their respective articles in *Annales ESC* 48, 3 (May–June 1993). See also Halls, *Politics, Society and Christianity*, 131–33.

34. Zuccotti, *The Holocaust, the French, and the Jews*, 169–70, 175–78, 190–93.

35. François and Renée Bédarida, eds., *La Résistance spirituelle 1941–1944: Les Cahiers du Témoignage chrétien* (Paris: Albin Michel, 2001), especially the articles of Nov. 1941 and Mar.–Apr. 1942, in addition to the June 1942 brochure.

36. Ibid. for the quotes, 212, 228.

37. Ryan, *The Holocaust and the Jews of Marseille*, chap. 5; Fernande Leboucher, *Incredible Mission* (New York: Doubleday, 1969), which details the network established by Father Benoît. Ryan cites the 4,000 figure.

38. Cretzmeyer, *Your Name Is Renée*, 130–34, 141–44.

39. Joutard, Poujol, and Cabanel, eds., *Cévennes terre de refuge* is the essential source for the Protestant effort to protect the Jews in this area.

40. Philip Hallie, *Lest Innocent Blood be Shed* (New York: Harper, 1978), 190 for Pastor Trocmé's estimate that 2,500 Jews passed through the town. Zuccotti, *The Holocaust, the French and the Jews,* 228–29 gives the figure of 5,000.

41. Peschanski, *La France des camps,* 156, 250–51, 255. The number of children in the camps dropped from 2,700 in Oct. 1941 to 661 in May 1942, due mainly to the actions of the Nîmes Committee.

42. Zucotti, *The Holocaust, the French and the Jews,* 213–14, 221–22; Renée Poznanski, "Résistance juive, résistants juifs: retour à l'Histoire," in *Mémoire et histoire: la Résistance,* eds. Jean-Marie Guillon and Pierre Laborie (Toulouse: Privat, 1995), 240–42; Caron, *Uneasy Asylum,* 350.

43. Gilbert Michlin, *Aucun intérêt au point de vue national: la grande illusion d'une famille juive en France* (Paris: Albin Michel, 2001); Cretzmeyer, *Your Name is Renée,* 191.

44. André Halimi, *La Délation sous l'occupation* (Paris: Alain Moreau, 1983), 42–43, 87–90.

45. Zuccotti, *The Holocaust, the French and the Jews,* 207–8; and Kaspi, *Les Juifs pendant l'occupation,* 339, for the statistics.

46. Kaspi, *Les Juifs pendant l'occupation,* 300–18; Poznanski, "Résistance juive," 235, 238–39.

47. The preceeding three paragraphs are based on Annette Wieviorka, *Déportation et genocide: Entre la mémoire et l'oubli* (Paris: Plon, 1992).

48. Peschanski, *Vichy 1940–1944,* 76, 108, 122, 133–34. See also Edward Mortimer, *The Rise of the French Communist Party 1920–1947* (London: Faber and Faber, 1984), 307.

49. Jean Le Bitoux, *Les Oubliés de la mémoire* (Paris: Hachettes Littératures, 2002), an intemperate work that contains the evidence regarding homosexuality in France during the war. The author maintains on page 221 that the French were complicit in the detention of Alsatian homosexuals because the police in Alsace had drawn up lists of suspected homosexuals, which the Germans used.

50. Denis Peschanski, *Les Tsiganes en France, 1939–1946* (Paris: CNRS, 1994), 21–34.

51. Ibid., 37–40, 45, 105–6.

52. Peschanski, *Vichy 1940–1945,* 487, points out that under Vichy the camps were never used "to reeducate the prisoner or to destroy his personality, not to mention exterminating him." This is true, but it does not make up

for the terrible fate that so many encountered as the result of Vichy's total collaboration with the Nazis.

53. For the quote see Bob Moore, *Victims and Survivors: The Nazi Persecution of the Jews in the Netherlands 1940–1945* (London: Arnold, 1997), 257–58. See also José Gotovitch and Pieter Lagrou, "La Résistance française dans le paysage européen," in *La Résistance et les français: nouvelles approches,* Les Cahiers de l'Institut d'Histoire du Temps Présent, no. 37 (1997): 156–58.

Chapter 5 Resistance

1. Quoted in Jean Lacouture, *De Gaulle the Rebel, 1890–1944,* trans. Patrick O'Brian (New York: Norton, 1993), 575; see also Gilles Ragache, *Les Enfants de la guerre: Vivre, survivre, lire et jouer en France, 1939–1949* (Paris: Perrin, 1997), 197–99, 226.

2. On this see Charles de Gaulle, *The War Memoirs of Charles de Gaulle: The Call to Honour (1940–1942),* trans. Jonathan Griffin (New York: Viking Press, 1955), 73.

3. Jean-Louis Crémieux-Brilhac, *La France Libre: De l'appel du 18 juin à la libération* (Paris: Gallimard, 2001), 68; see also Robert Paxton, *Parades and Politics at Vichy: The French Officer Corps under Marshal Pétain* (Princeton: Princeton University Press, 1966), 34, on the inability of French military officers to go against the chain of command, as de Gaulle did in 1940.

4. Crémieux-Brilhac, *La France Libre,* 109–10, 114–16, 122–23.

5. Pierre Laborie, *L'Opinion française sous Vichy* (Paris: Seuil, 1990), 239, who is cautious on the matter of French support for the British after Mers-el-Kébir, although he states that a majority supported a British victory. In contrast, see the report of the chief Paris reporter for the *New York Times,* Sept. 25, 1940, who claimed that everywhere he went in France he discovered support for the British and de Gaulle.

6. Lacouture, *De Gaulle the Rebel,* 280.

7. The account is based on Lacouture, *De Gaulle the Rebel,* 300–7 and on Crémieux, *La France Libre,* 210–21. See also Robert Frank, "Identités résistantes et logiques alliées," in *La Résistance et les français: nouvelles approches,* Les Cahiers de l'Institut d'Histoire du Temps Présent, no. 37 (1997), 80.

8. Lacouture, *De Gaulle the Rebel,* 324 for the quote. See also de Gaulle, *The Call to Honour,* 225–29.

9. Lacouture, *De Gaulle the Rebel,* 316–17, 328; Crémieux-Brilhac, *La France Libre,* 334, 377–81.

10. The quotes are from Crémieux-Brilhac, *La France Libre,* 275–76.

11. This paragraph is based mainly on the excellent account in Cremieux-Brilhac, *La France Libre.* But see also Frank, "Identités résistantes," 82–83, which claims that Anthony Eden was telling Churchill that de Gaulle was very popular among members of the French internal Resistance. Churchill did not believe this information, despite the fact that it came from British intelligence.

12. Pierre Péan, *Une Jeunesse française: François Mitterrand, 1934–1947* (Paris: Fayard, 1994), 175.

13. The above account is based on Péan and on François Mitterrand, *Mémoires interrompus* (Paris: Odile Jacob, 1996) in which Mitterrand attempted to correct Péan. The correct account may never be established but the general outlines are clear enough.

14. The Salle Wagram statement can be found in Péan, *Une Jeunesse française,* 281. For Mitterrand's denial that he was a Giraudist and his 1996 statement on the Resistance, see his account in his *Mémoires interrompus,* 133–34, 142–44.

15. This paragraph is based on John Hellman, *The Knight-Monks of Vichy France: Uriage, 1940–1945* (Montreal: McGill-Queen's University Press, 1997), who is somewhat hostile to the members of the school. More apologetic is Bernard Comte, *Une Utopie combattante: l'École des cadres d'Uriage, 1940–1942* (Paris: Fayard, 1999) and Michel Winock, *Esprit: Des intellectuels dans la cité* (Paris: Seuil, 1996). The quote is from Hellman, *The Knight Monks,* 56–57.

16. The Sartre quote is from Jean-Louis Loubet del Bayle, *Les Nonconformistes des années 30: une tentative de renouvellement de la pensée politique française* (Paris: Seuil, 2001), 457. Most of this paragraph is based on Hellman, *The Knight Monks,* but see also Roderick Kedward and Roger Austin, *Vichy France and the Resistance: Culture and Ideology* (London: Crown Helm, 1985), 173–75, 183–85 for a balanced treatment of Mounier and his gradual disillusionment with Vichy.

17. Jean-Marc Berlière and Laurent Chabrun, *Les Policiers français sous l'Occupation* (Paris: Perrin, 2001), 165–66.

18. This paragraph is based primarily on Henri Frenay, *The Night Will End,* trans. Dan Hofstadter (New York: McGraw Hill, 1976).

19. In addition to Frenay, *The Night Will End,* see also H. R. Kedward, *Resistance in Vichy France: A Study of Ideas and Motivation in the Southern Zone 1940–1942* (Oxford: Oxford University Press, 1978), 29–34, 46, 145–46.

20. François-Georges Dreyfus, *Histoire de la Résistance 1940–1945* (Paris: Fallois, 1996), 100–5.

21. Kedward, *Resistance in Vichy France,* 56–63, 92–94, 155–58, 171–75, 220–22, 241–42. On Marseille see Simon Kitson, "L'évolution de la Résistance dans la police marseillaise," in *La Résistance et les Européens du sud,* eds., Jean-Marie Guillon and Robert Mencherini (Paris: L'Harmattan, 1999), 259–60. See also Ollivier Vallade, "L'Enrancinement de la Résistance iséroise," in the same book.

22. See the articles in Jacqueline Sainclivier and Christian Bougeard, eds., *La Résistance et les français: Enjeux stratégiques et environnement social* (Rennes: Presses Universitaires de Rennes, 1995) on the sociology of the Resistance, villages, and peasants.

23. Among many accounts of the unification process see Claude Bourdet, *L'Aventure incertaine* (Paris: Stock, 1975), 164 ff.

24. Jean-Pierre Azéma, *De Munich à la Libération 1938–1945* (Paris: Seuil, 1979), 126–27. See also Diana Cooper-Richet, "Les Ouvriers, l'Église et la Résistance," in Sainclivier and Bougeard, eds., *La Résistance et les français,*138.

25. Jean-Paul Cointet, *Paris 40–44* (Paris: Perrin, 2001), 102–7.

26. See Jacqueline Sainclivier, "Les Débuts de la Résistance en zone occupée: essai de typologie," in *Mémoire et histoire: la Résistance,* eds., Jean-Marie Guillon and Pierre Laborie (Toulouse: Privat, 1995), 161–70.

27. François Marcot, ed., *La Résistance et les Français: Lutte armée et Maquis* (Paris: Annales littéraires de l'Université de Franche-Comté, 1996), 113–15.

28. Olivier Wieviorka, *Une Certaine Idée de la Résistance: Défense de la France* (Paris: Seuil, 1995).

29. Dreyfus, *Histoire de la Résistance,* 59–61, 106–8. For the OCM's anti-Semitism and pro-Vichy sentiments see Jacqueline Sainclivier and Dominique Veillon, "Sens et formes de la Résistance française," in *La Résistance et les français: nouvelles approches,* 97.

30. Pierre Brossolette, *Résistance (1927–1943)* (Paris: Odile Jacob, 1998). See also Crémieux-Brilhac, *La France Libre,* 684–87.

31. See Dominique Veillon, "Les Réseaux de Résistance," in Jean-Pierre Azéma and François Bédarida, eds., *La France des années noires* (Paris: Éditions du Seuil, 2000), vol. 2, *De la défaite à Vichy,* 407–37; Henri Michel, *The Shadow War: European Resistance, 1939–1945,* trans. Richard Barry (New York: Harper and Row, 1972), 216–17.

32. The evidence for this paragraph is extensive and old. See Alfred J. Rieber, *Stalin and the French Communist Party 1941–1947* (New York: Columbia University Press, 1962), 27–28, 32, 53, 58–60, 100–2. See also more recent studies such as Serge Wolikow, "Les Communistes face à la lutte armée," in Marcot, ed., *La Résistance et les Français: Lutte armée et Maquis.*

33. Crémieux-Brilhac, *La France Libre,* 1050, 1060; W. D. Halls, *Society and Christianity in Vichy France* (Oxford: Berg, 1995), 314–17.

34. H. R. Kedward, *In Search of the Maquis: Rural Resistance in Southern France 1942–1944* (Oxford: Clarendon Press, 1994), 56, 63, and 113 for the salient points in this paragraph. See also Georges Fournier, "Contestations collectives, résistances et Résistance: quelles continuités?" in Guillon and Laborie, ed., *Mémoire et histoire* for the reference to "primitive rebels."

35. This and the previous paragraph are based substantially on Lacouture, *De Gaulle the Rebel,* and Crémieux-Brilhac, *La France Libre.* The Leclerc quote is from the latter, 651.

36. The quote is from Lacouture, *De Gaulle the Rebel,* 493. See also, Charles de Gaulle, *The Memoirs of Charles de Gaulle: Unity, 1942–1944,* trans. Richard Howard (New York: Simon and Schuster, 1959), 79–150.

37. De Gaulle, *Memoirs: Unity, 1942–1944,* 85, 91.

38. See Paxton, *Parades and Politics* for the military and Resistance. On Michelin see John S. Sweets, *Choices in Vichy France: The French under Nazi Occupation* (New York: Oxford, 1994), 27.

39. See James D. Wilkinson, *The Intellectual Resistance in Europe* (Cambridge, Mass.: Harvard University Press, 1981), 25–106 and Michel Winock, *Le Siècle des intellectuels* (Paris: Seuil, 1999), 475 ff.

40. Quoted in Germaine Brée and George Bernauer, eds., *Defeat and Beyond: An Anthology of French Wartime Writing, 1940–1945* (New York: Random House, 1970), 331–32.

41. See, among others, the criticism of Herbert Lottman, *The Left Bank: Writers, Artists, and Politics from the Popular Front to the Cold War* (Boston: Houghton Mifflin, 1982), 168.

42. Dominique Veillon, *La Mode sous l'Occupation* (Paris: Payot, 2001), 112–15, 218.

43. See Margaret Collins Weitz, *Sisters in the Resistance: How Women Fought to Free France 1940–1945* (New York: John Wiley and Sons, 1995); Margaret L. Rossiter, *Women in the Resistance* (New York: Praeger, 1986); Claire Chevillon, *Code Name Christiane Clouet, A Woman in the French Resistance* (College Station: Texas A & M Press, 1995).

44. Philippe Buton, "La France atomisée," in Azéma and Bédarida, eds., *La France des années noires,* 2: 420–23, 441. See François Marcot, "Les Paysans et la Résistance: problèmes d'une approche sociologique," in Sainclivier and Bougeard, eds., *La Résistance et les français,* 255.

Chapter 6   Liberation

1. See the discussion of economic planning in Richard Kuisel, *Capitalism and the State in Modern France: Renovation and Economic Management in the Twentieth Century* (Cambridge: Cambridge University Press, 1981), 159–86. See also Henri Michel's pioneering work on the ideology of the Resistance, *Les Courants de pensée de la Résistance* (Paris: Presses universitaires de France, 1962).

2. Jean Lacouture, *De Gaulle the Rebel, 1890–1944,* trans. Patrick O'Brian (New York: Norton, 1993), 546 for the quote.

3. The figures on the Liberation army are for the period before D-Day. After D-Day the numbers increased greatly. See Jean-Louis Crémieux-Brilhac, *La France Libre* (Paris: Gallimard, 2001), 953–54.

4. Jean-Pierre Rioux, *The Fourth Republic 1944–1958,* trans. Godfrey Rodgers (Cambridge: Cambridge University Press, 1989), 10–11.

5. See Maurice Kriegel-Valrimont, *Mémoires rebelles* (Paris: Odile Jacob, 1999), 62–63, who maintained as late as 1999 that the Resistance had liberated France on its own, without much help from the Allied powers.

6. Michèle Cointet, *Pétain et les français, 1940–1945* (Paris: Perrin, 2002), 273.

7. See Charles de Gaulle, *The War Memoirs of Charles de Gaulle: Unity, 1942–1944,* trans. Richard Howard (New York: Simon and Schuster, 1959), 159–66, 189–90, 304–5.

8. Crémieux-Brilhac, *La France Libre,* 1087–89.

9. Ibid., 1100. See also Donna F. Ryan, *The Holocaust and the Jews of Marseille: The Enforcement of Anti-Semitic Politics in Vichy France* (Urbana: University of Illinois Press, 1996), 179 ff., 203–4 and John F. Sweets, *Choices in Vichy France: The French under Nazi Occupation* (New York: Oxford University Press, 1994), 214–17.

10. Most of this account is based on H. R. Kedward, *In Search of the Maquis: Rural Resistance in Southern France 1942–1944* (Oxford: Clarendon Press, 1994), 144–57. For the quote see Robert Zaretsky, *Nîmes at War: Reli-*

gion, Politics, and Public Opinion in the Gard, 1938–1944 (University Park: Pennsylvania State University Press, 1995), 240. See also the evaluation of the French historians, Christian Bougeard and Jean-Marie Guillon in *La Résistance et les français: nouvelles approches,* Les Cahiers de l'Institut d'Histoire du Temps Présent, no. 37 (1997), who see the Resistance in terms of historical memory, whether it be the Camisards, the Cathars, the Breton peasants, the Varois republicans in 1851, or communist workers. To them the Resistance relegitimized "the republican tradition in its popular and revolutionary aspects (if only on a symbolic level)." See page 44.

11. See Crémieux-Brilhac, *La France Libre,* 1119–42.

12. Ibid., 1179–91; Kedward, *In Search of the Maquis,* 134–38.

13. Cointet, *Pétain et les français,* 257–62; Jean-Paul Cointet, *Paris 40–44* (Paris: Perrin, 2001), 243–46, 267. In May 1944 the Allies carried out 1,284 bombing raids and, during a two-day period, killed 6,000 French. See Philippe Buton, "La France atomisée," in Jean-Pierre Azéma and François Bédarida, eds., *La France des années noires* (Paris: Editions du Seuil, 2000), vol. 2, *De la défaite à Vichy,* 424–25.

14. This is based on the account in Lacouture, *De Gaulle the Rebel,* 521–32.

15. See Hans Umbreit, "Les Allemands face à la lutte armée," in François Marcot, ed., *La Résistance et les français: Lutte armée et Maquis* (Paris: Annales littéraires de l'Université de Franche-Comté, 1996), 205–7.

16. See Crémieux-Brilhac, *La France Libre,* 1150–54, 1250–51. See also de Gaulle, *War Memoirs: Unity, 1942–1944,* 316, and Henri Michel, *The Shadow War: European Resistance, 1939–1945,* trans. Richard Barry (New York: Harper and Row, 1972), 123.

17. See Kedward, *In Search of the Maquis,* 162–201 for the details of a number of these uprisings against the Germans. See also Sarah Farmer, *Martyred Village: Commemorating the 1944 Massacre at Oradour-sur-Glane* (Berkeley: University of California Press, 1999), 24–25, 38–39, 44–45, and Jean-Pierre Azéma and Olivier Wieviorka, *Les Libérations de la France* (Paris: Éditions de la Martinière, 1993). But see especially the important article by Hans Umbreit, "Les Allemands face à la lutte armée," in Marcot, ed., *La Résistance et les français,* 205–8.

18. This account is based on Tzvetan Todorov, *Une Tragédie française, été 1944: scènes de guerre civile* (Paris: Seuil, 1994), who sees this incident as totally unnecessary and has little good to say about the Resistance.

19. Marie-Louise Osmont, *The Normandy Diary of Marie-Louise Osmont: 1940–1944* (New York: Random House, 1994), 67. See also H. R. Kedward and

Nancy Wood, eds., *The Liberation of France: Image and Event* (Oxford: Berg, 1995), 297–303 for the statistics and the conclusion that Liberation had not been worth the price. The same criticism of the war occurred in other cities such as nearby St-Lô that were heavily bombed in a futile and counterproductive effort to defeat the Germans. The author (Thomas) personally experienced similar hatred of the Allies in Le Havre in 1969, where the loss of life was also considerable.

20. Lacouture, *De Gaulle the Rebel*, 531–32, 549–51. See also Christine Levisse-Touzé, *Du Capitaine de Hauteclocque au général Leclerc* (Paris: Éditions Complexe, 2001), 180–83, 198.

21. This account is based primarily on Jean-Pierre Azéma, *De Munich à la Libération 1938–1944* (Paris: Seuil, 1979), 345–49.

22. This paragraph is based mainly on De Gaulle, *War Memoirs: Unity, 1942–1944*, 341–46.

23. Ibid., 355–57, 360–62. On the mass, see Michael Kelly, *The Cultural and Intellectual Rebuilding of France after the Second World War* (New York: Palgrave Macmillan, 2004), 79–80.

24. Most of this is based on Crémieux-Brilhac, *La France Libre*, 1275–80, 1288–91. See also Charles de Gaulle, *The War Memoirs of Charles de Gaulle: Salvation, 1944–1946*, trans. Joyce Murchie and Hamish Erskine (New York: Simon and Schuster, 1960), 29–30. Some of the statistics may not be totally accurate. Different sources quote different figures on the same subject. I have not tried to reconcile them. See Umbreit, "Les Allemands face à la lutte armée," in Marcot, ed., *La Résistance et les Français*, 210, for the German evaluation that the French played a major role in defeating them in Marseille and Toulon.

25. De Gaulle, *War Memoirs: Salvation, 1944–1946*, 156–78.

26. Most of this is based on Pierre Giolitto, *Histoire de la Milice* (Paris: Perrin, 2002; originally published in 1997), 370–71, 420–22, 453–44, 465–66. See also Philippe Pétain, *Discours aux Français, 17 juin 1940–29 août 1944* (Paris: Albin Michel, 1989), 325–26, 336.

27. This paragraph and the following two are based primarily on Henry Rousso, *Pétain et la fin de la collaboration: Sigmaringen 1944–1945* (Brussels: Éditions Complexes, 1984).

28. In addition to Rousso see Philippe Burrin, *France under the Germans: Collaboration and Compromise*, trans. Janet Lloyd (New York: New Press, 1996), 435–36, 455.

29. See de Gaulle, *War Memoirs: Unity, 1942–1944*, 329–30, and *Salvation, 1944–1946*, 12–15; Crane Brinton, "Letters from Liberated France," *French Historical Studies* 2, 2 (Fall 1961): 140–47.

30. Burrin, *France under the Germans*, 452–53.

31. This paragraph and the next one are based on Fabrice Virgili, *La France "virile": Les femmes tondues à la libération* (Paris: Payot, 2000).

32. The primary source for the purges is Peter Novick, *The Resistance versus Vichy: The Purge of Collaborators in Liberated France* (New York: Columbia University Press, 1968).

33. Jean-Marc Berlière and Laurent Chabrun, *Les Policiers français sous l'Occupation* (Paris: Perrin, 2001), 16, 25–26, 40, 247–49, 272–74, 281, 285, 321, 330, 334–35.

34. Novick, *The Resistance versus Vichy*, 79–91; Robert Paxton, *Parades and Politics at Vichy: The French Officer Corps under Marshal Pétain* (Princeton: Princeton University Press, 1966), 410–11; Henry Rousso, *Vichy: L'Événement, la mémoire, l'histoire* (Paris: Gallimard, 2001), 626.

35. Rousso, *Vichy: L'Événement*, 562 ff.

36. W. D. Halls, *Politics, Society and Christianity in Vichy France* (Oxford: Berg, 1995), 369–71, 377–78; Novick, *The Resistance versus Vichy*, 134–36, 138–39.

37. Olivier Wieviorka, *Les Orphelins de la République: Destinées des députés et sénateurs français (1940–1945)* (Paris: Editions du Seuil, 2001), 397–412.

38 Alice Kaplan, *The Collaborator: The Trial and Execution of Robert Brasillach* (Chicago: University of Chicago Press, 2000). The quotes are on pages 58, 173, and 181.

39. Ibid., 122–24. Only one of the four jurors in the Brasillach trial was a communist. The far right maintained that all of the jurors were members of the Communist Party. In reality, two of the jurors favored leniency for Brasillach before the trial took place. See 138, 140–42.

40. On Laval see Geoffrey Warner, *Pierre Laval and the Eclipse of France, 1931–1945* (New York: Macmillan , 1968), 409 ff. and also Jean-Paul Cointet, *Pierre Laval* (Paris: Fayard, 1993), 511–33.

41. Léon Werth, *Impressions d'audience: Le Procès Pétain* (Paris, 1995), for an eyewitness account of the trial plus a transcript of the proceedings. See also de Gaulle, *Salvation, 1944–1946* and Novick, *The Resistance versus Vichy*, 169–74.

42. Rousso, *Vichy: L'Événement,* 637–73.

43. Ibid., 500–46.

Epilogue

1. Jean-Pierre Rioux, *The Fourth Republic, 1944–1958,* trans. Godfrey Rodgers (Cambridge: Cambridge University Press, 1989), 13–25.

2. Jacques Marseille, *La Guerre des deux France* (Paris: Perin, 2005), 21, 35–37, 46–52, 67–68, 77, 89–92; Henri Mendras, *La France que je vois* (Paris: L'Aube, 2005), 15; Paul Krugman, "French Family Values," *New York Times,* July 29, 2005; Timothy B. Smith, *France in Crisis: Welfare, Inequality and Globalization since 1980* (New York: Cambridge University Press, 2004).

3. Marseille, *La Guerre des deux France,* 116–17, 136–37, 145–46, 149; Philip H. Gordon and Sophie Meunier, *The French Challenge: Adapting to Globalization* (Washington, D.C.: Brookings Institution Press, 2001), 24, 26, 31, 49, 83–84.

4. Henri Mendras with Alistair Cole, *Social Change in Modern France: Towards a Cultural Anthropology of the Fifth Republic* (Cambridge and Paris: Cambridge University Press and Éditions de la maison des sciences de l'homme, 1991), 15–22, 51–72; Mendras, *La France que je vois,* 88, 122, 131, 138, 161, 254, 263.

5. On the 2005 unrest see Alec G. Hargreaves, "An Emperor with No Clothes?" 28 November 2005, <http://riotsfrance.ssrc.org/Hargreaves/pf/ and the other papers posted at http://riotsfrance.ssrc.org.

6. Pierre Birnbaum, *La France imaginée: Déclin des rêves unitaires* (Paris: Gallimard, 1998), 359, notably.

Index

WORLD WAR II: THE GLOBAL, HUMAN, AND ETHICAL DIMENSION
G. Kurt Piehler, series editor

1. Lawrence Cane, David E. Cane, Judy Barrett Litoff, and David C. Smith, eds., *Fighting Fascism in Europe: The World War II Letters of an American Veteran of the Spanish Civil War.*

2. Angelo M. Spinelli and Lewis H. Carlson, *Life behind Barbed Wire: The Secret World War II Photographs of Prisoner of War Angelo M. Spinelli.*

3. Don Whitehead and John B. Romeiser, *"Beachhead Don": Reporting the War from the European Theater, 1942–1945.*

4. Scott H. Bennett, ed., *Army GI, Pacifist CO: The World War II Letters of Frank and Albert Dietrich.*

5. Alexander Jefferson with Lewis H. Carlson, *Red Tail Captured, Red Tail Free: Memoirs of a Tuskegee Airman and POW.*

6. Jonathan G. Utley, *Going to War with Japan, 1937–1941.*

7. Grant K. Goodman, *America's Japan: The First Year, 1945–1946.*

8. Patricia Kollander, with John O'Sullivan, *"I Must Be a Part of This War": One Man's Fight against Hitler and Nazism.*

9. Judy Barrett Litoff, *An American Heroine in the French Resistance: The Diary and Memoir of Virginia d'Albert-Lake.*

DATE DUE

5/10/15			

Demco, Inc. 38-293